HITLER'S
OLYMPICS

As guests of honour my daughters and I were deeply moved by the dignity of the commemorative act and by the gratitude that the democratic Berlin feels towards Jesse, because, looking back on the events of 1936 from today's perspective, the towering figure of Jesse and the admiration for him do eclipse Hitler.

Ruth Owens, 1993 in *Berlin 2000 Olympia GmbH*

HITLER'S
OLYMPICS

THE 1936 BERLIN OLYMPIC GAMES

CHRISTOPHER
HILTON

SUTTON PUBLISHING

First published in the United Kingdom in 2006 by
Sutton Publishing Limited · Phoenix Mill
Thrupp · Stroud · Gloucestershire · GL5 2BU

British Library Cataloguing in Publication Data
A catalogue record for this book is available from the British Library.

ISBN 0-7509-4292-4

Typeset in 10.5/14pt Photina MT.
Typesetting and origination by
Sutton Publishing Limited.
Printed and bound in England by
J.H. Haynes & Co. Ltd, Sparkford.

CONTENTS

ACKNOWLEDGEMENTS

Many people have helped in recreating the story of the Berlin Olympics but I must begin with the German National Olympic Committee – and particularly Bernd Roeder, their legal counsel, and Michael Schirp of the Press Office – for allowing me to use the 1936 Official Report, an immense and extremely detailed document. It acted as a pillar.

William J. Baker of the University of Maine very kindly gave me permission to quote from his book *Jesse Owens: An American Life* and, holidaying in England, he provided me with a penetrating, thought-provoking interview.

Margaret Lambert (formerly Gretel Bergmann) allowed me to use the letter telling her she was not selected for the German team and, at ninety-one, was a merry, youthful voice down the telephone from New York City, her home since before the Second World War. She gave a long, heartfelt and utterly candid interview about her life in the 1930s. She also sent a fascinating video of her life and allowed me to quote from her lifestory, *By Leaps and Bounds*. I have, incidentally, called her Gretel Bergmann throughout for simplicity. Christine Duerksen Sant allowed me to reproduce generous portions of her beautifully researched thesis, submitted to the Graduate Faculty of Wake Forest University, North Carolina, '"Genuine German Girls": The Nazi Portrayal of its Sportswomen of the 1936 Berlin Olympics'. Professor Yasuhiro Sakaue of the Faculty of Administration and Social Sciences, Fukushima University, Japan graciously allowed me to quote from his paper on 'Sport, Politics and Business' at the International Committee of Historical Sciences Congress in Sydney, July 2005.

Two duets – if I may use the word – had essentially the same invaluable idea: to let Olympians tell their stories in their own words. *Tales of Gold* by Lewis H. Carlson and John J. Fogarty carried interviews from American gold medal winners from 1912 to 1984; *'A Proper Spectacle': Women Olympians 1900–1936* was self-published by Britons Stephanie Daniels and Anita Tedder under their imprint ZeNaNa. It concentrated, as the title implies, on women. Both duets were happy to let me quote the memories of those who competed in Berlin.

For permission to quote I also thank Chris Rudge, Chief Executive Officer of the Canadian Olympic Committee and their *Canada at the XI Olympiad 1936 Germany*; Mike Tancred, Media Director of the Australian Olympic Committee for their Official Report; Lee Rogers and Toby Harris for *Jews and the Olympic Games* by Paul Yogi Mayer; Deborah E. Lipstadt, Dorot Professor of Modern Jewish and Holocaust Studies and Director, Rabbi Donald Tam Institute for Jewish Studies, Emory University, Atlanta, Georgia for *Beyond Belief: The American Press and the Coming of the Holocaust, 1933–1945*. Jerry Papazian, past president of the University of Southern California Alumni Association, allowed me to use his research on where the oak trees – given as saplings to gold medal winners – are today in America.

Terryl Asla and Matthew Walker of *I, Witness to History* in Wichita, Kansas were instantly helpful and Walker carried out an invaluable interview with a spectator at the Games as well as sending a little treasure trove of photographs taken by that spectator, Esther Wenzel (then Myers). Velma Dunn (now Ploessel), who won a silver medal in the diving, took me gently down memory lane. So did John Woodruff, who won the 800 metres and remains a man of enormous dignity.

Birgit Kubisch found two invaluable eyewitnesses and interviewed them – Fritz Wandt and Werner Schwieger – and their memories give little human touches which are so evocative. To her, and them, sincere thanks – and equal thanks to my neighbour Inge Donnell for translating all manner of German newspapers and documents.

For help: Jason Black, *Daily Courier*, Connellsville, Pennsylvania; Malcolm Fare, fencing historian, who took great pains to try and unravel several mysteries surrounding the women's event in Berlin; *The Journal of American History*; Terri Wykoff of *Frankwykoff.com*; Klaus Amrhein of the German Athletic Federation; Heather M. Gillette of Wake Forest University, Winston-Salem, North Carolina; Maren L. Read, Photo Research Coordinator/Archivist at the United States Holocaust Museum, Washington, DC; B.J. Folin of the Swedish Olympic Committee. Michael Salmon, Librarian at the Amateur Athletic Foundation of Los Angeles (aafla) responded wonderfully to every bizarre and obscure problem I threw at him. Randall Northam of SportsBooks Ltd, Worcester, England – an old friend – was generous with whatever background information I requested. Gustav Shrenk, German athletics historian, dipped into his records to find much invaluable information. Simona Rychtecky, Robert Bolton and Ross Arnold of the Olympic Television Archive Bureau were helpfulness and efficiency personified. P.K. Mohan and S.A. and M.A.R. Salazaar sorted out when the Indian hockey team left, opening the way to their journey to Berlin. Stan Salazaar pointed me towards the website www.bharatiyahockey.org, the internet home of Indian hockey where the full text of the evocative *The World's Hockey Champions 1936* by M.N. Masood can be found. I have used it extensively and many thanks to his son, Enver Masud, for permission to quote. The Deutsches Creditbank AG in Berlin are trying to revive the Olympic Village. Barbara Eisenhuth of the Bank helped with information about that and sent an invaluable booklet by VBN Verlag Bernd Neddermeyer GmbH.

I consulted and used the superb archival coverage of the *New York Times* throughout the book, but especially of their reporting team in Berlin; and also consulted *The Times*, London, the *Daily Express*, London and the *Los Angeles Times*.

The Internet has changed many facets of the historian's life. To be able to summon instantly such vast amounts of information on even the most arcane and obscure subjects remains slightly breathtaking. The trick for the historians of the future will not just be discovering information for themselves in musty libraries but penetrating the internet mazes and extracting what they want. In relation to this book, you will see to what extent I have used the internet in the footnotes.

Leni Riefenstahl's monumental two-part film record of the Games, *Fest der Volker* and *Fest der Schonheit* (Festival of the People and Festival of Beauty), (Videoyesteryear) remains revealing and compulsive viewing, not least because one can relive some of the great moments as they happened. I used it heavily in some re-creations.

The British Olympic Committee (thanks Amy Terriere) opened their extensive library in London to me, let me loose on their photocopying machine and treated me with their customary kindness.

Thanks must also go to Bow Watkinson who drew the maps on pages xi and xii.

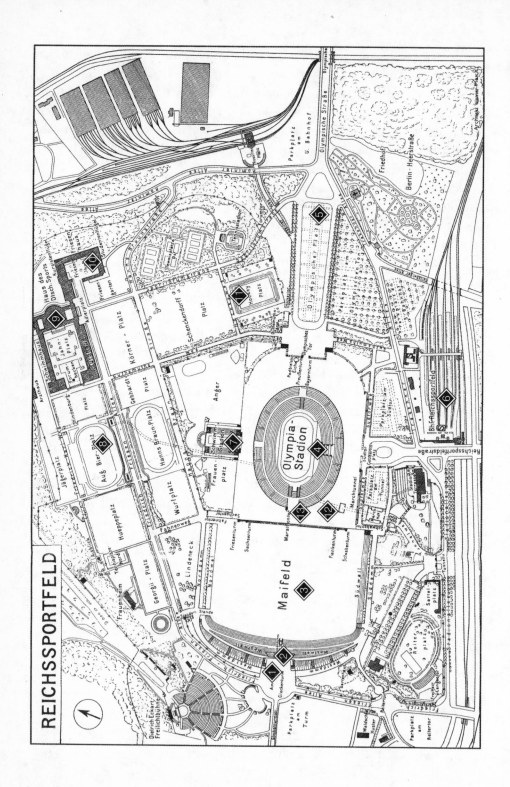

Opposite: Map 1. The scale of the Reich Sports Field astonished the world.

1. The *Platz* where Hitler arrived for the Opening Ceremony.
2. Bell tower.
3. The May Field where the competitors waited.
4. Olympic Stadium.
5. Olympic *Platz*.
6. Reich Sports Field station.
7. Swimming pool.
8. *August-Bier-Platz* where the gymnasts practised.
9. The House of German Sport and the Cupola Hall.
10. The *Friesenhaus*, the living quarters for the female athletes.
11. Hockey stadium.
12. Tunnel to the stadium.
13. Marathon Gate.

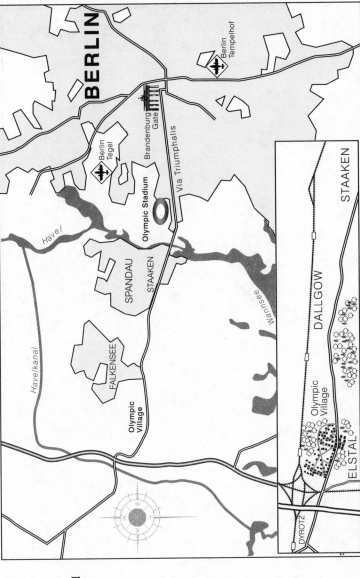

Map 2. The Olympic Village was in the countryside to the west of Berlin.

Map 3. The torch run from Olympia to Berlin.

Chapter 1

MAN AT THE CENTRE
OF THE WORLD

The German nation . . . provided the world with . . . its willingness to
co-operate in large international projects designed to further universal
peace.

Josef Goebbels[1]

T hat August day the city of heavy stone, the city with its new god,
waited. A million people, held back by 40,000 storm troopers,[2] stood
twenty and thirty deep all along the 3-mile route. Each of them knew
he would be coming in a moment from the enclosed Chancellory courtyard.

At the far end of that courtyard two statues of heroic naked men, one
symbolising the Party and the other the armed forces, guarded shallow steps
up to the Chancellory entrance. An open-topped Mercedes waited there. Two
bodyguards in dark uniforms sat on the rear seat, motionless.

He wore military uniform, knee-length leather boots and the peaked cap
designed for him. He wore a golden Party badge and his prized military
medal, an Iron Cross.[3] As he moved briskly down the steps, the Mercedes door
swung open and he stepped in. He stood and remained standing. He knew the
power of his physical presence over the millions and as he passed they would
all see him, feel that power. The Mercedes moved off towards the courtyard's
double doors at the instant the timetable decreed it should: 3.18 p.m.

A little drizzle had fallen from an overcast sky and, as the Mercedes
emerged and turned into Wilhelmstrasse, the road glistened. Four similar
Mercedes with more bodyguards followed, making a convoy with a symmetry
and a power of its own. The timetable decreed that the journey from here to
the great amphitheatre last 32 minutes.

At the intersection with Unter den Linden, a wide thoroughfare whose
buildings were draped with flags, the convoy turned left. The lime trees
populating the central area between two carriageways had been replaced by

swastikas 45 feet high. The crowd began cheering and, in great ripples, gave the stiff-arm Nazi salute. Along the 3 miles a voice echoed from loud speakers set at regular intervals '*He is coming, He is coming*'.

The convoy glided through the Brandenburg Gate, with its statue of a horseman on top, and was out onto the long avenue which stretched – rigid as a backbone, straight as a rod – away through wooded parkland. The avenue was so long it changed names several times, but people called it collectively the Via Triumphalis. It continued to the suburb of Charlottenburg and the amphitheatre.

Every moment brought him closer, every moment the ripple of cheering and saluting travelled with him, and from above the voice echoed '*He is coming now, He is coming now*'.

At 3.45 p.m. the amphitheatre gates closed; there were 100,000 inside.

At Charlottenburg the convoy turned off the avenue, moved towards a *platz* – deep crowds circling it – and the entrance. The convoy halted, he stepped down at 3.50 p.m. and passed through the entrance: an opened gate. He inspected a battalion of honour, walked briskly under a tall bell tower, passed four field guns ready to fire a salute and onto a vast field of manicured grass. The amphitheatre loomed at the far side of the field.

Two rows of dignitaries and officials waited for him and as he reached them a fanfare sounded in the distance. Now he faced a multicoloured panorama of some four thousand people arranged by nationality, half to one side of the field, half to the other. Some had spent weeks travelling half the world to be here. Some had come an exhausting journey by train, others caught trains quite normally. Some were in large groups, some came as individuals. Some brought pageantry with them: straw hats, naval caps, turbans, blue berets.

At 3.56 p.m. he walked briskly between them. He had 4 minutes to reach the amphitheatre. As he went, the dignitaries – military officers among them – fell in behind him, were towed along in his wake.

Two heroic statues of men holding horses guarded the amphitheatre entrance. Nearby young people in shorts, perhaps a thousand of them, jostled for their glimpse and raised their arms stiff in the salute.

He walked past a stone buttress with a huge iron tripod and crucible on it that would receive the sacred flame. As he descended stone steps, tier after tier of the 100,000 were on their feet raising a forest of arms in another ripple.

He crossed the reddish running track onto the circular grass of the infield. A tiny girl in white proferred a bouquet of flowers. He patted her, accepted it and reflexively she stepped back, gave the salute. He recrossed the track and at 4.05 p.m., as the timetable decreed, ascended to his private box cut into one of the tiers.

He had come.

The rest would be anthems and triumphal music, the hoisting of flags, the tolling of the bell, the march past of the nations who'd waited outside – programmed to last 46 minutes – and speeches.

Then he stood at the centre of the world for the first time in his life.

He held himself erect and said 'I hereby proclaim open the Olympic Games of Berlin celebrating the Eleventh Olympiad of the modern era'.

The field guns fired, a great host of pigeons representing doves of peace swarmed into the overcast sky and at 5.20 p.m. a runner bearing a torch with the sacred flame entered the amphitheatre, padded towards the stone buttress and the crucible.

The runner lit it.

The most controversial sporting event in history had begun.

Chapter 2

POISONED CHALICE

The German sports authorities have declared their intention of promoting the racial and anti-Semitic, the pagan and anti-Christian and other political policies of the German Government and the Nazi party . . . in the selection of the German Olympic team.

American Athletic Union resolution, 1935

I n May 1930 people could still speak the language of reason and normality. Adolf Hitler was nowhere near power and nobody except perhaps the man himself could imagine what he would really do if he got it. That month, to emphasise the normality, his autobiography *Mein Kampf* came out in a new English edition with all the profits going to the British Red Cross Society. That month, too, one of the regular Olympic Congresses met in the principal auditorium of Berlin University, giving the city a chance to lobby for the 1936 Games – the 1932 Games were already allocated to Los Angeles. The Congress comprised a wide group invited by the International Olympic Committee (IOC), the movement's governing body, and played a consultative role.

The city hosted a banquet in the town hall for Congress members and, there, the Municipal Corporation joined the application, as required by the Olympic Statutes.

The whole impetus created a favourable impression, enhanced by a glimpse of scale and efficiency: 2,000 rowing boats formed a procession on the proposed Olympic course. When the IOC met next, in April 1931 in Barcelona, the application would almost certainly be a formality and the Berlin bidders felt so confident they began to draw up plans to remodel the stadium they already had. They appointed an architect, Werner March, to work on it.

Far from being a controversial choice Berlin seemed a normal continuation of the great tradition stretching back into the very mists of time. Some historians dated the ancient Games to 900 BC, others claimed evidence taking it back several centuries further. Everybody agreed they lasted until AD 393 when the Roman emperor Theodosius banned them because winning had become paramount, inviting professionalism and corruption.

The Olympic idea did not die but remained dormant. In the nineteenth century various sports festivals around Europe included one at Much Wenlock, the scenic town in the English county of Shropshire. There a Dr William Penney Brookes founded an Olympic society in 1850 and campaigned for the Games to be reinstated.

In 1889 the French government wanted to study physical culture, and an all-round sportsman called Pierre Frédy, titled baron de Coubertin, became actively involved. He was already engaged on reforming the French educational system and believed passionately in the virtues of fitness and sport. De Coubertin went on a world tour to see what was happening elsewhere and, towards the end of it, met Brookes. The meeting seems to have been genuinely inspirational.

In 1892, during a lecture at the Sorbonne in Paris, de Coubertin put forward the idea of reinstating the Games and two years later he founded the IOC. He would be its president for four decades. The first Games of the modern era were held in 1896, appropriately at Athens, and thirteen countries sent 311 competitors.

Obeying the original four-year cycle, the next Games went to Paris in 1900 (twenty-two countries, 1,330 competitors) and women competed for the first time, in tennis and golf. St Louis, Missouri proved too far for many to travel (back to thirteen countries and 625 competitors), but the movement grew via Athens in 1906 (breaking and reinvigorating the cycle), London in 1908 and Stockholm in 1912. The 1916 Games were to have been in Berlin but the long shadows of the First World War crept across the Continent. De Coubertin and the IOC harboured the notion that having the Games might persuade the German people towards peace rather than alienate them: Germany, an Olympic stalwart, had sent teams to every Games from their reinstatement. Even when the First World War broke out in 1914, planning continued, no doubt helped by the general belief that the war would be over long before 1916.

Two men worked long and hard to make the Games happen, Dr Theodor Lewald, the chairman of the German Organising Committee, and Dr Carl Diem, the secretary. Lewald had been a central figure in German Olympics for a generation. Who knew, or cared, that his grandmother on his father's side was a Jew who'd converted to Christianity? Diem, only thirty, was 'a fine athlete, a scholar, an historian, an enthusiast for classical Greece, an expert on sport and sporting history the world over'.[1] He looked like an ascetic university professor.

The war quickly locked into a savage, brooding stalemate between trenches on either side of no man's land and, all else aside, that brought pressure within the IOC to take the Games elsewhere – America, perhaps, or a neutral European country. De Coubertin hesitated, feeling Germany would have to withdraw first but by 1915 the situation simplified itself – Berlin was now unthinkable. Meanwhile the IOC established its headquarters in Lausanne, physically safe from the buffetings of the twentieth century in neutral Switzerland.

The movement needed a second reawakening, this time at Antwerp in 1920, but the 'enemy' countries – Germany, Austria, Bulgaria, Hungary and Turkey – were not invited. 'Taking on the Games wasn't easy for the organisers in a country that already faced an enormous rebuilding task. Visiting athletes slept on cots in schoolrooms, but for the most part they accepted the accommodation and many of them even praised the food.'[2]

The movement grew. In 1924 the first Winter Games, at Chamonix in the French Alps, were added to the Games in Paris (Germany not invited again). De Coubertin, now in his sixties and decorated by a bushy white moustache, resigned as president after Paris and Count Henri de Baillet-Latour, a Belgian who had been a member since 1903, co-founded the Belgian Olympic Committee and helped organise the Antwerp Games, succeeded him. Baillet-Latour, hair receding and a wispy little moustache, looked like a doctor or a bank manager: a sympathetic face of character.

The 1928 Winter Games were held at St Moritz, the Summer Games at Amsterdam. There a team from Germany found acceptance again and quite normally an eighteen-year-old fencer, Helene Mayer, was chosen. She came from Offenbach of middle-class parents. Who knew or cared that her father, a respected member of the community with a general practice, was a Jew? Who knew or cared that her mother was not Jewish? As a young girl she'd liked ballet, riding, swimming and skiing but fencing attracted her more and more, and Offenbach was the centre for it. In 1924, and still only fourteen, she finished second in the German championship and won it a year later. Mayer considered herself German and looked stereotypically so – blonde hair, blue eyes. At Amsterdam she took the gold medal and became rightly famous.

The problem was that some people did know about her Jewish father and, however incomprehensible, they did care – manically:

While the daily German newspapers wrote in glowing terms of the success of the 'nice, blonde German girl,' the Jewish papers emphasised the Jewish origin of an athlete eminently suited to making all the anti-Semitic cliches seem absurd. Besides reporting her athletic achievement, the press drew attention to one other event: She had waved a little black, white, and red flag. While conservative newspapers . . . praised this as an heroic deed, liberal and left-wing papers criticised it as being in poor taste, a pathetic demonstration and a disavowal of the nation's colors. In . . . a Jewish paper the incident was dismissed as a mishap: the flag had been forced upon her by one of her fellow fencers. Helene Mayer was described as a 'simple girl, completely averse to any political activity.' . . . At any rate, although Helene Mayer was at the center of public attention, her Jewish heritage was totally ignored by the non-Jewish press.[3]

Some of the great and good of the day were at Barcelona for the IOC meeting and the attendance reads like a glimpse of a vanished world: counts and generals, doctors and professors, senators and councillors. It is true that human competition – essentially combat – on the scale of the Olympics inevitably produced drama and controversy, but these people in charge of it governed, as they thought, by right because then such people governed everything else as well. They did it on their own terms, calmly, without hurry and with a maximum of decorum. They made their decisions and they enforced them. It was the way the world was before Hitler got hold of it, bringing with it so many enormous pressures. Those pressures would almost engulf Baillet-Latour, humiliate Lewald and torment General Charles Sherrill, a former sprinter himself, from the United States, beyond endurance.

The Official Bulletin of the IOC did not reflect anything like this yet. It radiated precisely the calm and the decorum:

The first point brought forward was the fixing of the venue of the XIth Olympic Games in 1936. [The Italians] General Montu and Count Bonacossa stated that Italy waived their claim for the 1936 Contest at Rome but at the same time begged to be given the Olympic Games later.

Mr [Jules] de Muzsa [Hungary] asked that the Games of 1936 should be held at Berlin instead of Budapest but claimed a meeting at some future date.

Dr Lewald and the Count of Vallellano [Spain] spoke in favour of Berlin and Barcelona.

The meeting proceeded to vote.

Owing to the very small number present at the 1931 Session, and in order to take into account the number of written votes already received, the Committee decided to wait until the answers of the many absent members reached Lausanne.

The vote taken during the Session and those already received were sealed and deposited at Lausanne with the others.

In order to expedite the decision it was agreed to ask for answers by telegram. The IOC were informed of an application from Canada for the XIIth Games in 1940.

The voting was quickly accomplished, especially in those more leisurely times, because the Bulletin was able to report that Berlin received forty-three votes and Barcelona sixteen with eight abstentions. The Bulletin added that the 'German Olympic Committee has decided to exercise the right of priority reserved to the Country holding the Olympic Games by Article 6 of the Charter and will organise the Winter Games 1936. The venue will be chosen later.'

How could the great and good read the runes? How could anybody? William Shirer, an American correspondent in Berlin and later a celebrated author, wrote that 'the depression which spread over the world like a great conflagration toward the end of 1929 gave Adolf Hitler his opportunity, and he made the most of it. Like most great revolutionaries he could thrive only in evil times, at first when the masses were unemployed, hungry and desperate, and later when they were intoxicated by war.'[4] Who, however, could have predicted that into the 1930s? In 1931 his Nazi movement eyed power without any certainty that they would ever get it, but that October Paul von Hindenburg, a field marshal during the First World War and President since 1925, received Hitler. Within months Hitler would be debating whether to run for the presidency himself.

The German Olympic Committee, led by Lewald and Diem, set to work in July and put a model of their stadium on public display. It was to be situated in the Grünewald, the wooded area to the west of the city, beside a racecourse. Lewald and Diem did it against a political background which had begun to move perceptibly away from normality and the language of reason: German banks closed their doors to prevent a run on the currency and only opened them again when Britain, America and France agreed on renewed credits.

Two themes were running and would continue to run – sometimes parallel, sometimes veering towards each other, sometimes interlocking – until, in the late afternoon of 1 August 1936, they would be locked together forever. Helene Mayer, who concentrated on her fencing and won the European Championships, illustrated one theme perfectly: the self-contained, non-political world of sport. Adolf Hitler, who concentrated on winning Germany, *was* the other: politics red in tooth and claw.

In November 1931, just eight months after the Games were awarded to Berlin, the Nazi Party won elections in the state of Hesse. Hitler's hour was coming closer.

A week after the 1932 Winter Games in Lake Placid, New York State, he decided to stand against von Hindenburg for President. A patrician figure with a white, walrus moustache, von Hindenburg dismissed Hitler in a celebrated phrase as 'that Bohemian corporal' but received only 49 per cent of the votes (Hitler 30 per cent), forcing him into a humiliating run-off. He polled 53 per cent, Hitler up to 36. Von Hindenburg invited Franz von Papen, a relatively obscure member of the Catholic Centre Party, to become Chancellor and the incumbent, Heinrich Bruning, resigned. Von Papen formed a cabinet with no Nazis in it.

While the second day of the Summer Games was being contested at Los Angeles, in Germany Hitler won 230 seats in the parliamentary elections for the Reichstag, just short of an overall majority.

Two days later Mayer began her defence of the Olympic fencing gold. Described as 'the beautiful blonde Valkrie of the swords',[5] she moved through her pool to the final stages winning all her bouts. She radiated a great calmness and a certain sophistication, attracted male fencers and habitually greeted everyone on the fencing floor as friends. When California State Governor James Rolph, wearing a white linen suit and a gardenia button hole, arrived and asked her how she was doing she contented herself with pointing to the scoreboard . . . .

It went wrong in the final stages. She fought Mary Addams (Belgium) in her opening bout and they provided a stark sartorial contrast, Mayer in a white jacket and skirt, Addams in a black pleated skirt and white jacket. Mayer lost and afterwards sat motionless contemplating her defeat, her chin in her hand supported by an elbow on her knee. She ate an orange, thrust the peel under the chair where she sat. She fought Ena Bogen (Hungary) and lost a long, nervous, exhausting bout: 5 hits received to 4. She made her way back to the chair and shrugged her shoulders, perhaps discouraged or disconsolate.

Her pivotal moment came against Ellen Preiss (Austria), a great fencer in terms of skill and longevity – she would go on to compete at the Melbourne Games in 1956. Mayer led 4 hits received to 1 but Preiss, determined, came back at her and won it 5–4. Preiss had the gold, Mayer came fifth.

Diem and Lewald, by now a patrician figure of receding hair and a tuft of white moustache (white moustaches almost obligatory in that vanished era), were in Los Angeles to watch, record and learn. Lewald acted as the official figure taking care of whatever that entailed while Diem, energetic, was everywhere, taking notes and photographs, drawing sketches, even asking the cooks what kind of food the athletes preferred. Lewald and Diem had been sent with the instuctions to gain all the experience possible with the end in view of organising their own XIth Olympic Games. The Secretary-General of the Reich Commission for Physical Training [Diem] was especially requested to pay attention to the presentation of the Games in Los Angeles in order to derive useful knowledge for the great task facing Germany.

The Organising Committee for the Xth Olympic Games in Los Angeles had made its preparations in a most thorough manner and was able to provide Germany with well-ordered copies of all its printed matter and important documents as well as a comprehensive insight into the work carried out by the various departments, so that a complete survey of the American method of solving this huge task was possible.[6]

The Games had grown and thirty-seven countries attended, bringing 1,408 athletes (but not including the great Finnish runner Parvo Nurmi, excluded from the marathon amid accusations of professionalism occasioned by over-large expenses on a tour of Germany). Photo finishes were introduced although, wonderfully, the lap counter miscalculated in the 3,000 metres steeplechase and the runners covered an extra lap. A man with a truly glorious name, Volmari Iso-Hollo, won, continuing a strong Finnish tradition and suggesting they would be strong in Berlin, too, but another Finn, Lauri Lehtinen, was thoroughly booed when he twice baulked an American towards the end of the 5,000 metres. And the Brazilian water polo team were disqualified after being thoroughly rude to the referee when they lost 7–3 to Germany.

Purists within the Olympic movement disdain, or try to disdain, the nationalism of medals tables but after Los Angeles they held particular, arguably crucial, significance. The statistics demonstrate it.

	Gold	Silver	Bronze
America	41	32	30
Italy	12	12	12
France	10	6	4
Germany (8th)	4	12	5

Any Games without America would be devalued to the point of meaninglessness, which is one way of saying the Germans had to have the Americans in Berlin but, as the Los Angeles Games closed, there was as yet no reason whatsoever why the Americans should not be in Berlin.

Helene Mayer, who intended to join the German diplomatic service, visited Scripps College in California. The German Academic Exchange Service had offered her a two-year grant. She was formal in the German way and at her first meal bowed deeply to each dining table.[7]

Two weeks after Los Angeles, von Hindenburg lectured Hitler about the activities of his storm troopers on the streets.

In November the German Olympic Committee decided to form a special Organising Committee for the Games.

Von Papen resigned because he couldn't form a government. In Reichstag elections the Nazis shed 2 million votes although they remained the largest party.

In December initial plans for an Olympic bell were drawn up.

In January 1933 the Organising Committee met for the first time just days before von Hindenburg, confronting a breakdown of law and order as the storm troopers and communists fought daily street battles, appointed Hitler as Chancellor. His 'immediate task' was to 'quickly eliminate' anyone else holding some power and 'make his party the exclusive master of the State and then with the power of an authoritarian government and its police carry out the Nazi revolution'.[8]

Von Hindenburg remained head of state, of course, and accepted patronage of the Games because by tradition heads of state attend the Opening Ceremony and declare the Games open.

The Reichstag caught fire in mysterious circumstances and Hitler moved instinctively to exploit the event, using it as a bludgeon to crush his opponents.

At first he had shown no interest in the Games, dismissing them as 'an invention of Jews and Freemasons' and describing them as some sort of Judaistic theatre 'which cannot possibly be put on in a Reich ruled by National Socialists'. Whether Hitler concluded this because of Lewald's intimate connection with it – Lewald had a Jewish grandmother, of course – or whether he believed Jews and Freemasons controlled *everything* beyond Germany is not clear.

Goebbels, however, understood intuitively the potential propaganda possibilities, internal and external, and put it to Hitler something like this: 'We can make this the greatest advertisement for you and your Germany.' Goebbels also understood that the Germans had the first organised global press relations triumph within their grasp. He grasped it.

He made Hitler see the opportunity, too. Here was a pivotal moment because soon Hitler's word would quite literally be law and if he wanted a Games in Germany's new image he would get one. The normal constraints of personnel, budgets and logistics simply dissolved and, on Hitler's order, the formidable organising ability of the German psyche applied itself to creating something extraordinary.

The world would travel to what had been, such a short time before, a defeated, broken country – humiliated by the Treaty of Versailles imposed by the victors, ravaged by hyper-inflation so intense that people paid for their meals course by course as the currency devalued *while they were eating* – and would suddenly find themselves in a land of full employment, confident citizens and faces ruddy with health.

From outside Germany Hitler looked a combination of demagogue and caricature, a fundamentalist of his own religion – which was how Charlie Chaplin would be able to portray him so effortlessly on film – but the staging of the Olympic Games bestowed on him and his government legitimacy in a way nothing else could. They might, even briefly, make him seem benevolent, and Germany, too. Hitler met Lewald and the Mayor of Berlin, Heinrich Sahm.

[He] declared in response to Dr. Lewald's remarks that he welcomed the allotting of the Games to Berlin and that he would do everything possible to ensure their successful presentation. The Games, he asserted, would contribute substantially towards furthering understanding among the nations of the world and would promote the development of sport among the German youth, this being in his opinion of vast importance to the welfare of the nation. . . . An official statement printed in the German press informed the nation of the attitude of their Chancellor towards the Berlin Games.

The preparatory work could thus proceed on a firm foundation and it was carried forward with all alacrity in order that a complete plan might be submitted to the International Olympic Committee during its annual meeting at Vienna in 1933.

On the occasion of his conference with the German Chancellor, Dr. Lewald also had an opportunity of speaking with the Reich Minister for Propaganda, Dr. Goebbels, concerning the extent of the project and requested the support of the Propaganda Ministry.[9]

From this moment the twin themes – sport and politics – flowed towards 1 August 1936.

A week later the Reichstag, meeting at an opera house, passed an Enabling Act allowing Hitler to rule by decree, a terrifying prospect for the half-million Jews living in Germany, 160,000 of them in Berlin where their community dated back to 1295. Violence by storm troopers against them was already endemic. The government ordered a boycott of all Jewish businesses.

Lewald and Diem submitted their publicity plans to Goebbels and he gave consent for a special commission to handle their implementation. Meetings of the various German technical sporting commissions began.

Hitler appointed as Director of German Sports Captain Hans von Tschammer und Osten, a loyal supporter since the early 1920s who knew nothing about sport. His conduct as well as his ignorance ought to have disqualified him. Once a soldier received a beating for failing to salute him. Von Tschammer und Osten, with his hair swept across the crown of his head in perfect place and his neat-fitting uniform, certainly looked like a soldier although he had penetrating, dangerous eyes. His remit was to make young people mentally and physically fit to serve the Führer.

'German sport has only one task,' Goebbels said; 'to strengthen the character of the German people, imbuing it with the fighting spirit and steadfast camaraderie necessary in the struggle for its existence.' His statement remains a grotesque perversion and misuse of sport as well as the crudest violation of the Olympic spirit – if Josef Goebbels, club-footed serial adulterer, fanatic and distorter of all reality had ever heard of such a thing.

Von Tschammer und Osten was also appointed President of the German Olympic Committee. Lewald had earned international respect and his effective downgrading would provoke widespread misgivings about Germany so he remained as a consultant with the official title of President of the Organising Committee, by its nature a temporary post ceasing with the end of the Games and quite distinct from the presidency of the German Olympic Committee which von Tschammer und Osten held on to so tightly.

The Nazi government knew Lewald had his uses as a figurehead and that, having devoted so much of his life to these Games, he would do nothing to endanger them. They were compromising their rabid anti-Semitism by retaining him at all, a testimony to the forces now in play. What happened next demonstrated that. The Nazi government did not compromise over ordering all athletic organisations to be Aryan-only. That cast the leading Jewish athletes into the wilderness because the organisations had to expel them.

April was a cruel month. Thousands of Jewish bank accounts were seized, all non-Aryan officials dismissed and all Jewish teachers in Prussia deprived of their posts.

May was another cruel month. Trade unions were banned, their headquarters occupied and their leaders roughly handled. Some went to concentration camps. The Nazis began dabbling in eugenics, banning Jewish–Aryan marriages. Communist property was seized. Any books considered un-German were heaped onto a pyre outside the Humboldt University at the far end of Unter den Linden and burnt. A Race Council was established to search out mixed marriages and try to make sure Aryans married Aryans.

The shock waves reached Lausanne very quickly.

In June the IOC met in Vienna and Baillet-Latour gave a history of the negotiations that had taken place since Hitler came to power. He explained what the German delegates to the IOC had been saying, in order to be 'quite sure that the guarantees given by the Government in power in 1931 . . . could be considered as reliable, and that the application of the Olympic Rules dealing with the Committee of Organisation and the qualifications of participants would be scrupulously observed even though certain of our International Rules should seem to be inconsistent with recent orders laid down in Germany'.

Of necessity the IOC had to remain as far from politics as it could in a political world and it had a power of its own: *If you do not like our rules, you don't get the Games. You must understand that we make the rules, not you.* The movement would not have survived if it had adopted any other approach. When a Games is declared open the Olympic sites come under the control of the IOC for the duration and their rules apply. Hitler would discover this twice – once at the Winter, once at the Summer Games – and he would have to compromise. It may well be, at a personal level, these were the only times between his seizure of power in 1933 and his death in a bunker in 1945 that he actually did anything somebody else told him to.

The question of Jews in Germany was much more delicate and complicated. The IOC did not concern itself with a country's domestic laws unless they impacted on the Games. The banishment of the Prussian school teachers would be greeted by silence in Lausanne. The banning of Jewish athletes from their own clubs which, de facto, rendered them unable to train properly for the Games was quite different.

The Americans watched with mounting misgivings. The Jewish community in America had voice and influence. Would America send a team to a country which legally discriminated against Jews in the crudest, bluntest and most violent way? The weight of the Los Angeles statistics lay heavy: the Americans had accounted for 41 gold, 32 silver and 30 bronze medals – too sizeable a percentage to ignore.

Baillet-Latour, and the great and good around him, had no idea what was coming and if the German delegates kept offering assurances, what else could they do but accept them?

[Baillet-Latour] paid tribute to the Olympic spirit and to the loyalty of the German delegates who . . . had succeeded in putting matters sufficiently in order in time to allow the following statement to be published today:

The President of the International Olympic Committee asked the German delegates if they would guarantee the observance of the articles in the

Charter dealing with the Organising Committee and the Rules of Qualification.

On behalf of the 3 Delegates, His Excellency Doctor Lewald replied that, with the consent of his Government,

1 The German Olympic Committee has delegated the mandate, which had been entrusted to it, to a special Organising Committee as follows:

Dr. Lewald – President
Duke of Mecklenburg-Schwerin – Dr. Ritter von Halt
Herr Von Tschammer – President of the German Olympic Committee
Herr Sahm – Mayor of Berlin
Herr Diem – Secretary of the German Olympic Committee

2 All the laws regulating the Olympic Games shall be observed.

3 As a principle, German Jews shall not be excluded from German teams at the Games.

After this declaration Mr. [William May] Garland wished to have it known that the American Olympic Committee who were desirous of having the United States strongly represented at the next Olympic Games in Europe would have had to give up participation altogether if German Jew Athletes had not been assured the same terms as members of the same faith in other countries. General Sherrill added that the satisfactory statement made by the President would give great pleasure in the United States.[10]

Lewald made a report, fleshed out by Diem, on the preparations. One extremely important decision concerned the actual dates of the Games, which were set at the discretion of the German organisers. 'Following a careful study of weather charts and investigation of other circumstances, we chose the period between August 1st and 16th. . . . We were thus prepared to submit a printed memorandum dealing with the general programme, centres of competition and information on the accommodation for the athletes . . . this meeting with its complete approval.'[11]

Professor Jigoro Kano, representing Japan, hoped that an Olympic Village would be organised because of its importance for teams 'sent by distant countries'. Lewald explained that the Village was intended to be in military barracks at a little rural place called Döberitz. The barracks, about 20 kilometres from the stadium, were new and comfortable and intended to be in service after 15 July 1936.

The Bavarian resorts of Garmish and Partenkirchen were awarded the Winter Games in the February, the exact date to be decided.

The twin themes reached out and touched a vivacious nineteen-year-old in the little town of Laupheim, near the city of Ulm in the south. She was called Margaret Bergmann, nicknamed Gretel, and all her life she adored sport. She started early at Laupheim's sports club, competed from the age of ten and developed into a high-jumper so promising that by 1931 she needed specialist training. She dreamed of the Games quite normally, as so many others did.

Bergmann came from a prosperous Jewish family, something else quite normal because Jews had been merchants, industrialists and craftsmen in Laupheim for a hundred and fifty years. A completely assimilated community of some three hundred people, they defined themselves as Jews and were seen as Jews, but it never mattered. They were all Germans.

Bergmann did not receive a religious upbringing. She spent three years at a Jewish elementary school then moved to a municipal secondary school. She applied to the German College of Physical Exercise in Berlin, which accepted her. They withdrew their acceptance when they discovered she was Jewish. On 12 April, her nineteenth birthday, the Ulm sports club of which she was a member expelled her. During a business trip to London her father Edwin made enquiries about her studying there. In October she went to the London Polytechnic on a language course; the Polytechnic did not hesitate to recruit one of Europe's leading high-jumpers to their team.

In July the German Olympic organisers drew up a new constitution and a plan to finance the Games, but Hitler rendered all that irrelevant. In the autumn he decided to have a look at the new stadium, taking with him Reich Minister of the Interior Wilhelm Frick and von Tschammer und Osten. Hitler inspected models of the new buildings, the remodelled stadium and the entire area. He asked

why the necessary enlargement of the stadium to a capacity of 80,000 spectators was to be achieved through increasing the depth of the stadium rather than expanding it. Dr. Lewald explained that according to the lease contract with the Berlin Racing Association the stadium might not extend over the racecourse or obstruct the view. This led to the second question as to whether the racecourse was essential, to which Dr. Lewald responded that he did not believe this to be the case since Berlin already possessed two . . . and the Grünewald course had been operated during recent years at a great loss. The German Chancellor then made the significant decision that the racecourse must disappear and if necessary be reconstructed at another location, while the entire Grünewald premises should be given over to the construction of a sporting centre. The Chancellor expressed the wish to have a large open-air amphitheatre included in the construction programme.[12]

He intended to construct a monument to his Germany which would last a millennium. If he felt the racecourse obstructed this he had no need to consult anyone, even the owners. If he wanted an amphitheatre on the site instead, accommodating 100,000 spectators, that is what he would get. Werner March was commissioned to do sketches for the new project which was to extend over an area of 325 acres. Diem, who was abroad, was summoned back by a telegram to help. They worked fast.

Five days after Hitler's inspection he told a meeting – Goebbels and Secretary of State Hans Pfundtner among those attending – that because 'practically all the nations of the world' would be at the Olympics the 'New Germany must provide evidence of its cultural accomplishments and ability'. In addition, Berlin needed 'spacious facilities for the assemblies and traditional festivals which are an important feature in Germany's modern development'. Was there anywhere better than the racecourse?

Lewald said he didn't think so.

Hitler decreed that the Games required a lot of the land under lease by the racecourse and it would be taken over. The owners were offered compensation.

At that moment, the 1936 Olympic Games found their home.[13]

March brought Hitler a topographical map and showed him an area big enough to accommodate half a million people for assemblies, festivals and processions. Hitler was pleased, but a curious problem arose: that of symmetry. If they abandoned the old stadium and sited the new one 150 metres away it would be parallel to the rod-like avenue from Unter den Linden out to Charlottenburg and the countryside. Hitler liked symmetry and said *do that*.

The new stadium could be built vast enough to accommodate however many spectators Hitler wanted. No doubt for further reasons of symmetry – and practicality, because every spectator had to be able to see the events – the number 100,000 felt right.

March broached the subject of a gigantic Olympic bell to toll the beginning and end of the Games, and do so from a bell tower so tall it would be visible from many points in the city.

The Reich was now in charge of the whole construction project. The entire direction of the execution of the tremendous project was in the hands of the Minister of the Interior [Pfundtner]. It was necessary, first, for the Minister to create the legal prerequisites necessary for the commencement of construction. Then, as construction chief, he had to ensure that the new structure should blend harmoniously with the architecture of Berlin. He was responsible for the athletic organisation, the building of the approaches, and the technical equipment. He was furthermore entrusted with the task of welding these parts into a pleasing, artistic and organic whole. His most important responsibility was to make sure that this tremendous programme was carried out within the short time before the beginning of the Olympic Games. This would require the utmost efforts on the part of all concerned. State Secretary Pfundtner devoted himself untiringly to the negotiations for the acquisition of the necessary grounds. Within the surprisingly short period of eleven weeks, he had clarified all legal points.[14]

Pfundtner had a rounded face, all jowels, with a tuft of hair peeking over the back of his head. He couldn't help looking like a thug.

Hitler provided the broad sweep, kept an eye on the detail and the whole project went on to something resembling a war footing. Its scope, character and extent *were* the same as waging a war.

The main entrance, the Olympic Gate, was to have fifty-two turnstiles for the paying public and the two wings beside them would contain 'every possible provision for the reception and the care of the spectators'. This would include 'one large office for replying to enquiries and giving information, one office for the exchange of tickets, one medical station for giving first aid, one police office, a room for the checking of the tickets sold, accommodation for the control officials and the cleaners, and three dwellings for the officials of the stadium administration'. The south entrance would have twenty-eight turnstiles. Cumulatively, the 100,000 could buy tickets and enter within an hour.

The new stadium's central area, where the competitions took place, would be excavated far below ground level giving it a deceptive appearance from the outside: because of the excavation it was much bigger than the external walls suggested. Shaped like an enormous oblong bowl, it would be divided into two 'rings', one dug 13 metres down, the other rising 16 metres. That would allow the comings and goings of the 100,000-strong crowd to be carried out 'in two distinct halves in half the time required if only the surface arrangement were available. The division of the spectator traffic is helped further by the twenty gangway stairs to the upper ring and the twenty passages to the lower ring arranged round the oval at equal distances from each other. The stream of spectators is still further divided by means of the colonnades within and outside the arena. In order furthermore to restrict the unnecessary crossing of the streams of spectators to a minimum there have been placed in these colonnades, for each block of seats, public conveniences, refreshment rooms, and stands for the sale of programmes.'[15]

A tunnel 65 feet wide took officials from outside the stadium to the central arena. Another tunnel, named for the Marathon, would be used by the marathon runners at the end of their event, by Hitler, by marching groups like the national delegates at the Opening Ceremony and for the transport of what the organisers termed apparatus and implements.

In November, Döberitz, far out into the countryside along the Hamburg road, was confirmed as the site for the Olympic Village for male competitors.

A month later Hitler approved plans for the whole area around the stadium, to be known as the Reich Sports Field. It would comprise a big swimming pool, hockey pitches, a stone-clad House of German Sport for the indoor events, a vast, open space called the May Field and all harmonised into the landscape. Never before had a sporting event been catered for on such a scale. The women competitors were to be accommodated in another stone-clad building beside the House of German Sport.

We decided to follow the example of our 1932 predecessors in solving the problem of providing quarters for the women competitors. The Americans had placed one of the finest hotels at the disposal of the women. Although this hotel was wonderfully situated, equipped and managed, it still did not please all the women competitors who lived in it. This, however, was not due to any deficiencies in the hotel, but merely to the fact that after long and intense training, women are very high strung immediately before difficult contests. We wished the quarters to be separate from those of the men and also outside the radius of the metropolitan traffic. We were fortunate enough to possess an entirely new, large students' dormitory, the 'Frisian House' [Friesenhaus] in a part of the Reich Sports Field far away from traffic.

The women thus had quarters much nearer to the contest sites and to the streets of the city than the Olympic Village. They could reach the centre of the city in a few minutes. The most beautiful athletics fields and training grounds were directly in front of their doors. At the same time this dormitory was surrounded by woods. Despite the proximity of the principal contest sites, it resembled a secluded island.[16]

The Official Report came (no doubt unwittingly) close to humour when it added: 'We could do nothing to change the rather barrack-like impression which the large structure made on some girls. The resounding noise in the corridors, which disturbed many of them, was due, however, more to the way some of the women competitors walked than to the construction of the building.'

Invitations to compete went out to the various countries' National Olympic Committees and nine days later Finland and Italy became the first to accept.

In January 1934 Goebbels formed a committee to look after the more general publicity, a euphemism for the sophisticated, meticulous portrayal of Hitler and his Germany. The Organising Committee handled the normal traffic of Olympic news. Subcommittees dealt with the press, radio, film and art. The latter was particularly important, no doubt because Hitler regarded himself as an artist, a judge of art and believed art was important. A second meeting, chaired by Goebbels, discussed how 'to emphasise and develop the artistic aspect in decorating the Capital City for the Games, to enlist the talents of German artists for the designing of posters, diplomas and medals, and to combine the Olympic Art Exhibition with a large national display which would bear the title "Germany"'.[17]

During this meeting someone raised the possibility of having a torch relay from Greece to Berlin. It must have seemed like just another item on the agenda, novel and worth some consideration. Those round the table surely cannot have understood they had hit upon something of such simplicity and profundity that it would become a defining symbol of the whole Olympic movement, carefully preserved at every subsequent Games; that the arrival of the flame would bring every host city into physical contact with Greece and the Games' very origins; that the ritual act of lighting the bowl in the Olympic stadium with the flame of the final runner would represent an instant of light in an often dark world.

The political theme sharpened. A mass meeting at Madison Square Garden, New York, condemned Hitler and the direction Germany had taken. A mock trial convicted him; the indictment read: 'We declare that the Hitler government is compelling the German people to turn back from civilisation to an antiquated and barbarous despotism which menaces the progress of mankind towards peace and freedom, and is a present threat against civilised life throughout the world.' Timed to mark the first anniversary of Hitler's ascent to power, it attracted a wide range of people including former Mayor Fiorello LaGuardia, the editor of a Jewish paper and Samuel Seabury of the American bar who put the case against Hitler in a great, echoing oration.

Gustavus Kirby, the American Olympic Committee's treasurer, described the official German policy of discriminating against Jewish sportspeople. When he said, in condemnation, that the swastika, an overt political symbol, was being associated with the Games, the audience booed and hissed in his support. When he demanded that Jewish sportspeople be allowed to try and qualify for the German teams he was loudly applauded.[18] The big question was alive now: to go to Berlin or not?

In April the International Amateur Athletics Federation approved plans for the stadium's arena.

The IOC met in Athens and Baillet-Latour gave a progress report. 'The two most important questions appearing on the agenda of the session last year,' he said, 'were the concession of the guarantees, demanded from the German Olympic Committee, which have permitted the holding of the Games of the XIth Olympiad in Berlin, and the study of the means of combating semi-professionalism. The repeated assurances that these guarantees are being respected, given to certain National Olympic Committees both by our German colleagues and by the Sports Director of the Reich, allow us to reckon on the participation of all countries and it is with the hope of a brilliant success that your Executive Committee have pursued, with the Organising Committee and the international federations, the study of the programme of the Games which will be submitted to you.'

Baillet-Latour described a visit he had made to Rome where he had the honour of an interview with Mussolini who gave him 'the opportunity of judging for myself the care which the Duce takes in providing "l'Education Physique" in Italy with the most perfect resources. The progress attained in the realm of sports in Italy is but the just result of a marvellous organisation.'

Baillet-Latour found himself trapped among the competing ideologies of the 1930s which veered hard right and left. Germany had embraced Nazism, Italy Fascism, Spain was turning Fascist, and Stalin was applying brutal coercion in the construction of a communist state – and he was not alone. Who knew how to cope with the present? Who knew what the future would bring? Baillet-Latour could not and did not because there were no precedents. Better, perhaps, to salute Mussolini's supposedly wholesome fitness programme and leave it at that. Baillet-Latour would find holding the middle ground harder and harder.

Lewald reported on the state of preparations, covering the demolition of the racecourse, the erection of new buildings beside the stadium, progress on the Olympic Village and the swimming pool, the organising of the yachting at Kiel on the Baltic coast. He raised the idea of the torch relay from Olympia to the Marathon Tower at the stadium. If it was approved, he asked the Olympic Committees of the countries it would pass through – Greece, Bulgaria, Yugoslavia, Hungary, Austria and Czechoslovakia – to organise athletes to take part.

Without any warning Hitler struck at the heart of the 2 million storm troopers who were threatening to get out of control. Their leader, Ernst Röhm, was dragged out of bed and shot, and so were countless others in what became known as the 'Night of the Long Knives'.

Gretel Bergmann, in London, will never forget that day. Enrolled on a language course, she competed in the high jump at the British Championships and won. Her father travelled over to watch. 'We celebrated and had a wonderful time. My father invited a few of my friends for lunch and then we went back in a taxi and on the way we saw evening newspaper placards: *Extra! Extra! Extra!* We asked the cab driver what this was all about and he said "It's the Nazis killing each other off." It was the day when Hitler had I don't know how many SA men shot, it was 30 June, and we thought it might be the beginning of the end of the Nazi regime. Then we got to the hotel.'

Once in his room her father gave her a chilling message – although from which body is not clear – that she should return to Germany. 'He said I had been asked to go back and I said, "No, I'm not going." He said, "I'm not forcing you to do anything but just listen to what I have to say." And he told me what they had told him. He said that they were *hinting.* I don't think they were absolutely telling him, but hinting at it – and in Germany then a hint was enough. You did what you were told or else.'[19] In her own words she had been 'blackmailed under threats to my family and the whole Jewish sports movement. I had absolutely no choice but do what I was told. I packed my bags and sailed with him the next day.'[20]

At this stage the idea 'that I might have to represent Nazi Germany sickened me and yet I desperately wanted the chance to compete. My motivation was different from that of any other athlete and not at all compatible with the Olympic ideals. I wanted to show what a Jew could do, and I wanted to use my talent as a weapon against Nazi ideology.'

The Germans had their token Jew and, like Lewald, would exploit her as they liked, holding her up to counter international and IOC misgivings about anti-Semitism by saying she was training for their Olympic team! Between now and the Games Gretel received at least four standard letters instructing her to go to the big German national training camp at Ettlingen, near Karlsruhe. 'I figured I'd better go or else.' None of this extended to a reversal of the 'Aryan paragraph' covering membership of athletics clubs.

Training when I got back from Britain? That is a very interesting thing. I was so completely unaware of anything like this – you're Catholic, you're Jewish, you're this, you're that – it didn't matter. There was never any unpleasantness in any of the clubs that I belonged to. We all got along beautifully and then – bingo.

I was an official member of the German Olympic team and I was not allowed in any stadium or a gym or anything because I was Jewish (except once at Hanover in 1934, twice in 1935 and once at Ettlingen). And the only time I had training was when they sent us to this Olympic training camp for three days or four days once a year. It was a very bad time and, you know, every time I had to go to those training camps there were always different people involved, different girls, so they tried out everybody. I thought, "Maybe this bunch will hate me, maybe this bunch will call me a dirty Jew", and it never happened. We got along so well it was unbelievable.

[Apart from that] I could train in the corner of a field: we tried to get an acre of land where we could but after a while everybody was so concerned about what was going on that that was not important anymore. We played field handball on it for a little while but it died off very quickly.

I couldn't train at all until I was invited to come to Stuttgart where there was an organisation set up by Jewish soldiers from the First World War and it branched off into a kind of sports organisation. They allowed me to train there so I travelled to Stuttgart a few times every month but there was no coach there. Between 1930 and 1933 I used to go to one of the best coaches in Germany for training and of course I had a great crush on this guy and tried to do as well as I could to impress him – but, after the Nuremberg Laws, nothing for any Jew. We were not allowed in even as spectators. You could not be in any public place.[21]

Behind all this hangs a tale, one of the most astonishing in all Olympic history.

A high-jumper called Dora Ratjen was, Bergmann says, 'always at the training camps and she was always assigned to be my room-mate. I never suspected anything. I just said "she's kind of weird" but she was a nice kid, we got along very well. I never looked when she undressed or most likely she never got undressed in front of me completely. We had this huge shower room and we all took our showers in there and she never came in, she always went into this little room which had a bath. That was supposed to be off-limits to us but she went in there.'

Dora Ratjen was a man. How the Nazis came to coerce him into competing as a woman will be explored later. 'Maybe she/he shaved in there, I don't know. All the girls thought she was a little unusual. Pretty deep voice, and they made fun of her.'[22] The surviving film of Ratjen jumping gives an ambiguous impression, because if you already know the truth you look for confirmation (and doubtless find it), but if you don't know there are precious few clues. His legs were slender and the muscles show under stress, but then women's do, too. He wears a blouse and appears to have small breasts. His face is slightly square, slightly mannish and appears much more so in head-and-shoulders photographs. His mop of dark hair is distinctly unfeminine but it isn't particularly masculine either. In sum, there is not enough visible evidence to decide it either way, and so the status quo was maintained. Picked as a woman, he was able to compete as a woman.

Afghanistan became the thirtieth nation to accept Germany's invitation.

The Games were to be people-friendly, with air and train fares reduced for athletes and spectators, and a competition for Olympic poster designs.

In August, von Hindenburg died at the age of eighty-seven and Hitler waited no longer than three hours to abolish the office of president. He decreed that from this moment he would be known as Führer,[23] Reich Chancellor and Supreme Commander of the Armed Forces. He put this to a national plebiscite and received a 90 per cent endorsement. Germany had delivered herself into the hands of a primitive man with strange powers.

The patronage of the Games passed to him as the new head of state, which is how he threw a tantrum about the stadium of glass and said he wouldn't open the Games in a place like that (see n. 13).

On 29 September America accepted their invitation.[24]

The first plans for the torch relay and its route went out:

Greece	(Olympia–Athens–Saloniki)	1,108km
Bulgaria	(Sofia–Zaribrod)	238km
Yugoslavia	(Nis–Belgrade–Novisad)	575km
Hungary	(Szeged–Budapest–Oroszavar)	386km
Austria	(Karlburg–Vienna–Waidhofen)	219km
Czechoslovakia	(Tabor–Prague–Teplice)	282km
Germany	(Dresden–Liebenwerda–Berlin)	267km
		Total 3,075km

The route was divided into sections of 1 kilometre and a different runner would be assigned to cover each, the flame being passed from one to the next and forming a great chain extending across Europe. The Olympic countries taking part 'were authorised to make special provisions such as increasing the stretches in thinly populated sections or allowing more time for traversing difficult districts. To ensure the smooth progress of the run, each participant was required not only to be acquainted with his own stretch but the following one as well so that he could continue in the case of an unforeseen emergency.'[25]

The flame had to stay alight. Expert historical advice was sought and initially it seemed the original Greek method – using only fagots of a certain wood found at Ephesus, whose pith retained fire – might be the solution, but these fagots didn't burn for long enough. In an emergency, a runner would be covering 2 kilometres and that meant the flame had to burn for 10 minutes. The problem was exacerbated by the fact that various different torches could not be carried in the open and keep burning whatever the weather – 'heat, rain, storms' – never mind for 10 minutes.

The German Organising Committee commissioned their own magnesium torches, each containing two fuses so that if one failed the other would reignite it. The top of the torches contained a special substance enabling rapid ignition in the flame's transfer from runner to runner.[26] Sample torches were sent to the six Olympic countries for trials.

The Olympic flame in the stadium posed a much bigger problem because it had to burn throughout the Games – 363 hours – once it had been lit by the 3,075th and last runner. The organisers wanted the flame to be very visible and settled on a height of 3 metres. They intended to use lighting gas from the Berlin Municipal Works but that didn't give the right flame and to get enough of it would require construction of a pipeline to the stadium costing 300,000 Reichsmarks: a Volkswagen car was 1,000 Reichsmarks, the average weekly wage 35 and, even with Hitler's backing, 300,000 was a fortune. Worse, this ordinary gas contained chemical and oil substances that created smoke, giving rise to the potential scenario of thousands of spectators coughing even if they could see through it. Attempts to use oil pressure burners, coal tar and benzol all failed. To get the height of the flame right and sustain it needed from 350 to 400 tons of heavy benzol, costing 36,000 Reichsmarks. Eventually a company in Hannover solved the problem by providing new liquid propane gas.

In October 1934 the official Olympic poster was selected and the warrior at the Brandenburg Gate became an enduring icon.[27] Hitler visited the Reich Sports Field and the stadium to inspect progress and keep his eye on the details, expressing 'several wishes for slight changes'. There was no mistaking the subtext: Hitler was watching. More than that he had the sort of mind which remembered what he had asked for, and if you had not done it, he would not forget.

The promotion of the Games within Germany started with a touring exhibition in an Olympic caravan designed to generate interest for the event in every citizen under the slogan

OLYMPIA, A NATIONAL MISSION

'It was intended that no German should feel himself merely to be a visitor at the Games but that everyone should share in the responsibility of presenting them.'[28]

Goebbels knew his craft and, club-footed or not, was just getting into his stride.

Chapter 3

NO JEWS OR DOGS ALLOWED

Removal of the Games is possible in case agreements are not kept. Hitherto such a case has never occurred in the history of the Olympics.

Count Baillet-Latour, President, IOC

I n the winter of 1935 the national Olympic Committees received details of the accommodation for the Games. An Olympic exhibition opened in Berlin, and remained open until the spring. An Olympic Publicity Week, run by a Nazi leisure organisation, preferred 'Strength Through Joy'. Training areas were being selected for the athletes before and during the Games. A news service charted progress in fourteen languages.

The pace was quickening and that kept the twin themes of sport and politics flowing in something approaching tandem. It does not make for a smooth narrative because the staccato sequence of events in both strands were not themselves smooth.

By now Hitler held Germany in an iron grip. All news was heavily censored so that an ordinary citizen had no informed perspective about anything. German cultural and artistic life, once so wonderfully vibrant and challenging in so many spheres, lay dead; in its place Hitler put his hatred of Jews and communists. And he had begun to rearm, something in theory under the control of the Treaty of Versailles. So he did it in secret.

In early March 1935 Britain's Ambassador in Berlin, Sir Eric Phipps, a man who understood the nature of Hitler and Hitlerism perfectly well, told the Foreign Office in London he had confidential information: inside a month the Germans expected their air force to be stronger than that of France, and within a year their army to be stronger than the French army. Nor would they stop there. Phipps added that his confidant 'expressed intense surprise that France had allowed Germany to get so strong'.

On 15 March the French government doubled military service to two years and next day Hitler summoned Phipps to say that in response conscription would be introduced in Germany immediately, and that the country would have half a million men under arms.

At the end of the month in the Saarland, the coal-rich area on the French border taken over by the League of Nations after the First World War where France was allowed to exploit the mines for fifteen years as reparations, 99 per cent of the population voted for reunification with Germany – more, William Shirer noted, than anticipated, although he felt most voted for it in case anyone found out they hadn't. Shirer added: 'Hitler has said, and repeated in a broadcast, that the Saar was the last territorial bone of contention with France. We shall see . . .'.[1]

Arguably, and in hindsight, the inevitability of a world war began here, because Hitler had got away with it. From 1933 many did not need hindsight to see through him, but there was a problem with that. Since the Western powers had surrendered the Saarland he sensed weakness: for all the sane reasons so soon after the slaughter of the First World War, they preferred appeasement to confrontation. That gave him room to manoeuvre, and he'd created a disciplined, subservient, heavily militarised nation to use as an instrument to exploit it.

America's Ambassador, William E. Dodds, had studied in Leipzig and arrived in Berlin hoping to bring the two countries closer but, like Phipps, he understood Hitler. Over the next four years his frustration mounted to the point where he felt open bitterness and hostility to the Nazis and resigned. Ignoring all conventions about customary farewell for such dignitaries, the Nazis completely ignored his departure. Albeit he had tried to do so on an almost daily basis, Dodds had not been able to convince Washington of what Germany was actually doing and what it meant. Hitler was left with a free hand.

The Olympics provided beautiful international camouflage, because they seemed to show that Germany was *not* really like that at all while, at the same time, making Germans feel good about themselves and their Führer. Meanwhile, the British Foreign Office took care not to become enmeshed in the question of whether a British team should go to the Olympics, and the British Olympic Committee was nothing to do with the government, anyway (as Margaret Thatcher was to discover in 1980 when she tried unsuccessfully to get a British boycott of the Moscow Games).

The IOC met in Oslo and Baillet-Latour, anxious to reassure all concerned, said Dr Diem had methodically

carried out the preparatory work that has enabled him to present you with the complete programme much earlier than his predecessors have been able to do.

He has profited from the experiences of Amsterdam and Los Angeles and you can be assured he has set up a perfect organisation. . . . . Athletes are training enthusiastically on land, in water, on ice, on the snowy slopes of mountains, and even in the air. Painters, sculptors, engravers, musicians, men of letters and poets are working equally to bring to the fete of physical strength a contribution of the arts and of letters imbued with the athletic ideal. Regional Games have permitted the new countries to cherish the hope of sending their representatives to mingle with those of older countries. . . .

God grant that the XIth Olympiad may be the dawn of an era of peace marked by an 'entente cordiale' between the youth of all nations working together to assure in the future the prosperity and happiness of their homes.[2]

Hitler moved into Saarbrücken, symbolically as well as physically repossessing the town on a wet day when, surrounded by military officers, he strode forward smiling to take a review of the troops. He had made himself room for manoeuvre: fomenting a breakdown of government in Austria to bring it into the Reich, reclaiming the German minorities in Czechoslovakia for the Reich, provoking trouble round the Danzig corridor in Poland.[3] Rational people could not believe they were being carried towards another war and instinctively recoiled into something approaching denial.

This is the conflicted position in which Baillet-Latour found himself. He never did find a way out of it. Yet the various national Olympic Committees, unable to live in ethical isolation however hard they aspired to it, had to reflect the growing unease in their own countries – not about another, un-thinkable war but whether to go to Berlin or not for a sporting event meant to celebrate the antithesis of the Nazi creed.

The Americans had already given strong voice to such misgivings in the New York meeting. Now others were, too. The Czechoslovaks, harbouring doubts from the beginning, said publicly they would not send a team, although eventually they did; the same went for Yugoslavia. The initial French reaction had been not to go. The Swedes were torn, a forceful movement developing against. Many Swedes thoroughly disliked German National Socialism, which was utterly alien to their way of thinking and living. Several South American countries hesitated and that perplexed the Germans because their governments seemed so pro-German. Brazil compensated by sending two distinct teams. In December 1934, Great Britain had decided to go, but political pressures compelled the British Olympic Committee and the government to hold a review. It confirmed participation, although a sense of unease persisted and would not go away.

As the time shortened to the Games, now only a year away, a third theme became evident as competitors all over the world prepared regardless of what their governments and Olympic Committees said. They could do nothing else and there is not much evidence that they wanted to do anything else.

That is how in St Louis, Missouri, a tall, strong teenager called Helen Stephens from Fulton quite naturally entered the long jump, the shot-put and the 50-metre sprint at the American Athletic Union's championships. She won the long jump and shot, itself remarkable for an unknown seventeen-year-old, but the sprint subsequently assumed international importance. In it Stephens met a runner known as Stella Walsh. Born in Poland, her family emigrated when she was two although in international competitions she always ran for Poland because repeated attempts to secure American citizenship failed. She therefore won the 100 metres as a Pole in the 1932 Games and would compete as a Pole again in Berlin. Stephens had Stella's picture on the wall for the purpose of sticking pins in it.

As they prepared Stephens felt nervous. She wore a blue gym suit made for her by her mother, grey sweat pants from a boy in her high school team, running shoes from another boy. Despite her nerves she was confident – and won the race. She'd claim that Walsh called her 'a greenie from the sticks', that Walsh said she had jumped the gun, and that she said to Walsh, 'Come to Fulton and I'll run against you even across a ploughed field.'[4]

Walsh didn't.

They would run against each other again but not until one August afternoon in 1936 in the stone-clad stadium, and when they did, something much more than a bitter Olympic rivalry was born. Both were accused of being men.

In the spring Jews were excluded from the 'gardens of Bad Dürkheim, the swimming pools and baths of Schweinfurt, the municipal baths of Karlsruhe, Freiburg, Gladbach, and Dortmund. Even the streetcars of Magdeburg were closed to Jews.' In spite of this the President of the American Olympic Committee, Avery Brundage, insisted that Germany would abide by its 'unqualified assurances of non-discrimination'.[5] Brundage, a controversial figure, had competed in the 1912 Games, graduated from the University of Illinois with a degree in civil engineering and founded a construction company which did a lot of work around Chicago. Autocratic by nature, he showed no interest in the middle ground but trenchantly maintained a pro-German position.

Brundage said he had heard nothing of discrimination in Germany and there were no 'reports whatsoever, official or otherwise, that Germany has failed to give Jewish athletes a fair opportunity'. As long as Germany adhered to its promises, the American Olympic Committee had no right to 'interfere in its internal political, religious, or racial affairs'.[6] The US Embassy, reporting to the State Department, contradicted Brundage and

> by this time the Germans had managed by deft manipulation and sheer terror to transform the question of Jewish participation into a theoretical and not a practical matter. Many Jews who were potential competitors had left Germany because they knew they would not be able to train in the manner demanded of an Olympic contender. Lacking financial means and communal support, two critical components of Olympic preparation, those who remained faced such substantial psychological and personal handicaps that qualifying for a berth on a team became a virtual impossibility.[7]

Brundage's position could, and ought, to have been viewed as disingenuous. The Americans would not have been interfering if they said they didn't propose to go near it and, anyway, IOC member General Charles Sherrill would certainly interfere – but not yet. At this stage, however, Sherrill was quoted as saying he wasn't concerned 'one bit the way the Jews in Germany are being treated, any more than lynchings in the South of our own country'.

Frederick W. Rubien, secretary of the American Olympic Committee, was quoted as saying that 'Germans are not discriminating against Jews in their Olympic tryouts. The Jews are eliminated because they are not good enough as athletes. Why, there are not a dozen Jews in the world of Olympic caliber.'[8]

Brundage had his supporters including Sigfrid Edström, Swedish delegate to the IOC who wrote to him that he was against the persecution of the Jews but something had to be done because 'a great part of the German nation was led by the Jews and not by the Germans themselves. . . . They are intelligent and unscrupulous . . . they must be kept within certain limits.'[9]

Germany was rearming, Britain was rearming and, unusually, the Swiss parliament met in Bern in summer session. Although the congressmen agreed on a budget of 34 million francs for the country's defence they refused 36,000 to finance the Olympic team for Berlin. The conservative Swiss press rounded on the 'reds' for doing this and the German press rounded on the Swiss, accusing them of supporting a boycott as a protest against Nazi Germany. The Swiss Olympic Committee was in favour of going, the Swiss Workers' Federation of Gymnastics and Sport (Satus) against. They said:

> Its members would like to open the eyes of public opinion to the dangerous totalitarian and racist politics of the Third Reich. From international sporting meetings, they have met German workers' sporting associations

and learnt of their situation since Hitler came to power: interdictions, imprisonment etc. For the Satus activists, to take part in the Games is to work within the Nazi propaganda game.

From the 1930s sport has been used by the Fascist regimes as a cult for the national image. Hitler wants to use the Berlin Games to prove to the world the superiority of the Aryan race. For its part, the International Olympic Committee supports the streams of Nazi propaganda to assert its supremacy in the world of sport.

In Zurich, the IOC met the Swiss Olympic Committee and reiterated the assurances given by the German Olympic Committee.[10]

In Berlin 156,000 copies of the official poster were printed in four languages and circulated for free while in July, with the Games just thirteen months away, advance ticket sales began. In nineteen days they reached 1 million Reichsmarks. The Olympic housekeeping went on, every mosquito at the Olympic Village exterminated by the end of the month.

In athletic terms, Germany had sixteen districts each with their own championships. Württemberg was one and Bergmann competed in June, winning by jumping 1.56 metres. The following month the best German Jewish athletes, men and women, were told to attend a 'one-week training course in Ettlingen, and this must have been when I competed against Elfried Kaun – one of three times I was allowed to compete agaist Aryans'. Bergmann felt the move was 'strictly grandstanding on the world stage' because, while she could perform at the highest level and might nurse realistic hopes of an Olympic gold medal, the others were nowhere near that standard 'and the Nazis knew it'.[11] However, the week proved productive in different ways. Because they were all Jews they had a great deal in common and friendships were forged. Briefly, because they were together, they could 'forget the troubles of the outside world'. Bergmann came across a medical student who had ambitions as a sprinter. It seemed just another friendship but it wasn't. She would marry him and still be married to him half a century later. By then she'd have forgotten most of her German and have a New York accent.

In August the *New York Times* reported that foreign correspondents in Berlin were being officially obstructed in reporting because the government feared losing the Games and even felt some of the correspondents wanted that to happen. In fact, as the newspaper pointed out, correspondents helped the Organising Committee with translation work. A day later the paper reported that Bergmann had been excluded from the high jump in the German Championships, an important step to Olympic selection. Von Tschammer und Osten offered the classic *Catch 22* defence. Because she was

Jewish she couldn't belong to the German Athletic Association and because they ran the championships she could not take part. In the strictest terms the German Olympic Committee remained true to their promise: her exclusion was for non-membership.

A short while later the *New York Times* highlighted how the Germans were getting away with this.

NAZI OLYMPIC VOW KEPT TECHNICALLY.
In Theory Even Jews May Try For Team,
But All Except Hitlerites Are Handicapped[12]

Speaking in Vienna, Baillot-Latour adopted his fixed position. He explained that

removal of the Games is possible in case agreements are not kept. Hitherto such a case has never occurred in the history of the Olympics. I cannot imagine the German sports authorities not fulfilling their obligations. If it happened however that von Tschammer restricted training possibilities for 'non-Aryans' in the same way he did for the national championships and other sports competitions then the International Olympic Committee could – and would be compelled to – order the removal of the Games from Berlin. But I cannot believe things will develop in that direction, and hope the Olympic Games will go through in 1936 without any friction.[13]

Baillet-Latour must have known what was happening. Gretel Bergmann's experience highlights the public nature of anti-Semitism, the park signs ordering 'No Jews or Dogs Allowed', the people she knew who suddenly wouldn't talk to her, the feeling of 'being reduced to nothing'.

Diem, speaking in Paris, took up his stance. In the newspaper *France Soir* he said 'we have made a promise and you can rest assured we will keep it. That promise was that we will not make any distinction between race or religion during the Games. Jewish athletes will be received the same as others.' You needed to read that carefully because he did not say *German* Jews, a completely unsustainable claim. Of course the Jews in other teams would be received, for propaganda purposes and because a refusal to receive them would make the Berlin Games themselves unsustainable.

At Boston, Massachusetts, 1,500 people representing the town's Jewish organisations met at a hotel and laid down a resolution: 'This conference urges upon the Amateur Athletic Union to rescind conditional American acceptance of Germany's invitation to participate in the 1936 Olympic Games as a solemn obligation in defense of the spirit of sportsmanship and fair play and the principles of racial and national equality upon which the Olympic Games are founded.'

Far in the background, and quietly, the president of the north-east Ohio division of the Amateur Athletic Union, Lou N. Bloom, said that one of their leading sprinters, Jesse Owens, was to be summoned over allegations concerning his amateur status, a very serious matter. The principle of absolute amateur status for participants held athletics and the Olympics in a rigid vice – hence Baillet-Latour's preoccupation with it at the IOC meetings where it was given equal importance with the Berlin problem. Rumours circulated that Owens received money for work he hadn't done, because of his athletic ability. He worked for the Ohio House of Representatives and was paid $3 a day but received $159 between 9 June and 31 July as an honorary page.

On 15 August, Hitler banned German–Jewish weddings and a day later the London *Times* correspondent in Berlin, Norman Ebbutt, was expelled in retaliation for the British government's expulsion of some Nazi journalists. Ebbutt had been 'hated and feared for years because of his exhaustive knowledge of this country and of what was going on behind the scenes', Shirer wrote. In a touching farewell, some fifty foreign correspondents assembled at the Charlottenburg Station to see him off, although Nazi whispering warned them against it. Shirer found himself amused to note the correspondents *not* there, including a couple of well-known Americans. He watched as the platform crawled with Gestapo agents 'noting down our names and photographing us. Ebbutt terribly high-strung, but moved by our sincere, if boisterous, demonstration.'[14]

The Olympic bell was cast in the town of Bochum and, like the Olympic poster and the torch run, was a matter of enormous importance for the Organising Committee and the government. In early September a senior member of the Organising Committee covered the entire route of the proposed torch run in an enormous recce.

At Nuremberg Hitler announced a series of decrees which reduced Jews to subjects without rights and barred them from holding jobs in public services except the law and medicine. The Nuremberg Laws, as they became known, could scarcely be misunderstood.

The debate about the Games now spilled over from the [American] sports pages, where it was first raised, to the editorial pages, and from the meetings of the Amateur Athletic Union to the Congressional floor. The presence of an American team at the 1936 Olympic Games became a matter of national significance and remained so until the day the team set sail for Germany. In the twelve months preceding the Games reporters, columnists, sports writers, and editorial boards debated how an American presence at the Games would be interpreted and what was more likely to violate America's neutrality: boycotting or participating in the Games.[15]

Perhaps the view expressed by the *Norfolk Pilot*, Virginia, was typical of the domestic American mood. It wasn't 'the function of the Olympic Games to distribute clean bills of political health. Too many glass houses are involved.' That view held until the paper discovered anti-Semitic signs were decorating Garmish. The *Pilot* wanted a boycott.[16]

The twin themes converged on Helene Mayer, teaching at a fashionable girls' school in Oakland. Classified as a 'half Jew', her club in Offenbach had barred her under the 'non-Aryan' rule. The German Academic Exchange Council withdrew her grant but she came from a wealthy family, continued to live and fence in America and won the national championships from 1933 to 1935.

Like Bergmann, she could be exploited.

The *New York Times* reported the IOC had received a 'purported text' from the German Organising Committee inviting her to join the German fencing team. Von Tschammer und Osten claimed there would be two Jews, Mayer and (presumably) Bergmann, and as a consequence promises were being kept. However, Mayer sent a telegram to an official at the German Jewish Men's League in New York saying 'Have not received any such invitation from German Olympic Committee'.

If the Nazis intended to exploit Mayer, she intended to exploit them. Both sides knew the respective strengths and weaknesses of their positions. Their dispute became, in an exquisitely appropriate way, a fencing match complete with tactical advances and retreats, hits and misses, and many, many feints.[17]

An American magazine cabled her asking if she had been invited, whether the American team should go to Berlin, if she regarded herself as a refugee and would she comment on the Nazi newpapers that regularly reported her suicide. She replied sardonically that she had not received an invitation, couldn't answer as to whether Americans should go – none of her business – and certainly did not regard herself as a refugee. She added a feint, 'My suicides amuse me.'

Lewald journeyed to America to promote the Games and said he would be inviting her to the German trials in February 'with all expenses paid'. He said he hoped she had kept her form as a leading fencer – perhaps he was unaware of what she had done in the championships – because they wanted Jewish athletes of Olympic standard but 'we have none'. He was sure Americans would not want the Germans to have token Jews . . .

Mayer said that she had not received any communication from Lewald. Von Tschammer und Osten sent a letter to Sherrill reiterating that Mayer and Bergmann had been invited and would be given the same treatment as any other 'candidates' for the team 'although they are Jewesses'. He enclosed a copy of the letter that had been sent to Mayer although this might have been *the* letter to her and not a copy at all, meaning it had not been sent to her.

Mayer said she had not received any letter and added that she didn't believe a letter had been or would be sent.

That autumn Brundage and Sherrill journeyed to Germany and met Hitler. Sherrill insisted that the German Olympic team be open to Jewish athletes with, presumably, the implication that if it wasn't, American participation would come into question. Sherrill told the *San Francisco Chronicle* that he had gone to Germany with 'the purpose of getting at least one Jew on the German Olympic team'. Sherrill faced a delicate problem, as many others would, because, as he said, he would not countenance Germans lecturing him on the 'Negro situation' in the United States. He had not therefore discussed any 'obstacles' German Jewish athletes faced but only the principle of picking at least one – Mayer. The delicacy did not end there. Sherrill knew an American withdrawal risked a domestic anti-Semitic backlash. 'If our Jews force us to stay out of the Olympic Games they will be taking a great chance with their own comfort,' he said.

Still Mayer had received no invitation.

The German tactic seemed to wear her down and make her refuse to return – the ideal solution for the Nazis, simultaneously absolving them and removing the problem. Mayer seems to have seen that particular feint quickly and clearly.

Sonja Branting, the daughter of a former Swedish prime minister, told a meeting of the Manhattan division of the Women's International League for Peace and Freedom in New York that sending a team would be a dangerous step, not least because they would be subject to the 'most insidious Nazi propaganda'. A resolution opposing the team going was carried unanimously.

The President of the American Athletic Union, former Supreme Court Justice Jeremiah Mahoney, firmly against, spoke at a dinner with five hundred guests in honour of Branting. He described how some people 'went to Germany with the intention of keeping their eyes closed'. Pressed if he meant Brundage and Sherrill he said 'I didn't mention any names', although a little later he spoke of 'my dear friend Sherrill [who'd] spent four days with Hitler and patted him on the back and said "Old Sport Hitler"'.

Mahoney, of course, was not an athlete and had a very different perspective. He'd discover that from Benjamin Washington Johnson, a black freshman and sprinter (known, inevitably, as the Colombia Comet). In 1932, Johnson qualified for the American Olympic trials but his family were so poor they couldn't afford for him to go. It took a local appeal to raise the money. Since then he had proved good enough to beat Jesse Owens in a 60-yard dash and Ralph Metcalfe in a 100.

Mahoney went to Columbia University to gather support for a boycott but after he had spoken Johnson said he was for going: the conditions of blacks in the South were just as bad as those for Jews in Germany. 'It is futile and hypocritical that Judge Mahoney should attempt to clean up conditions in Germany before cleaning up similar conditions in America,' said Johnson.[18]

Mahoney remained undeterred. He wrote to Lewald in Berlin saying that if Germany did not have Jewish athletes of Olympic standard might that be because they are 'either dead, exiled or barred?' Of the Mayer case, he stressed it was not important whether she made the team but it *was* important that she be allowed to compete in the trials. He also pointed out that publicly she had been invited four times but actually she hadn't been invited at all.

Lewald tried to parry by saying Mayer had accepted the invitation and brandished a telegram from California which read 'Sickness delayed answering you and Tschammer [*sic*]. Acceptance left yesterday. Love'. It was signed 'H'.[19]

What moves lay behind all this – Mayer's biographer speaks of obfuscating 'lies and pointless statements by many spokesmen'[20] – have disappeared from the record, but Mayer felt she now had the force with her and made a thrust. She demanded restoration of her full German citizenship, lost under the Nuremberg Laws, as a condition of returning. The Laws stated: 'An individual of mixed Jewish blood is one who is descended from one or two grandparents who, racially, were full Jews . . . Full-blooded Jewish grandparents are those who belonged to the Jewish religious community.' Mayer had the grandparents but had never belonged to a religious community. She sought out the German Consul-General in San Francisco and asked him to negotiate a compromise, assuring him she felt in no way Jewish.[21] He recommended she be granted citizenship despite the grandparents factor.

Maybe pressure of unpleasant consequences was brought to bear on the family. Her mother cabled her saying her brothers were considered German citizens and so she was, too. One report suggested she had been obliged to disassociate herself from her Jewish father and say she was the product of her Aryan mother and an illicit affair with an Aryan father. Another report hinted that some test had been carried out and she had only 25 per cent Jewish blood.[22]

She would go to Berlin.

Fritz Wandt was eleven and his family were farmers at Dyrotz, a tiny place within walking distance of where the Olympic Village would be. They'd moved about a bit but his father considered Dyrotz 'as his elixir of life' and they came back in 1935. He leased land and literally made hay. At the military camp nearby 'there were a lot of horses and they needed hay and so we took ours and sold it to them. The Olympic Village was already under construction. We could see it when we came past it with our loads of hay. As early as this time, it was possible for all the nations that were going to take part in the three-day event to have their horses there and exercise on the military training area – very similar to the Olympic course. As a little boy you could get into the stables and watch the horses. I remember that the Swedish team – I think it was, or it may have been the Swiss – had their horses. That was the beginning of it for me, the beginning of my Olympic enthusiasm.' [23]

In September, a German football team called Ratibor played a Polish team in Upper Silesia – part of Germany, of course – in front of 50,000 people. After the game a member of that crowd, a Polish Jew called Edmund Baumgartner, was reportedly beaten to death by some Nazis. The facts remain disputed because other sources suggest Baumgartner played and when his team took the lead the crowd invaded the pitch, and he was beaten to death on it. Whatever the truth, newspapers spread the story far and wide, and the stark brutality of it seemed to encapsulate the Nazis. That it happened at a sporting event provoked its own kind of disquiet, heightened because the German team was due to play England on 4 December at White Hart Lane, London – the home of the Tottenham Hotspur team, which had wide Jewish support. The ominous mood heightened further with the announcement that the Germans would be bringing 10,000 of their own supporters.

Hitler intended to use the behaviour of the 10,000 as living proof that the Nazi regime was humane, normal and sporting. This might help to head off any boycotts of the Olympics, as would the presence in London at the time of the match of von Tschammer und Osten, Lewald and Diem. They would be lobbying hard.

On 5 November, three months to the day before the Winter Games opened, Baillet-Latour visited Hitler and had a long conversation with him. Judging the nuances of it, recapturing the hard and soft moments, is very difficult. Baillet-Latour pointed out that Munich newspapers worked under censorship and carried stories about signs at the Garmish recreation hall saying 'Jews Are Forbidden to Enter', words that violated the spirit which the Germans had assured the world they would respect. Hitler promised the signs would come down there, in Berlin and from centres of foreign tourists, but gave no promise about the special glass cases on the streets which displayed the rabidly anti-Semitic *Der Stürmer* magazine for people to read.

The German newspapers did not carry any of this and the Propaganda Ministry refused to issue a statement. The news emerged when Baillet-Latour met foreign correspondents and answered their questions. He was asked about a reported official German news service announcement that 'in future the winners of athletics contests in the Third Reich may only be those who master the Nazi ideology and who make known not only in athletic contests but also in national life that they stand up for that ideology'. He responded that the IOC did not concern itself with 'such details'. He condemned those in America who demanded a boycott. That led to a question about the Lake Shore Swimming Club of Chicago, in Berlin the month before to take on the provisional German team, who had found signs on all entrances to the pool 'Jews Are Not Wanted'. Baillet-Latour gave a politician's answer: what might have happened in the past did not interest him, only the future. He pointed out that a recent Germany–Hungary fencing match in Munich passed without incident and the Jewish fencers in the Hungarian team had been received with cordiality.

He was asked about the letter Mahoney had written to Lewald and said crisply: 'Mr Mahoney has demonstrated his lack of arguments by having recourse to personalities. It is of no value.'

Baillet-Latour restated his fixed position by issuing a declaration which began:

I have the honour to bring to your notice that the meeting I had with the Chancellor of Germany has convinced me that nothing will prevent the Games. The required conditions by the Olympic Charter have been respected by the German Olympic Committee. Visitors and participants can be assured they will receive a perfectly cordial welcome without the risk of experiencing anything which might offend their principles. The boycott campaigns . . . are political . . .

The President of the Maccabi World Union, an international Jewish sports organisation, wrote to Baillet-Latour from London in response to an earlier letter:

I am perfectly in agreement with you that the Olympic Games should not be confused with any political issues but would remark that I, in common with all other Jews and many non-Jews, look upon the state of affairs in Germany today from the point of view of general humanity and social decency.

The Maccabi Movement has never attempted to question the decision of the IOC as to the venue of the Olympic Games, but we certainly do wish to urge all Jewish sportsmen, for their own self respect, to refrain from competing in a country where they are discriminated against as a race and our Jewish brethren treated with unexampled brutality.

As a sports Organisation, we hope we understand the meaning of the words 'sport' and 'sportsmanship'! It is for this reason that we cannot as Jews accept lightly the situation created by the Olympic Games being held in Germany.

Finally, may I thank you for your sympathetic letter and express the hope that our attitude in this matter will not be misconstrued?

I am, Sir,
Yours faithfully,
S. Brodetsky
PRESIDENT

Baillet-Latour, now back in Lausanne after his visit to Hitler, responded.

I thank you for your letter of the 12th of November and am very happy about the Maccabi World Union's and the IOC's understanding of the meaning of the words 'sport' and 'sportsmanship,' and [am] in perfect agreement that the Olympic Games should not be confused with any political issues [and] share the same opinion on a question which has been misunderstood by so many others who have interfered in this matter.

The Maccabi World Union does not, as you say, question the decision of the IOC as to the venue of the Olympic Games.

The IOC holds the view that no athlete can be prevented from taking part in the Games but admits that nobody can be forced to go to Germany if he does not wish to do so.

As a proof I will quote what I wrote a few days ago to Mr. Avery Brundage, President of the American Olympic Association: 'It goes without saying that the IOC, respecting the individual liberty of everyone, does in no way wish to coerce those – Christian or Jews – who, for personal reasons, which obviously concern them alone, may possibly object to go to Germany.'

You may be assured that your attitude in this matter is not misconstrued.

In full agreement with you, I remain

Yours sincerely
Baillet-Latour

The England *v.* Germany match caused consternation and controversy. There was a poster campaign against the match by the British Anti-Nazi Council, the Foreign Office and the Home Office tried to offload the problem on to each other, demonstrations were promised and many people adopted a traditional stance: politics and sport must be kept apart. Others thought the match would be a chance to improve relations with Germany. In the event, the 10,000 came and behaved impeccably, the match was played quite normally and Germany lost 3–0. Von Tschammer und Osten made gracious speeches complimenting England and talking of the spirit of sporting friendship that existed between the two countries while Lewald pointed out that work on the Olympic Village proceeded apace.

Johnson, Owens and Metcalfe wrote to Brundage saying they wanted the American team to go. Another sprinter, Marty Glickman, approached it from a different angle, and he was a Jew. He insisted his perspective was more typical: he was an athlete not a politician and of course he wanted to go, no question. The Olympics had been his goal from the earliest days when he first understood his sprinting ability. Bigotry against Jews had been going on for a long time and was, he knew, going on all over the place including America.[24]

The whole question demanded a proper resolution by the Amateur Athletic Union, whose officers duly met at the Hotel Commodore, New York, to debate a resolution for a boycott. It became a battlefield fought over so fiercely that only hunger and exhaustion beat down those attending. They retired to dinner with a gentleman's agreement that they would not continue until the following day.

Five hours after battle did resume – amid all manner of accusations of double-crossing, trickery and compromises – a vote was taken which Mahoney lost. He withdrew the resolution and, feeling his position as head of the American Athletic Union no longer tenable, resigned. Brundage was nominated as his replacement and unanimously elected. In his victory speech he set out again his fixed position: he would devote all his energies to getting the American team to Berlin.

As President of the American Olympic Committee as well, Brundage had moved into an immensely strong position. It was one he would occupy for the rest of his life.[25]

On 21 December Jewish doctors in Germany were forced to resign their posts in private hospitals.

The New Year began with news that advance ticket sales had reached 2 million Reichsmarks but it was the Olympic bell that grasped everyone's attention. It was cast,

16.5 tons of molten steel being necessary. Following the cooling, polishing, chasing and tuning, all of which required several weeks, the Olympic Bell was finished. It was pitched in E of the minor octave, and the first overtone lying in the interval of the minor third of the main tone was pitched in G so that the total effect was a minor tone. The plainly audible overtones resulting from the strokes of the clapper combined with the mighty undertone to produce a rich, full sound.[26]

It had a diameter of 9.10 feet, a height of 8.78 feet and weighed 21,197 lb. Between 16 and 26 January it was transported from Bochum to Berlin and its slow but imperious progress created enormous interest. At Bielefeld it was 'escorted into the town by a squadron of the National Socialist Motor Corps as well as runners. Members of the Municipal Administration and of the Reich Association for Physical Training made speeches of welcome, characterising the Bell as the herald of Olympic peace and honourable competition.'

At Brunswick 'a festive reception was arranged on the Market Square, the band of the Air Force providing music and Municipal Councillor Mehlis delivering an address of welcome. The radio broadcasting stations in Western and Central Germany informed their hearers about the transportation of the Bell to Berlin, and the festivities and demonstrations which were held in various towns along the route. The sirens of the factories were blown and church bells pealed in greeting.'

On the way to Potsdam, the town on the outskirts of Berlin, a wooden bridge had to be reinforced. In Potsdam, 'the band of the Labour Service, political organisations and thousands of people thronged the streets to greet the Olympic symbol, the police department having installed special lighting effects on the large town square'.

The bell inched into Berlin to an official reception. 'Accompanied by large crowds of pedestrians and cyclists and joyfully greeted from all sides', the procession moved past 1,600 members of the Hitler Youth while '45 youths from the Reich Association for Physical Training awaited the arrival with flags and pennants'. It progressed to the Brandenburg Gate and went down Unter den Linden to a square where it 'was presented with fitting ceremony to the Organising Committee'.[27] The bell stood as a symbol of the Games, together with the five rings, the oath and the flame. On it bystanders could read the great, historic Olympic call: 'I summon the youth of the world' which had been forged into it.

On 6 February, Hitler declared the Winter Games at Garmisch open. The picturesque Bavarian resort, dwarfed by the Alpspitz mountain at 2,628 metres with the Zugspitz further away rising 2,966 metres, lay clad in snow. Hitler, sitting in the grandstand with Goebbels beside him, leant down to receive notebooks, postcards and pieces of paper from those entreating him for his autograph. He smiled broadly.

These fourth Winter Games were very much the younger sibling. Alpine skiers made their debut, taking their place among the skaters, Nordic ski racers, curlers, two- and four-man bobsleigh teams, speed skaters and ice hockey teams. Therein lay a paradox.

Rudi Ball, regarded as Germany's best ice hockey player, was a Jew who had fled the country as the anti-Semitism became a political reality. Officially invited back, he returned a month before to lead the team. That this happened without provoking much comment or affecting potential boycotts of Berlin can only be explained by the humble status of the Winter Games.

During the Garmisch events a lot of people in military uniform milled around and a lot of people gave a lot of Nazi salutes. Berlin would be just the same. At the Opening Ceremony, as the parade of nations entered the main stadium, most of the crowd gave the salute, as did many of the competitors. Germany's Maxi Herber and Ernst Baier won the pairs skating and, at the medal ceremony, stood on the top rung of the podium, saluting ostentatiously.

Internal IOC politics reared its head, too. Commodore Lee Jahncke, an American member and one-time assistant secretary in the US Navy and by ancestry a German Protestant, held strong views against Berlin. He had been exchanging postal broadsides with Baillet-Latour and, when the IOC met at Garmisch, Baillet-Latour

after having spoken on the campaign being conducted in the United States against American participation . . . informed his colleagues about the intervention . . . of Mr Lee Jahncke, who by a public announcement, proved that he was opposed to the opinions unanimously held by Members of the International Olympic Committee. The President read the letter which he had written to the American Members, the letter of Mr Lee Jahncke and his own reply.

The Members, who objected strongly to the attitude of Mr Lee Jahncke in view of the fact that he had clearly infringed upon the Status of the International Olympic Committee in betraying the interests of the Committee and in failing to preserve a sense of decorum toward his colleagues, unanimously requested the President to make known to all Members the correspondence which had taken place between himself and Mr Lee Jahncke in order that a decision might be reached regarding the matter at the first Meeting in Berlin.[28]

In the restrained terminology of the time this represented strong stuff and before Berlin Jahncke became the only member in IOC history to be expelled. Brundage replaced him, consolidating his own power base.

At the meeting Lewald gave a progress report on Berlin and said the current estimation for officials and competitors was about ten thousand.

The timetable to Berlin and the Opening Ceremony there on 1 August ticked insistently now, each week bringing it closer.

On 13 February, Helene Mayer boarded the luxury liner SS *Bremen* in New York, bound for Germany and her family. She had not seen them for four years, and not been in the country since Hitler got hold of it.

The twin currents of sport and politics flowed into one another, as they had always been destined to do.

After Garmisch the official word went out to the German media that 'no comments should be made regarding Mayer's non-Aryan ancestry or her expectations for a gold medal at the Olympics'. Rudi Ball's presence had not made much difference to the ice hockey team because Great Britain took the gold, Canada the silver and America the bronze, but Mayer might be more problematical.

In March the torches were distributed to the countries through which the relay runners would pass.

In Paris some leading French sports people met and passed a resolution requesting the French government not to provide funds for the team. A former minister presided and one speaker claimed the Nazis were both exploiting the Games for propaganda and using them to raise money for themselves.

The French cycling authority, La Commission Sportive de l'Union Vélocipédique de France, allocating resources for 1936, decreed that their professionals would compete for a total of 107,000 francs in prize money but their Olympic team would receive no funding.

In Sweden 6,000 people prepared to go as spectators while their Olympic Committee prepared to send a large team (150), but two teams of gymnasts, each 600 strong, were also going to take part in non-competitive displays and the Swedish Olympic Committee made negative noises about that. After strong words they disclaimed all responsibility for them. 'They will receive no pecuniary support, will not be members of the Olympic team and may not stay in the Olympic village.'[29]

Thereby hangs a tale and one, no doubt, among many. Werner Schwieger, born in 1913 in the Wedding district of Berlin, would take part in these gymnastic displays. In 1927 he went to art college and was taught to paint in watercolours. He went twice a week on a sort of scholarship. He worked, however, as a foundry pattern maker, creating wooden and metal patterns for industrial machines.

From the age of twelve he had been a member of his local gymnastics club before moving on to the club for all Berlin, where he also did track and field sports. He *also* went to a class painting the animals in the Natural History Museum and after more than a year the teacher said, 'You can come and take part in my nude painting class.' Schwieger was delighted because not everybody received invitations and he had visions of beautiful models. When he arrived for the first time he saw the model was aged between forty-five and fifty and had hanging breasts. He took his easel into a corner of the room and began to paint. After half an hour the teacher inspected his work and found Schwieger had been diplomatic. 'Good Lord, what did you paint there? You are supposed to paint the breasts and behind as they are.'

From their members, sports clubs chose those whom they thought to be the most suitable for the gymnastics events and sent their names forward to the organising body. At twenty-three, Schwieger and his discretion would be among them. From his club 'there was only me. The clubs were asked to nominate their best sportsmen and they wanted to name my friend Edmund because he was better than me but for some reason he did not go. So I did.' He'd take part in the torch run, too.[30]

In Stockholm trade unions were enraged that some Swedish sailors, distributing anti-Nazi leaflets in German sea ports, had been given five years' hard labour. The unions formed a committee to force a boycott and the Social Democrats asked any of their members who were competitors not to go; if they did, they risked losing their union membership.

The *New York Times* noted that the process of taking down offensive posters, as at Garmisch, had begun in Berlin and added cryptically that perhaps the way to get proper treatment for Jews would be to hold the Olympics every year and in Germany. Hitler, the newspaper concluded, normally ignored what the world thought but was sensitive to it while he had the Games.

The Olympic Village was almost ready and we have many testaments to its scale, efficiency and mode of working. Suffice to say here that it comprised single-storey brick cottages for the teams, a welcome building, a building for meetings, a restaurant, a lake and sauna, swimming pool and training track, all harmoniously blended into the countryside.

Local lad Fritz Wandt recalls:

from 1 May to 15 June the Olympic Village was opened to the public for sightseeing. There were double-decker buses that came from Berlin according to a fixed schedule and during that time about 400,000 people visited, including me. There were guided tours of the Village, carried out by *Ehrenjungs* [boys of honour]. Some time before, 400 boys and 200 girls were chosen from track and field associations and were sent to a school to be trained. They all had to pass an exam and of the boys 170 remained, of the girls 70 or 80, I think. They were to look after the sportsmen in the Village throughout the Games, run errands and they also did the guided tours. They were all dressed in white.

The tours lasted about 90 minutes. It was very detailed. I can remember that the tour started at the entrance and then we went along to the Waldsee [forest lake], and I can remember that the boy who did the tour – he was seventeen or eighteen – told us there had always been a little murky pool there. When it was enlarged and all the old sand and mud taken out they found gnats and dragonflies and other insects, and all were registered meticulously. The excavated earth was used to raise the level of the upper and lower village green in the middle of the Village. At the far end of the lake there was a Finnish sauna that had not been planned initially, but when the Finns asked for one it was built there.

After 15 June it was closed except, of course, for the people who worked there, gardeners, telephone people and others who had to do the rest of the construction work.[31]

The bell had been taken to the stadium on a flat railway truck and, at 7 a.m. on 11 May, the laborious process of hoisting it into position got under way. This was a quiet and, for some reason, secret operation with only about a hundred people present. 'In order to reduce the weight, the different parts of the Bell (bell, yoke, clapper) were elevated separately.' An electrical 5-ton winch accomplished this and at 7.55 a.m. it reached the top of the tower. By 9 a.m. it rested in its place, the 'successful completion' relayed to the Reich Minister of the Interior.[32]

It didn't do to fail in Hitler's Germany.

Chapter 4

STORMY WATERS

The train trip to Paris, with six in a second-class carriage, was none
too comfortable but the Team took it in good part, knowing that
sleepers were out of all reason, as the cost in Australian money was
about £5 each.

Australian Olympic Committee report

O n Wednesday 13 May the Australian team left Sydney for Europe on
the steamer *Mongolia* to a rousing send-off. They'd travel via Hobart,
Melbourne, Adelaide and Fremantle (to visit neighbouring Perth).
The German Organising Committee presented the ship with an Olympic flag
and she flew it whenever she was in port, somehow bringing distant Berlin
physically closer.

The great gathering was under way and between May and 1 August,
competitors from forty-eight other countries from all over the world would
board ships and trains for Berlin.

One of the Australian swimmers, Pat Norton, felt 'very conscious of taking
part in a politically motivated Olympiad. Though only seventeen I was very
politically minded, which was cultivated by the turbulent Jack Lang days,
when I would join the crowd while the budding politician was pleading his
case.[1] The wit and heckling was great! My trip to Berlin was to develop my
international politics.'[2]

The sea stayed calm to Hobart which they reached on Friday the 15th.
There, the rowers rowed and 'the athletes gave exhibitions during the interval
at a football match. The Lord Mayor tendered the Team a farewell and visits
were made to the Cascade Brewery, Elswick races, and Mount Wellington. We
were presented with two cases of apples, and to ensure that we would have
ample fruit on the voyage 12 cases were purchased and put in the ship's
freezer for use on the voyage.'[3]

On the way from Hobart to Melbourne, which the Australian team reached
on the following Monday, the boxers, wrestlers and rowers 'worked together'.

That night at a farewell dinner the Prime Minister proposed the health and success of the team. Next morning the Lord Mayor of Melbourne gave a further farewell speech and the *Mongolia* slipped her moorings at 1 p.m. As the ship moved away and headed towards Adelaide arrangements were made with the ship's officers for 'training facilities. A complete rowing machine to accommodate eight men was set up on the emergency bridge deck aft and a portion of the deck was set aside for the wrestlers, athletes, cyclists, etc. Rubber mats were purchased in Melbourne so that the athletes could train on deck without jarring their legs; a wrestling mat was available, as also high jump standards. The ship's hospital was made available as a massage room.'

The sea didn't stay calm.

The *Mongolia* docked at Freemantle on Monday, 25 May where the team were greeted with more ceremony and farewells. Six members of the New Zealand team, also on the *Mongolia*, were included in the ceremonies and someone gave the Australians a small kangaroo as a mascot. 'The Team was then motored back to the steamer, which sailed at 6.00 p.m. and again we received an enthusiastic send-off. As we left Australia we felt we carried with us the hearty good wishes of the Government, the public and the sporting bodies, which had been made manifest to us on our trip round the Australian coast.'[4]

While the *Mongolia* churned forward, in Berlin the multi-language publication *Judenkenner* (Observer of Jews), which tried to spread anti-Semitism throughout the world, was suspended, although with the expectation it would resume publication after the Games.

As we have seen, propane gas proved the answer to the great problem of keeping the Olympic flame burning at the stadium for the two weeks, despite needing 55lb of it a day. On 28 May it was successfully tested there.

Special attention was paid to the colour and volume of the flame in the fire-bowl as well as to the development of smoke. The attempts were completely satisfactory and it was discovered that smoke and soot from the 10-foot flame could not be detected for more than a distance of 50 feet.

In providing a fire-bowl, a deviation was made from the system used in Holland [Amsterdam, 1928] and America [Los Angeles, 1932]. A 7.15 feet high tripod constructed according to a Greek pattern was placed in the centre of the deep opening at the end of the Stadium. This supported a round fire-bowl which was fashioned of 0.16 inch steel plate. The bowl was filled with broken fire-clay in order to ensure a good distribution of the flame. A weatherproof room was constructed in the immediate vicinity . . . and the regulation of the gas supply as well as the supervision and adjustment of the flame was carried out from here.[5]

Another flame would burn at the Lustgarten, an old pleasure garden situated at the far end of Unter den Linden from the Brandenburg Gate, although the Nazis had 'expressed their perverse understanding of the word "pleasure" by ripping up the trees and bushes and transforming the compact space into a parade-ground'.[6]

Malta became the fifty-third and last country to enter.

The sea grew calm as the *Mongolia* churned up to Colombo and the Australian team trained, although one of the boxers, hit in the eye by the elbow of a sparring partner, needed stitches. Fancy dress parties helped to pass the time. The ship docked at Colombo on 3 June.

The Indian Hockey Federation announced that they had enough money to send a team to Berlin. 'To compete in the Olympic Games, defend the very proud title of world champions, and see Europe – could anything look brighter to us in the world?'[7] Eleven of the team met in Delhi on 16 June – others would join later – and, after an afternoon of rain, played a Delhi Select XI at 6 p.m. losing 4–1. Taken in context, this was a genuine sensation and news of it spread far and wide very quickly. The Indians knew that their great rivals, the Germans and Dutch, would have noted it – it 'seemed that the Indians were not invincible after all'. After the defeat they embaked on an extensive country-wide series of preparatory matches.

The *Mongolia* steamed on making the usual calls at Bombay, Aden, Port Said and Malta, with a little sightseeing at each, before she reached Marseilles on 19 June. 'We arrived . . . in the middle of the French strike, and as we had quite a large amount of baggage we could not get through the customs in time to catch the boat train at 7.30 pm and had to spend the evening in Marseilles, catching the train at 11.30 pm. We saw the city under martial law but there were no disturbances.'[8]

That evening Pat Norton remembered popping 'into a Newsreel' and watching 'a short [film] on Herr Hitler – interesting and threatening. It showed a white map of Europe with boundaries in black. Then a section of Europe was blacked out – it looked like Poland – then came Hitler's photo and another section of Europe was blacked out. And so it went on until the whole of Europe disappeared into black except a section of France. The reality of Hitler and the situation rising in Germany hit home. The irony of this, an Olympic team on its way to Germany, watching their host making threatening overtones to another community.'[9]

The train trip to Paris, 'with six in a second-class carriage, was none too comfortable but the Team took it in good part, knowing that sleepers were out of all reason, as the cost in Australian money was about £5 each.'[10]

The day the *Mongolia* docked at Marseilles, Germany's Max Schmeling met and felled the hitherto unbeaten Joe Louis at the Yankee Stadium, New York, for the world heavyweight championship. Louis, knocked out in the twelfth round, had a similar background to Owens. The seventh son of an Alabama sharecropping family, he took up boxing when he moved to Chicago. Schmeling was white, of course, a heavy puncher and could – against his will – be presented as an example of Aryan mastery. Louis was black, of course, and could – against his will or not – be presented as an example of what a man of his colour and background could achieve. When he went down in round 12 it may be that his whole community went down with him and, when they rose, they swivelled their gaze of hope towards Owens.[11]

The year before, in 45 minutes during a meeting in Ann Arbor, Michigan, Owens equalled the world 100-yard record and broke three world records: long jump, 220 yards and 220-yard low hurdles. It made him as famous as Louis, so famous that now, as the trials for the Olympic team drew near, he recorded how things were happening too fast and how he felt a reverse kind of shock looking at a photograph of himself on the front page of a newspaper.[12] He suddenly realised that being on a front page had become normal.

Owens recorded a dialogue between himself and his wife Ruth.

Owens said he would like them to go to church before he got on the boat.

Ruth said she was glad because he hadn't said that for a long time.

Owens thought out loud, 'Can't this morning – Got to meet Coach Snyder at ten. Maybe next Sunday morning, but I've got that press conference and got to get in my practice sometime . . . .'

Each busy moment melted into the next.[13]

The coach, Larry Snyder, advised Owens and was well placed to do so. A pilot instructor in the First World War he 'did some stunt flying in the early 1920s before enrolling at Ohio State University'. He served as head track coach from 1932 until 1965. During this time 'his athletes set 14 world records, won 52 All-American certificates and eight Olympic gold medals'.[14] He hammered home to Owens that success brought obligations and responsibilities, that he must be careful what he did and that he must promote good interracial relations.[15]

Owens was not, of course, the only sprinter anticipating Berlin. A whole clutch of other Americans were, too, and at the two-day Canadian trials Howie McPhee, dubbed the 'quiet spoken, beautifully muscled Vancouver boy', set three Canadian records. During a pre-Olympic meeting in Vancouver he equalled the Olympic record. What might he do to Owens – inflict another defeat, à la Schmeling?[16]

Spain withdrew from the Games – the country faced civil war – and Brazil caused problems of another kind altogether by sending two teams. The

Official German Report said dryly that an 'especially difficult situation arose' because Brazil 'possessed two National Federations for athletics, rowing and swimming, one of which was affiliated with the International Federations, the other with the National Olympic Committee'. Which represented Brazil? Nobody knew.

The first competitors, five Japanese swimmers, arrived in Berlin after twelve days on the Trans-Siberian railway. They seem to have been both swimmers and an advance party for the full team of 191. 'For all those who watched the gradual development of the Olympic Village, it was an unforgettable moment when these five Japanese entered to the tones of the Japanese national anthem and the flag of Japan, followed by that of Germany, was unfurled for the first time.'[17] The Japanese took to going out onto the grass beside their cottage in the early morning for callisthenics. They approached these exercises very intently and the Germans watching said openly that none of their competitors would have been able to stand the strain. The swimmers were secretive and their coach did not want them observed when they began training. If he saw anyone at the pool timing any of his team, he would order his swimmer out of the water immediately.

The majority of the Japanese team, one of the strongest the country sent abroad and including seventeen women, trained and acclimatised at Helsinki for several weeks. They, too, guarded their privacy. No doubt they had an extra incentive to impress the world, because Tokyo had been awarded the 1940 Summer Games and Sapporo the Winter. The Japanese contenders would not be coming to Berlin yet.

The Australian team spent a night in Paris and reached Cologne the following day. They were given a conducted tour of the city before boarding the Berlin train at 10.20 that night.

The Indian hockey team's tour went on. They played a tense match against All-Madras in front of a big crowd, winning 5–3, and left Madras at 9.30 that night on the Bangalore mail train. They arrived at 6.45 next morning, Tuesday, 23 June, and that evening beat Bangalore 4–1 before boarding the Bangalore passenger train for Bombay and departure for Europe.[18]

The Australians arrived in Berlin at 7.55 a.m., six weeks after leaving Sydney. 'The bands struck up our national anthem, "God Save the King." We were given a great ovation.' They were met by, among others, Lewald and 'we were driven through enthusiastic crowds to the town hall, where the Lord Mayor welcomed the Team as the first to arrive in Berlin.'[19] A gold key, presented to the team leader, symbolised 'that the City of Berlin was thrown open to the Olympic athletes'. They were driven to the Olympic Village and the Australian flag raised to another rendition of 'God Save the King'. They made their way to their cottage, named after the German city of Worms. Pat Norton recalled how she had felt a sense of relief at arriving because in Australia 'we were very worried we would not get to the Olympics as there was much talk of war. We were the first team to arrive in Berlin, great reception, but surprised at all the military uniforms.'[20]

The man in charge of the Olympic Village, Staff Captain Wolfgang Fürstner, no longer wore his. Widely praised for his work there, he took pride in every detail even down to having dentists available. The timing is lost now but he was found to be a *Mischling* – a half-Jew – something he might not even have known. That led to his dismissal from the job and the army. It broke his heart. He served under his replacement Lieutenant Werner von und zu Gilsa throughout the Games, but as a man he was little more than a shadow. Fürstner joined Lewald, Mayer and Bergmann in being tolerated and exploited.

The Indian hockey team reached Bombay at 9 a.m. on Thursday 25 June and stayed at the Taj Mahal Hotel, built in 1903, opulent and described as an 'architectural marvel' because it combined Moorish, Oriental and Florentine styles. The Bombay Hockey Association and the Bombay Olympic Association gave them a luncheon and during it a cry went up for the captain, the legendary Dyhan Chand, to make a speech. He didn't. That evening a dance for the team at the hotel proved so popular that there was hardly room to take the floor. Then the Mayor of Bombay wished the team good luck.[21]

On Friday 26 June the forty-nine-strong Argentinian contingent entered the Village, including swimmer Jeanette Campbell.

My future husband, Roberto, belonged to the same swimming club as me and we both . . . broke South American records. Roberto had gone to Los Angeles in 1932. We always trained together. We both worked in those days so only swam a while in the evening. He was named in 1936 to go to Berlin but the cash didn't stretch, so I had to go alone. The trip there was not so much fun as I had to sit at a table with the directors and trainers. They always had problems and were always squabbling, but when you crossed the Equator there was always a fancy dress dinner. We dressed up, but changed sexes. I was in shorts (not worn in those days), a dinner jacket, coat and hat, and my bride was our fencer in my sister's evening dress. Not having been at the dinner very long, the Captain of the ship stood up and came over, carrying a lovely little baby doll which he placed in the fencer's lap.[22]

Norton and Campbell struck up a friendship. They decided to try and get into the stadium to have a look although that was forbidden until the opening day of the Games. Only tourists were allowed. They mingled with a group of tourists and did get in but a storm trooper chased them. They managed to get up a flight of steps and have a look – and there it was, not just the vast bowl but the cinder running track which would cause so many problems for the Australian athletes, accustomed as they were to grass. Their feet and legs would take a terrible pounding.

On 27 June the Indian hockey team 'with our mackintoshes on our arms and our luggage in the custody of the agents of Thomas Cook & Co.' left the hotel for a free day before they gathered at the Ballard Pier, originally a small pier but which became a centre of industry as well, for embarkation. Reportedly the 'simple boys like Ronak Singh and Akram Rasool', who had not been to the city before, found themselves literally a little lost.

The team reflected all India: 'a great variety of ages, colours and appearances. We had among us ages ranging from twenty to forty, skins in all shades of white and brown, heights varying from 5 feet to 6 feet, beardless and bearded, from no moustaches to moustaches of every description, from leanness carried to extremities to muscles bulging out of blazers, Aryan, Dravidian and Mongolian features, bare-headed, hats and turbans. What a variety in appearance! And still greater by far in thoughts, habits, temperament and general outlook on life.'[23]

Bergmann's exploitation would be finessed this same day because she was allowed into the final trial at Adolf Hitler Stadium in Stuttgart. She remembered 'all the Nazi flags and all the officials saluting and I jumped like a fiend. I always did my best when I was angry. I never jumped better; I didn't miss a jump.'

She did 1.60 metres, equalling the German record. Now she prepared to go for the record, with all that that involved: not least making a case against her Olympic selection arguably impossible even in Nazi Germany.

'I thought this would be a slap in the face to the Aryans. What would they do to me? Would they break my legs? Would they kill me? What would they do to my family?' Under this pressure 'I just fell apart. I couldn't really lift myself again.'[24]

The Indian hockey team left Bombay on the P & O line steamer *Ranpura* – they ought to have left a day earlier but the ship was late. This was the monsoon season and as the ship moved into the Arabian Sea the weather battered it. Two players suffered such acute seasickness that they 'made frantic appeals to the managers to send them back' to Bombay immediately. Hardly anyone could eat.[25]

South and Central American teams came in almost daily, Bolivia and Peru on 1 July.

A twenty-year-old teacher from Kansas, Esther Myers, sailed to Europe as part of a student group spending a summer abroad. They went to Berlin for the Games. She met team-member Harold Manning, who invited her to have a look at the Village. 'He said "You can bring some of your pals with you."' Women 'could come into the courtyard and see the buildings but not enter the lounges, dining area, exercise rooms or dormitories. It was a privilege for me to be invited into the gated courtyard for a visit. That was a highlight of the Games for me.' Manning met them at the 'reception entrance. He was as glad to see fellow Kansans as we were to see him. After a picture taking session, Manning told us we were fortunate to be there as the three Bolivian athletes arrived. We watched a welcoming ceremony in front of the complex. The official representatives of that country gave a speech, a German band played as they ran up the colors of Bolivia. It was an impressive ceremony.'[26]

The *Ranpura* fought on through heavy seas, and reached Aden in the early hours of 2 July. The Indian hockey players were delighted to get their feet on terra firma although Aden itself, encircled by barren mountains and lacking any sort of greenery, did not interest them. They did not like the steaming hot wind off the desert, either. They had breakfast and disembarked hoping to find somewhere to practise. 'An open-air cafe in the marketplace, noisy and dimly lit, faces pale and haggard over cups of coffee or iced-water,' was a sight they'd never forget. Aden was part of the British Empire and a regiment from the Punjab, stationed there, offered their regimental field for the practice and provided Indian food. Then, 5½ hours after arriving, the *Ranpura* sailed on towards Marseilles, with stops at Port Said and Malta en route. The sea was now so calm that the players, who'd spent the trip so far in their cabins, frolicked on the deck.[27]

In Berlin, Mexico arrived on 4 July, Uruguay the day after.

The Maharaja of Mysore travelled on the *Ranpura* with a large retinue – he was going to Britain for medical treatment. Despite His Highness's exalted status he mixed easily with the team and a great affection for him grew, was literally fed because he had his own supplies of food and daily plied the team with 'curds and Indian vegetarian dishes'. At Malta journalists came aboard to interview the Maharaja.

The final seat numbers were being painted, the last gates set in place and the cinder track 'tilled'! At the stadium, testing and rehearsing began of the transport facilities, the police traffic controls and the thousands of light-blue uniformed ushers who would be showing visitors to their seats. A 'crowd' was assembled to find out if they could hear announcements over the stadium's loudspeakers clearly. The best positioning for music and choruses was selected to eliminate echoes. The Olympic bell was rung so that the 'penetrating quality' of its tones could be judged.

Another task which required time and patience was the training of the stadium personnel. The arena had to be changed rapidly for different competitions, the running track measured off, lanes marked and the apparatus set up rapidly and removed without loss of time. A special staff was engaged for the 30 feet high scoring tower. This work covered both day and night, since during the night hurdles and barriers were set up and the fields for shot-putting and discus-throwing constructed and removed. We even provided rest rooms in the stadium for these workers in the event that they succeeded in obtaining a few hours' rest.[28]

The numerous cleaners needed to be 'organised and instructed . . . which was performed during the noon hour and at night. Scarcely had the last spectator left the stadium than the uniformly dressed columns of cleaners . . . descended upon the stadium and swept diligently under the illumination of the gigantic searchlights so that all was spotlessly clean when the visitors arrived on the following morning.' A special group tended and repaired the field where the polo matches and dressage would be held. Advance ticket sales reached 5 million Reichsmarks.

Not everyone was going to Berlin. Canadian welterweight champion Sammy Luftspring looked a likely medal winner but as a Jew felt he could not attend, and he persuaded Norman 'Baby' Yack, a fellow Jew, to withdraw from the Olympic trials as well.

Luftspring wrote an open letter of explanation:

We desire to advise you that we have decided not to take part in the boxing trials to be held in Montréal to select the Canadian Olympic team. It is a matter of keen disappointment to us to turn down the opportunity of trying for the great honor and privilege of making a place on the Canadian team. However, we have gone into the community, and find that we cannot act differently from what we have decided. We know that we, as Canadian boys, would be personally safe, and perhaps well received in Germany. But can we forget the way the German government is treating the Jewish boys in Germany? The German government is treating our brothers and sisters worse than dogs. Can Canadian sportsmen blame us for refusing to take part in a meet sponsored by people who would humiliate and degrade and persecute us too, if we did not happen to have the great fortune of being

Canadians? We are making a personal sacrifice in refusing the chance and we are sure that all true Canadian sportsmen will appreciate that we would have been very low to hurt the feelings of our fellow Jews by going to a land that would exterminate them if it could. We wish the Canadian team every success.[29]

Two other Canadians, speed skater Frank Stack and walker Henry Cieman, had refused to go.

On the evening of 7 July a train pulled out of the central station at Los Angeles for New York with sprinter Wykoff on it bound for the Olympic trials at Randall's Island. The local newspaper had been instrumental in raising money to send him and the sports editor, Frederick Graham, wrote that they had only managed to collect enough just two days before. People from all walks of life made donations, some for what they could spare: $1.

The *Ranpura* reached Malta in the early hours – so early that the Indian hockey team were asleep and unaware she spent two hours unloading cargo before sailing on.

The American trials began on 11 July. The tension tormented Marty Glickman, only eighteen and younger than his fellow competitors, in the week before. That and hellishly hot weather meant he had not had much sleep. Randall's Island sits between Manhattan, Queens and the Bronx. Before a capacity crowd of 21,000 and in the truly appalling heat some astonishing things happened, not least that world record holders failed to make the team in the 800 metres, 1,500 metres, pole vault and high jump.[30] This did not prevent the *New York Times* from judging the team the strongest the country had ever sent to any competition,[31] a judgement based squarely on the fact that two other high-jumpers, Cornelius Johnson and Dave Albritton, both broke the world record; Owens broke the world 200 metres record; three pole vaulters broke the Olympic record and various other records went in the steeplechase, the 400 metres hurdles and the 110 metres hurdles.

The 100 metres proved particularly tense, America's clutch of top sprinters pitted directly against each other. By tradition the first three finishers qualified for the Berlin 100 metres and the next four made up the 4 × 100 relay with the fall-back position that, in emergency, they could be deployed as substitutes. At Randall's Island the three best finishers from two heats went into the final but, because the 100 metres and relay needed seven sprinters, the seventh place would be decided by a run-off.

Glickman had Owens and Sam Stoller, a Jew from the University of Michigan, in his heat and came third to them. Ralph Metcalfe, 25-year-old Foy Draper from the University of Southern California and Mack Robinson, a quiet black from Pasadena – a junior college sprinter and barely noticed by anybody before the Games[32] – qualified in the second heat while Wykoff won the run-off. He demonstrated the depth of his ability. Another sprinter from the University of Southern California, he had won gold in the 4 × 100 relays at the 1928 and 1932 Games and, in 1930, became the first man officially timed at 9.4 seconds for the 100 yards. And he was now seventh.

Glickman tried to compose himself before the final by standing in the locker room where the fierce heat couldn't get at him. Ordinarily the immediate build-up to a race made him feel light-headed but now he made his way to the start in something like a trance, nerves so taut he thought he might be sick. The lanes were allocated by draw. From Lane 1

> Robinson
> Draper
> Wykoff
> Owens
> Glickman
> Metcalfe
> Stoller

Before the introduction of starting blocks, runners dug holes with trowels to give their feet grip for the start. Glickman did that – Randall's Island a cinder track – but nerves made his leg shake so violently he could hardly get his foot into the hole. The other six assumed their positions and for a long, terrifying moment he thought the leg wouldn't stop shaking. He'd never felt anything like this in his life before.

He knew the starter, who noticed the leg and aborted the start, called Glickman over and told him to limber up for a few moments to calm himself. When they went to their marks a second time he felt better.

The judges stood on steps at the finish to see who finished where: no photo finishes, of course.

Glickman held Owens and Metcalfe towards half distance before they pulled away. He thought he'd got past Wykoff for third but couldn't be certain. He loosened his shoelaces and walked near the finish as the judges milled about, consulting and deliberating. They decided: Owens, Metcalfe, Glickman.

Glickman was doing a radio interview when Dean Cromwell, a coach from the University of Southern California, moved in and started promoting the cases of Wykoff and Draper, both from the University. The judges revised their positioning, pushing Wykoff up to third and Draper fourth. Glickman felt strongly conflicting emotions but at least he was going to Berlin.[33]

| 100 metres | Owens, Metcalfe, Wykoff |
| 4 × 100 relay | Draper, Glickman, Stoller, Robinson |

That evening the *Ranpura* docked at Marseilles but passengers had to struggle with their own luggage because the dock workers were still on strike. This took so long that the Indian hockey team missed their Paris train and retreated to a cheap hotel. They were astonished to discover that the French drove on the right and needed some time to convince themselves it could be as safe as driving on the left.

They were woken by bells at 5 a.m. and, sleep in their eyes, had a tea or coffee and boarded a bus for the railway station. It bustled with activity although the French stopped and gazed at the wondrous and no doubt exotic host before them. The team took their seats in third class. The Marseilles–Lyons–Paris express pulled out at 6.40, heading north. The restaurant car tempted them but they did not have enough money for anything but a 'meagre breakfast'.[34]

In Paris a representative of the travel company Thomas Cook was waiting for them at the station. He organised overnight accommodation and the next day they took the tourist tour – the Eiffel Tower, Notre Dame, the Arc de Triomphe and the Follies Bergères. That delivered a culture shock. 'Young girls, some twenty in number, a piece of silken cloth around their loins, were dancing in pairs. They were almost naked, as the silken cloth which might have been put on to avoid an infringement of some law, concealed nothing to the hungry eyes of the passionate.' The hockey players stayed for about 30 minutes drinking lemonade and keeping their gazes firmly averted downwards. That amused the girls, who did not hesitate to taunt them as they left. Then they caught the night train to Berlin via Cologne but it was so busy they only just managed to get third-class seats. They slept in those. It was very cold.

At Cologne an official of the Organising Committee came on board and accompanied them to Berlin where a large crowd assembled to greet them. Diem welcomed them and the British national anthem was played – India was a British colony, of course. And the team encountered their first volleys of *Heil Hitler!* and the stiff-arm salutes. After a ceremony in the town hall they were driven out to the Village by bus. They became the eighth country to come in. Their house, 131, was called 'Elbing' and the name seems to have been chosen deliberately because the city had evidently made trains which were exported to India. The facilities, the cleanliness and their two stewards impressed them. One, Otto, knew India and could speak good English because he'd been a sailor but the other, Schmidt, was not so fluent.[35]

That was 13 July.

The German Olympic trials were held in Berlin (but not at the Olympic stadium) and produced some disappointing performances. Before previous Olympics the Germans competed a great deal but this time competition had been carefully rationed. By a bizarre twist this would impact directly on the American sprinters.

The *New York Times* considered that the German women's team offered their country the best chances of medals, something the macho men of the Reich might find hard to live with and perhaps explains why, in the domestic media build-up, the women were given less publicity. If the Nazi creed led them into a moral maze over the Jews, their beliefs about the role of women led them into another.

A special edition of the illustrated magazine, *Berlin Illustrierte Zeitung*, had a spread entitled, 'Promising German Sportsmen and Women.' In a host of pictures and short biographies, the magazine only featured one woman, swimmer Martha Genenger. Similarly, another publication, the 128-page book, *Die Olympischen Spiele*, had just two pages on the women's competition, an article written by track star Gisela Mauermayer assessing the German women's chances in track and field.

In publications that did feature more about the women, by far the most attention was showered upon Mauermayer, who[m] journalists routinely portrayed as a shoo-in for the gold medal in the discus. In its pre-Olympic issue, *The Young Socialist* trumpeted, 'who would beat her? She is known throughout the world for her discus throwing.' Likewise, a journalist in *Der Angriff* proclaimed in mid-July, 'This Gisela Mauermayer! Who can beat her?'[36]

Statuesque and graceful, Mauermayer represented the Nazi ideal of womanhood with her blonde hair but the talk of certain victory disconcerted her, and understandably so. 'In every milk bar and at every kiosk, I must have heard that the gold medal was a sure thing for me.' She found herself thinking that she *had* to win rather than her customary thought, that she *might* win[37] – always a dangerous state of mind.

Others tipped to do well were hurdlers Doris Eckert and Anni Steuer, high-jumper Elfriede Kaun, javelin thrower Tilly Fleischer and the 4 × 100 relay team. The swimmers, however – 'known as "Nixen" (mermaids or water nymphs)' – did get media attention. One, Hanni Hölzner, appeared on the cover of *Berliner Illustrierte Zeitung* in her swimming costume with the caption 'the fastest breaststroke swimmer in the world'.

[Coverage] suggested the idea of 'Aryan supremacy' in a number of ways when reporting on the women's team. Most blatantly, the press drew attention to 'Aryan' physical characteristics when applicable. Publications took note of the sportswomen's hair color, if it was light, when relaying information about the competition. They described Ruth Halbsgut and Tilly Fleischer, for example, as blond, and Anni Steuer as dark blond. In addition, publications indicated whether an athlete was of tall stature. Steuer and Fleischer happened to be given both the 'tall' and 'blond' designations.[38]

Gretel Bergmann was not invited to compete in the German Championships. Dora Ratjen won but was disqualified – the reason lost in the mists of time – and the next three girls, led by Kaun, did 1.54 metres. Since Bergmann had done 1.60 metres at Stuttgart she clearly merited a place in the Olympic team, something highlighted by the fact that in virtually every event the Germans fielded three competitors but in the women's high jump only two.

Bergmann thinks she 'only found out in the 1990s, when I got connection again with Elfriede Kaun. We met for the first time when I was in Germany in 2001, 2002 and they got her to come to Berlin and we met again. It was very emotional. I'm not a crying person but when I think of that meeting tears come to my eyes. I knew only two women had been picked but I didn't know why. She told me that they were told "Bergmann is injured and we are keeping the place open in case she recovers." They didn't want to put anybody else on the team to show their manoeuvring.'[39]

A much greater highlight to absurdity was coming soon.

The media paid particular interest to the American women's team, 'mainly because journalists considered them to be the toughest competition. Showing them as such allowed the German press to make winning or losing against them seem more meaningful.'

[The media] perceived some of the American women, especially the swimmers and divers, as having 'star-like' qualities, which their readership may have found appealing. Before the Olympic trials in the United States, for example, *Der Angriff* ran a photograph and short piece on some of the swimmers titled, 'Seven beautiful girls from the USA,' in which the reporter commented that, 'one only wishes that all of them will be at the Games.' . . . Diver Dorothy Poyton Hill, for instance, appeared in German periodicals wearing various custom-made swimsuits and was described as the 'lovely' gold medallist from the 1932 Los Angeles Olympics and as 'pure grace.'

Another American woman the German press singled out was the 1932 winner in the backstroke, Eleanor Holm Jarrett, dubbed 'the Diva' by reporters. Publications featured her as 'the pretty swimmer,' who was also an actress, singer, and the wife of a popular musical group leader. *Der Angriff*, for instance, devoted a full page to Jarrett – more space than they gave to any of the German women. Likewise, [the] *Berliner Illustrierte Zeitung* hailed her as America's 'surest mainstay' for Olympic gold.[40]

Holm would lose no time in drawing a great deal more media attention to herself, just hours after the American team sailed from New York on 15 July.

Meanwhile, the US Football Association wrestled with the dilemma of whether to go or not and decided in favour, 'despite the unpalatable political situation. However, heavy snowfall during the winter of 1935–36 wreaked havoc with attempts to raise money for team preparations and it was only three weeks before the Olympics that Joe Barriskill, the USFA secretary, transferred just under seven thousand dollars to the Olympic Committee to fund the team.'[41]

The American track and field team stayed at the Hotel Lincoln on Eighth Avenue (1,400 rooms from $2.50 up) before sailing. Many slept little the night before and the day of departure started early. Helen Stephens, the sprinter of awesome potential from Fulton, stayed up late talking to her room-mates, woke around 6 a.m. and ate breakfast quickly. One report uses the word 'hysteria' to capture the mood of excitement. They were already down in the lobby before the dawn shift of porters and clerks started work.

Some competitors carried instructions with them. Forrest 'Spec' (Freckles, shortened to Spec) Towns, 100 metre hurdler and son of a railroad man, was being coached by Weems Baskin at the University of Georgia, and Baskin told him to ignore whatever one of the Olympic team's coaches, Lawson Robertson, said. 'You know what you have to do', Baskin concluded. 'Do it.'[42]

They were to sail on the steamer SS *Manhattan*, a five-year-old ship whose funnels were appropriately red, white and blue, moored at the pier at the end of West 20th Street. It regularly plied the route to Hamburg via Cobh – the cove of Cork, a place with deep resonance for many Americans because thousands of Irish people emigrated from there – then on to Plymouth (another place of resonance because the Pilgrim Fathers had sailed from there to Massachusetts), Le Havre and up the North Sea coast.

The *Manhattan* departed at midday and shuttle buses from the Lincoln began to transport the American teams at 9 a.m., but in their eagerness the boxers took taxis and were the first aboard. From 9.30 a current of competitors flowed up the gangplank and some, to oblige the photographers, even did it twice. Autograph hunters had their favourites, mainly Eleanor Holm and Owens. The *Manhattan* had other, commercial passengers and the autograph hunters noted actresses Mary Astor and Helen Hayes boarding. When Owens appeared, looking dapper in his only suit, a dark-blue pinstripe, the photographers, reporters and autograph hunters swarmed.

Stephens had never travelled by ship before. When she arrived she saw one of her teachers in the crowd. The teacher gave her a small, cherry-red leather-bound travel diary and said she should record all the exciting events of the trip. Stephens promised she would. Then she went to Cabin 35 on Deck 6.[43]

Velma Dunn, a member of the diving team, 'had never been out of America. I'm from California and I went to New York by train, about four days at that time. I don't think I had been to New York. I had been to Chicago. It was a huge adventure.'[44]

The competitors had their bunks on the two decks below the waterline and Owens made his way to Room 87 on Deck D, in the hold of the ship.

Archie Williams, the 400 metres runner, found the black athletes were to room together because, as someone said to him, 'Well, you guys want to be with your own kind.' His cabin mate was James LuValle, who had been his hero but now represented a direct threat in the 400. Williams thought whoever allocated the cabins simply did not realise two rivals might indulge in 'heavy psyching' although, he'd claim, he himself was 'too dumb' to be subtly undermined.[45]

Williams, from California, studied at Berkeley for a degree in mechanical engineering, the first member of his family to go to college. Study had taken preference over preparing for the Olympics, not least because athletics was 'an end in itself' rather than opening the golden door to money. Wrong era. And when he arrived at Berkeley his counsellor queried the engineering degree because, even with it, no big company would be hiring a black man. Wrong era again.[46]

On board the *Manhattan*

physically segregated by a sealed door were a few wives and parents who were making the trip, whose section divided male from female athletes. Regular passengers nearly filled the two upper decks to capacity. Among them were American Olympic officials and coaches, who traveled first class. To one of their own members, they seemed like 'a bunch of junketeers taking the gravy that should have gone to the athletes.' Unaccustomed to anything different, most athletes scarcely noticed the contrast.[47]

The sleeping arrangements did not suit Eleanor Holm, bunked with two young swimmers, at all. 'I had been around – I was no baby,' she said. Evidently she had tried to pay for her own passage across first class but Brundage forbade it. That didn't suit her, either.

Betty Robinson, twenty-five, competed in the 1928 Games as a 100-metre sprinter, but injuries from a plane crash three years later meant she could not assume the crouch position for the start of the race, so she went to Berlin as part of the relay team. Kathlyn Kelly from Seneca, South Carolina, was 16 years and 309 days old when she qualified for the Olympic high jump, which still makes her the fifth youngest high-jumper to do so.

Twenty minutes before the ship sailed a vast white flag with the Olympic rings was hoisted to the top of a mast by five female competitors and visitors were asked to go ashore. One official had two bags with him, one for soiled clothing and the other clean. His wife, who disembarked, took the wrong one leaving him without so much as a razor.

Three tugs backed the *Manhattan* away into the Hudson. As she went the competitors stood behind the ship's white railings and shouted 'Ray! Ray! for the USA' with, as a sort of echo, 'A–M–E–R–I–C–A!'

As the United Press reported, the team sailed aboard the 'gaily be-flagged *Manhattan* in a bedlam of bon-voyage cheers from more than 10,000 well-wishers and an ear-splitting din from the tied-down whistles of harbor craft'. Aeroplanes and small airships 'soared and dipped' and the whole spectacle became 'a virtual tornado of massed joy'. After all the bitter wrangling over whether to go or not, only one anti-Olympic picket came and the placard he carried was an advertisement for a book he had written.

Owens would later say that as the shoreline receded and disappeared a simple thought held him: the next time he saw it he'd have won or lost, with all that those two possibilities implied.[48] He gazed at the expanse of the Atlantic and wanted to get on his knees to thank God for this chance. But he didn't. He wondered if he didn't because of his team-mates around him, or because 'there was a stranger inside of me now'.[49]

The *Manhattan* had 1,064 passengers, 688 in the Olympics entourage (344 competitors, the rest were officials, coaches, journalists and relatives) while most of the remaining 376 were going to the Games as spectators and supporters. A further forty-eight competitors completed the team, some – yachtsmen, equestrians and two baseball players – were already in Germany, and the ten canoeists were to follow a week later. Taken together, United States had never sent a larger team. It contained eighteen black athletes (sixteen men, two women), three times the number at the Los Angeles Games four years earlier.

The *Manhattan* churned on into the Atlantic and the passengers prepared to settle down to the rhythm of shipboad life, whatever that brought. For 400-metre relay sprinter Harold Smallwood it brought appendicitis and confinement to his quarters wearing an icepack. While Smallwood underwent surgery the ship slowed dramatically, making people think it was to keep it steady, but the captain explained over the PA that he was trying to avoid a school of whales.[50]

The rest were fit enough to eat 700lb of beef, double the normal amount for the ship and bringing the possibility of rationing by banning second helpings.

The delicate matter of race relations has spawned two conflicting testimonies.

The first: Owens went to his assigned table 'only to find all three of his dining mates to be outspoken, wisecracking Southerners. . . . All were whites, and to Jesse their necks appeared red. For all his easy-mannered adaptability, he could not cope with that situation. He found another table.' Afterwards, one of them teased Owens 'for his prejudice against white Southerners'.[51]

The second: Towns remembered that he, shot-putter Jack Torrance and Glenn 'Slats' Hardin, a 400 metre hurdler – three white Southerners – had been assigned a table for the voyage. Owens came up and hesitated but Hardin, who knew him, asked if it was his table, too. Owens said yes and Hardin said, 'Well, sit your ass down here.' Towns claimed that Owens ate with them all the way across and it didn't bother them at all.[52]

John Woodruff says 'there was no discrimination amongst the athletes on the team'.[53]

After dinner the competitors watched a film or danced to live music.

That night the competitors were settling to life on board. Some had already been seasick but evidently Helen Stephens was not affected as she covered eight 'laps' of the deck after dinner.[54]

In Berlin the radio links with foreign countries were tested 'after the removal of many international difficulties which ordinarily exist. The authorities in the different countries concerned gave every assistance to the German Broadcasting Company.'

In Laupheim, Gretel Bergmann waited in a kind of nightmare to hear if she had been selected. 'I didn't know what was going on, I had no idea. I didn't think they were going to let me compete. I mean, how can 100,000 people look at a Jewish girl high-jumping for Adolf Hitler? Nobody will know what psychologically I went through. Day and night I was thinking: *What am I going to do if they let me compete?* I had this idea that the madder I got the better I jumped and I said, "*Am I going to have to give the Hitler salute?*" All these things were weighing on me and I didn't want to talk about it to my parents because I didn't want to make their lives harder than they already were. It was a horrible time. Horrible. Psychologically I don't know how I got through it. By being a normal human being, I think! If I hadn't had my sense of humour I don't think I would have.'[55]

An official letter from the German Reichs Union for Sport in Charlottenburg, dated 16 July, settled it. For months the German team trained at Ettlingen. Jewish athletes had much poorer conditions and might or might not be invited to regional qualifying competitions. Bergmann, by contrast, had been to Ettlingen and there found no discrimination among her fellow athletes, particularly from fellow high-jumper Elfriede Kaun – as we have seen.

The letter, delivered quite normally with the post to Bergmann's home in Laupheim, read:

The Reichssportführer, who has selected the team for the Olympic Games, has not been able to include you in the team representing Germany during the time of 1 to 9 August in the Olympic stadium. For each competition – except relay – only three competitors could be chosen. Due to your recent performances you yourself probably did not reckon on being selected.

But Dr. von Halt [of the German Olympic Committee] is prepared to reward your willingness and hard work by offering you, free, standing tickets to the track and field week, including the Opening Ceremony, for the days 1./ 2./ 3./ 4./ 5./6./ 7./ 8./ 9 August.

Should you intend to make use of this offer please let us know. The tickets will be sent to you immediately. Unfortunately travel and living expenses cannot be included.

Heil Hitler!

Tschammer

'I opened it and I cursed my head off. I used every word I had ever learnt and that was a lot because I was the only girl in my class – we were thirteen, I think, and I was the only girl. They cursed and I learnt. I was absolutely stunned.'[56]

The letter made no mention of the fact that she was joint holder of the German record or that only two competitors had been selected for the women's high jump, Kaun and Ratjen. To pass up a likely gold medal for anti-Semitic reasons is startling enough, even in Nazi Germany. To have selected Ratjen the man instead was far more than startling. Ratjen, first name Hermann, was a member of the Hitler Youth and had been threatened with *consequences* if he did not agree to compete. The reasoning: a man has to beat the women, and he'll have Bergmann's gold.

The Bergmann and Ratjen cases, contrived as they were from a blind adherence to Olympic ideals, represent a neat insight into insanity.

It was measured insanity, too. Again as we have seen, Bergmann and Ratjen were ordered to be room-mates during training because, Bergmann insists looking back, as a seventeen-year-old male with testosterone pumping he might have been tempted by an Aryan girl but would never dare touch a Jew. It cut the other way, too, because she, as a Jew, would never have dared denounce Ratjen the Aryan even if she had discovered his real gender.

Bergmann 'could never figure out' who signed the letter dismissing her from the team – the signature is an indecipherable scrawl.[57] 'Tschammer was the overall boss, I guess. But you know this is a letter that was sent, I am sure, to all the people who didn't make the final team. That wasn't just a letter to me, this was just a form letter. To so-and-so-and-so, then the text, so-and-so-and-so, you didn't make it. This had nothing to do with a personal letter to me – but I am convinced that that letter went out much earlier to the others, mine got sent at the last minute after the American ship sailed. I never had any proof of this but I said, "If that's a coincidence, I'll eat my hat." I was joint German record holder: of course it is nonsense to say I wasn't good enough. I did that four weeks before the Olympics, *four weeks before*.'[58]

Once the *Manhattan* set sail, with her coveted cargo of American competitiors, the Nazis judged it safe to dump Bergmann without fear of repercussions, even explaining away her absence to the German Olympic team by claiming she was injured. Bergmann said this was the first time 'I really realised my candidacy as an Olympic athlete was all a sham.'

As a 'half Jew' Mayer received quite different treatment. Her physical appearance was that of a stereotypical Aryan: blonde hair and fair-skinned in contrast to Bergmann's dark eyes and hair. By one grotesque irony among so many, years before the Ministry of Propaganda had described Mayer as a perfect Nordic woman – but that was before they discovered her Jewish ancestry. The Ministry now ordered that 'coverage should not mention there are two non-Aryans [Mayer and Bergmann] among the women on the team'. The presumption must be that Bergmann's continued public 'inclusion' was intended to prolong the pretence even after she had been ditched. Whether the German public could see through these manoeuvrings – the word 'posturings' has been used – in a situation of tight censorship seems highly unlikely, although a day later *Der Angriff* explained that, apart from the two high-jumpers selected, no others were world class.[59]

The Ministry held daily press briefings at noon to exercise the censorship. That involved control over what would be printed and what omitted as well as identifying subjects to be given particular prominence. If newspapers and magazines did not have a reporter present, confidential directives were sent to editors and section editors. These directives had to be kept in a safe place and destroyed at regular intervals.

Hans Bollmann, the head of the Nazi sportswriters association, insisted journalists reporting the Games should be totally committed to National Socialism, drawing, he wrote, on the Nazi imperatives of '*Volk* [people], race, blood, and soil'.

On 16 July, the Turkish and Brazilian contingents arrived at the Olympic Village.

The *Manhattan* maintained her course for Europe. On board, most competitors, American officials noted, went 'through their training program almost as they would at home' (although Stephens lapped the deck again). Space had been allocated on several decks for training and it gave the ship 'the appearance of a floating gymnasium'.[60]

In the afternoon Brundage addressed the team. He said the deeds accomplished in Berlin would make these Games long remembered and some of the men's track team shouted their approval so rowdily and clapped so loudly that Brundage halted. Once they had settled down again he explained that each of them would have to take the Olympic Oath at the Games and he read it out. He also explained that the team did not have the facility to provide each competitor with their own coach but added that the competitors knew what to do anyway. He wished them luck.

Brundage added that when he sailed to Stockholm for the 1912 Games he saw 'several of his comrades destroy their chances by eating too much. Exposure to the unlimited menus on shipboard was fatal to some,' he said: medals had been lost at the dinner table.[61]

That raised a problem for many because, by definition, they were active or hyperactive and bored by the shipboard rhythm. The diary Helen Stephens kept is extremely eloquent about how mundane things filled most people's days. They certainly couldn't train as they would have on dry land, burning off the calories, and they discovered what every seasoned transatlantic passenger knew: on a ship the food is rich, plentiful and a too-tempting way to pass the time.

Wykoff, an experienced competitor, understood exactly what Brundage was getting at because on the ship to Amsterdam in 1928 he'd put on 10lb and was determined not to make that mistake again – especially since he found the food on the *Manhattan* 'swell'. But Donald Ray Lash, a 5,000-metre runner from the University of Indiana, put on 1lb a day – 10lb over the duration of the voyage – and would have a disastrous run in Berlin, finishing thirteenth.

Louis Zamperini beat him but only by six places, having himself put on 12lb. Being a kid from the Depression, Zamperini had never even bought a sandwich from a drugstore and here he suddenly was taking the train from California to New York and the *Manhattan*. The adventure of the travel seemed more exciting than the prospect of the Games themselves and the food more exciting still: it was free and with his bacon and egg at breakfast he'd have about seven sweet (say, cinnamon or caramel) rolls. 'My eyes were like saucers.'[62] Williams remembered having the sweet rolls before breakfast, then breakfast from the menu, lunch, a tea break, supper and at 10 p.m. more food which passengers could 'pig out' on. He estimated he gained 8 or 9lb during the voyage.

Ellison 'Tarzan' Brown, a Narraganset Indian and marathon runner, put on 14lb, suffered an Achilles tendon injury because of the extra weight and got no further than 2 miles into the marathon. Owens, by contrast, dealt with 'his boredom, homesickness and anxiety by sleeping, not by eating foolishly'.[63]

There were things to do. Gertrude Wilhemsen, javelin and discus thrower, remembered that Owens 'asked me to be his shuffle board partner on the ship. I was thrilled! A green farm girl being a team mate of Jesse Owens! Jesse was my hero and I gave up a chance of meeting Hitler to see Owens compete in his events.'[64]

After Brundage had spoken, an official handed out a list of conduct rules and mail from home then four of the girls, including Stephens, had to don their running gear and go on deck for a photo shoot.

That night the ship hit a storm and several athletes were very seasick, including Owens. Velma Dunn remembers, 'The voyage was a little rough because ships in those days were not stabilised, but other than that it was fine. I met Jesse Owens on the ship but I didn't make too much of him at that time because being a diver I wasn't into track and field so he was just one of the athletes and nobody knew what he was going to do in Berlin.'[65]

On Friday 17 July, a coach, Dee Boeckmann, seemed preoccupied. The athletes gathered to watch film of the Olympic trials and afterwards Boeckmann asked Stephens to come by her cabin. There, Boeckmann wanted to know if Eleanor Holm was 'influencing' any of the other girls by stirring up trouble. Evidently, Stephens had received protest letters about anti-Semitism in the German team and Boeckmann said Brundage wanted to see them because they could auger trouble in Berlin.[66]

Through it all the *Manhattan* kept on coming.

The torch relay was being prepared. German broadcasters made their way towards Olympia for the start but the rough roads and tracks slowed them down, to 10 miles an hour.

The Egyptian team arrived at the Village.

Fritz Wandt recalls:

[there was a building called] the Bastion, a small round kiosk in the middle of the Village where the sportsmen could meet at night and have a (non-alcoholic) drink for which they had to pay. From that Bastion they had a wonderful view of the Village, the forest, the lake with the sauna or to the reception building or to the Speisehaus der Nationen (restaurant of the nations).

Some of the dining halls were for up to 150 persons – for the bigger national teams. The Americans were more than 300 and they couldn't eat all at the same time, of course. The dining halls all looked out onto the terrace. Only the sportsmen from a few countries were allowed to have alcoholic drinks, like the Dutch and the Belgians who drank beer and the Italians and the French who preferred wine.

The sportsmen also met in the Hindenburghaus where 500 to 600 people could sit each night in the great hall and watch cultural events. The most famous artists would come from Berlin and present singing or dancing programmes.

And there was a ring of birches around a small paved area next to the Bastion where orchestras – Navy, Air Force or other military – would play each day. They came from all over Germany. At noon they played at the Speisehaus and, in the evenings, in the ring of birch trees. They played all sorts of music.[67]

In Berlin a 'Laughter Week' ordered 'jollity and cheerfulness' to help the citizenry prepare for the rigours of the Games. They were instructed to wear friendly faces for all the Olympic guests due any moment now.

From the *Manhattan* Wykoff wrote a letter to Frederick Graham, sports editor of his local paper, the *News-Press*, in Glendale, California expressing thanks for all he had done. He said that thus far everything had been perfect and added, delightfully, a request to be forgiven for the state of his handwriting: he was not, he insisted, drunk; it was the result of the motion of the *Manhattan*.

Later that day others were to be much less sober than Wykoff. Eleanor Holm discovered the ease of moving between the classes on the ship and found a bar in First Class on A Deck, a haunt of reporters, which suited her.

She fell in with a journalist and playwright who, recently remarried, was escaping a feud with his first wife. He liked a drink, she liked a drink, journalists like a drink and they had a party that Friday night. One report suggests the owner of the ship invited her and it began as a cocktail party.[68] At one point someone approached her at the bar, where she was drinking champagne, and said she really ought to go to bed. 'Oh, is it really bedtime? Did you make the Olympic team, or did I?' The party lasted until 6 a.m. when Holm was seen being carried back to her cabin.

This became one of the biggest stories of the whole Games and Velma Dunn gives it some perspective.

[Holm] was from Los Angeles and she trained at the Los Angeles Athletic Club, so did I and she was one of the most generous persons I have ever known for giving her time and helping others. Let's say somebody was a backstroker. If they were there for practice and having a bit of trouble with their stroke or something she would spend her time helping them. She was very good looking in a provocative way. That would be fair to say. Sexy, that's right.

You have to remember she was married at the time and she was a nightclub singer. Part of her life was singing and drinking and many of her friends were on the ship same as we were, except that they were up in First Class. She thought nothing of going up to First Class at night and being with her friends. That wasn't my life! I'd never done that! But it was her regular life. I think that to anybody working in a nightclub liking a drink would be part of it.

If she had competed it was a kind of foregone conclusion she would have won a gold medal because she was just an excellent swimmer. She was a natural swimmer. Many of us had to work for whatever we got.[69]

Holm was not alone in flouting the team rules about training and curfews; members of the hockey and fencing squads drank and stayed up late, too.

The American Olympic Committee members on the ship faced a crisis. Failure to act would likely lead to a breakdown of discipline and a minority wanted the offenders removed from the team immediately. Instead, warnings were issued that anyone offending again would be put ashore at Cobh. At this stage no competitors were named although subsequently Brundage confirmed he had offered Holm a second and final chance.

Brundage comprehended the difficulty of having a rigid set of rules for the conduct of so many competitors, ranging in age from thirteen to forty. 'We are making all reasonable allowances. We are not prudish nor do we have any objection to a glass of beer or smoking by athletes who know how to behave generally and not disrupt the team's morale and discipline. Now it's up to the members of the team to show they mean business.'

In the Olympic Village, with so many athletes already arrived, training schedules caused problems because the time for each team's squads at the stadium and pool had to be limited. At least the weather improved, the cold and damp giving way to something like a heatwave. The South Americans, so unused to the cold, welcomed this although the Peruvian team suffered problems acclimatising from the altitude of home. They caught colds and tonsillitis.

The Japanese continued to be secretive and inscrutable. Their football team scaled the perimeter fence of the Village at 4 a.m. one morning to practise on a pitch a mile away.

India would play eight practice hockey matches before the competition proper began, but they lost the first of them 4–1 to a German select team. The contrast in styles was marked, the Germans direct and robust, the Indians relying on 'short passes, dribbling and planned movement'. The Indians consoled themselves with the thought that although the Germans were strong, they had time to improve.[70]

On Saturday 18 July the competitors on the *Manhattan* attended the Captain's Ball, a lively occasion which seems to have pleased those who went. The athletes behaved impeccably so that, as a reward, the 10 p.m. curfew was extended to midnight. Brundage said publicly the matter of the rule breakers was closed.

Eleanor Holm did not say anything publicly – yet.

Sometime during the voyage – perhaps this Saturday, perhaps the day after – the Secretary-Treasurer of the American Athletic Union mentioned to a gathering of athletes plans for a post-Olympic tour. With so much already on their minds they almost certainly did not understand the significance of this and, anyway, with each day bringing them nearer Berlin, who could conceivably be looking beyond the Games?

On Sunday 19 July, as the *Manhattan* finally drew towards the Irish coast the athletes were doing light training. Some attended church services.

Owens had caught a cold bad enough to make him visit a doctor but by this fifth day he was feeling better, however much the shipboard confinement and routine bored him. He even slept one whole afternoon.[71]

The day's amateur hour parodied a well-known radio programme and shipboard fun featured a variety show in the evening with spoof weddings and funerals. Two boxers brought the house down with a dance routine, gymnasts yodelled and a female hurdler sang the blues. Eleanor Holm was no prude but certainly shrewd and, as she watched, she may well have concluded the spoof weddings provided her with ammunition.

The twin themes – politics raw in tooth and claw, the youth of the world preparing to play – flowed on. In Spain, General Franco arrived in Cadiz at the head of Spanish foreign legionaries, an event that highlighted a sad little footnote to the Berlin Olympics. Spain attempted to set up an alternative to the Nazi Games, in Barcelona, from this day to 26 July. Trade unions, communists and socialist parties from all over the world offered their backing. Free room and board were promised but competitors had to get there under their own steam. Apart from sport the programme included chess, musical and theatrical events. Teams from the USA, Britain, France, Germany and Italy did attend – almost exclusively communists in exile and socialists. The alternative Games did happen, however low key, and were even more subdued because with the Spanish Civil War tightening its grip on the country Republicans and Nationalists were exchanging fire all over Barcelona. Canadian boxers Luftspring and Yack intended to compete but when they reached Dieppe they heard they had been cancelled.

The workouts on the *Manhattan*'s hard deck damaged Stephens's shins, requiring treatment and rest.

On Monday 20 July the Finns arrived at the Village and by now the viciously anti-Semitic newspaper *Der Stürmer*, its pages until then on display in glass cases on street corners all over Berlin, had disappeared. Rumours suggested that Goebbels' Propaganda Ministry or even Hitler himself might have bought it to soften its tone or ordered it off the streets altogether. Some of the glass cases came down, others were being used for different publications.

The torch relay was due to start at noon at Olympia from the first Olympic stadium, among olive groves and pine trees and ruined temples. To ensure the torch's smooth journey, nothing had been left to chance.

Certain delays had to be allowed for, and for this reason an additional two-hour period was inserted for each 80–100 kilometres, these intervals being utilised in the larger cities for special ceremonies. In the case of slight delays, such a programme could continue until the runner arrived with the Olympic Fire. In every case the runners had to depart punctually and the entire relay run had to be organised so that the final torch bearer would enter the Olympic Stadium [in Berlin] at the proper moment during the opening ceremony.[72]

The special ceremonies 'constituted an effective introduction to the Olympic Games'.

A model programme was sent to each town to be used as a general basis for the ceremonies. This programme included the following events: arrival of the runner, ignition of the Olympic Fire, singing of the hymn, 'Burn, Olympic Flame,' address by the Mayor, general singing, gymnastic exercises by the men, women and children, sporting demonstrations, singing of the Olympic Hymn, festive address dealing with the Olympic Games, folk dancing, folk songs, preparation for the departure of the next runner, words of consecration, singing of the national anthem, departure of the runner, pealing of the bells. Outlines for the address were also prepared in various languages.[73]

Beyond this, the National Committees could make whatever arrangements they wanted for these ceremonies.

While the whole world watched, the German Organising Committee felt that each of the 3,075 runners believed they were a living expression of the Olympic ideals, each would understand the symbolic importance of it, and each feel the link between ancient and modern.

At Olympia, buglers welcomed the day and dignitaries from all over Greece gathered. Thirteen Greek maidens 'in short, belted smocks of rough serge' supposedly resembling robes worn by ancient priestesses, entered the stadium through a covered passageway.[74] A magnifying glass, positioned on a stand, refracted sunlight creating a fire into which one of the maidens dipped her torch. In procession, the other maidens followed her to a Fire Altar outside the stadium where the dignitaries and the first runner, Kyril Kondylis, waited. She lit the fire on the altar.

The German Chargé d'Affaires watched, as did a crew from the German Broadcasting Company, journalists from far and wide, and film-maker Leni Riefenstahl. A favourite of Hitler and already well known for recording a Nuremberg rally, she was embarking on a lavish documentary of the whole Games. The local mayor and a Greek government representative spoke, a message from de Coubertin was read. It praised the relay run and requested the 'youth assembled in Berlin accept the heritage of my work – that the bond between the physical and intellectual forces may be sealed eternally for the progress and honour of humanity'. A gun was fired and ancient instruments accompanied a hymn.

As the moments ticked towards noon and reports reached the German Organising Committee that the run was generating mounting anticipation in all the countries and places through which it would pass, Kondylis, dressed in shoes and shorts, came forward and prepared for the solemn moment that would unite past, present and future.

The broadcasting crew preparing to cover the moment comprised three radio reporters, three engineers and three drivers. They had flown to Athens while a heavy cross-country transmitting car, adorned with the five Olympic rings, and a saloon car went by rail. Now microphones were set up.

At noon Berlin called.

Kondylis lit his torch from the altar.

In Berlin, the loudspeakers relayed the commentary from the transmitting car into the crowd that had gathered in the broad square in front of the town hall.

Kondylis turned and set off on the first of thirty-seven handovers to a place called Pont Ladon. The relay would pass through there at 3.15 p.m., and so on through fifty handovers to a place called Vytina, and with each footfall the sense of anticipation increased. The radio crew departed immediately for Athens and from then the supply of hourly bulletins heightened the excitement.

The Greek route was prepared in a most thorough manner. The runners were conveyed to their posts in motor-coaches, and those who had completed their stretch were collected by a following car. At other times an automobile preceded them, depositing the fresh bearers at their posts and taking in those who had completed their stretch. This system was used wherever changes had to be made on the highways or in streaming rain so that the runners would not have to wait in the open. Since sporting clubs existed only in the larger cities, peasant youths from the districts through which the Fire passed were usually enlisted as torch bearers. They had enrolled in the lists circulated by the Greek Olympic Committee and ran in their national costumes, which included the short, full skirt or 'fustanella'.[75]

The broadcasting crew faced difficulties because Greece had no radio network to plug into. More than that, the crew recorded their broadcasts onto disks for posterity and the temperature began rising towards 122 degrees Fahrenheit. The disks became so soft the recording needle cut into them. In all the laboured, seemingly meticulous planning and rehearsing, the consequences of the fierce heat of a Greek summer, had been overlooked. The crew stepped outside the box: they used their initiative and poured their drinking water over the disks to keep them cool. It worked, just the way forward planning sometimes doesn't and human initiative usually does.

The *Manhattan* kept on coming.

Chapter 5

LIGHT MY FIRE

I refer to the mock marriage and mock trial ostensibly given as an entertainment feature but so shocking that many athletes walked out of the social hall. The trial was presided over by Gustavus T. Kirby who so handled the dialogue having to do with marital situations that it was open to questionable interpretations and altogether unsuitable for youthful ears.

Eleanor Holm, US swimmer

The city of heavy stone had a population of over 4 million, making it the third largest in the world behind London's 8 million and New York's 7. It had its own accent and its own irreverent, quick-fire humour like any Cockney barrow boy, self-respecting New York cab driver or Parisian barman. Hitler never felt comfortable with the Berliners and a lot of them never felt comfortable with him.

Albert Speer recorded how, during the nations' march past at the Opening Ceremony, the Berliners' open enthusiasm for the French team, which they applauded long and loud, 'jolted' Hitler.[1] He sensed 'a popular mood, a longing for peace and reconciliation' with France which was not what he had in mind after the humiliation of the Versailles treaty. Their reaction, Speer thought, disturbed Hitler.

Berlin's stone-clad facades, the imposing avenues and ornate palaces, the squares and museums, the ponderous streets of three- and four-storey apartments with their secluded communal courtyards, gave the city its public face. It had another. The 1920s had been gloriously decadent, especially the city's nightlife with the nude reviews, upper-class brothels, homosexual haunts and artists' quarters (one club/restaurant even had phones on the tables so one customer could proposition another by ringing their table). Whatever the puritans in the Nazi movement did to this they did not get their way all over the city. Entire working-class districts remained staunchly communist and would do for generations. Berlin was not a placid capital, unifying the aspirations of a people with their politics. Right and left lived their principles not as matters of academic debate or fuel for ballot boxes but as something to fight and die for.

The city, squatting so heavily on the flat Brandenburg plain, could be arctic cold in winter and jungle hot in summer. Despite that, outdoor café life flourished and Berliners loved to walk their Sundays away in the woodlands close by or lie along the shore of Lake Wannsee. They even called the fresh air – *Die Berliner Luft* – their own because, they claimed, it invigorated and refreshed.

A visitor peering out of a carriage easing into any of Berlin's railway stations with their beguiling names – Schleisser, Gorlitzer, Anhalter, Potsdamer, Lehrter, Friedrichstrasse, Zoologischer, Charlottenburg – immediately sensed that they had arrived somewhere important, that the city felt like a capital. Now it prepared to open its arms to embrace the Olympic Games and, by extension, the attention of the world. Big, old capital cities know how to do that.

The difficult part is trying to reconstruct this assumption of welcome, or rather the apparent truth of this assumption. There is no easy evidence to the contrary, that any residents of Berlin thought the whole thing a waste of time and money; no easy evidence that the nightlife people made cutting asides about how horribly healthy they thought the whole business of the Games; no protests about disruption to daily life, especially traffic; certainly no sense that there were questions raised about value for money or, more sensitively, about what was really being done to the purity of the Olympic movement; no mention of any of the other questions one would be tempted to ask, especially anyone who loathed everything the Nazis represented. The ultimate question – 'Do you want this?' – was never asked, either. All the black-and-white pictures of crowds show herd-like groups, but what else would they be? About the Games, the cynical Berliner – sharp, perceptive, living in the current of the moment – remains silent. The rest comes to us as caricature, which is precisely what was intended. Powerful people would make simple, obedient, normal people enact the rituals which the powerful people demanded. And that is just what happened.

The Nazi machine orchestrated a unified Olympics, the same front of unified approval cloaking the Führer and everything else.

There were a couple of chinks in this presentation of unity in the form of cartoons. The publication details are not clear because both were potentially very dangerous to anyone associated with them. One shows the Brandenburg Gate with Nazi flags and figurines giving the salute. A slogan is scrawled across the Gate: '*Jews Warmly Welcome*'. A sign nearby reads: '*Jews Out!*', but the '*Out*' has a line through it and '*In!*' is written above. The second shows a pygmy Goebbels, his club foot evident, holding a Nazi flag in his left hand and strings to the five Olympic rings, each through the nose of a runner as if he is pulling them all along, in his right. The caption, in Berlin slang, says '*The Point of the Whole Thing*'.

There is a further insight into the Berliners' true feelings provided by Werner Schwieger, speaking in 2005. 'You know, things were not like they are today, at least as far as I can see it. The population was not so much interested. Of course, the stadium was crowded, they came from all over Germany, from all over Europe. Even from America.' By this he means the population may have liked – even thrilled at – the idea of hosting the Games without necessarily wanting to follow them event by event.

Clearly the vast majority of Germans did favour the Games because by mid-July ticket sales exceeded 6 million Reichsmarks. What is not recorded are the views of those who did not dream of buying a ticket, not least because these Olympics had to be viewed as the Nazi regime incorporating the Games into its own forms of pageantry, co-opting them for the purpose of endorsing the vision of a united Germany; nor were those mentioned who thronged the Olympic venues and oggled artefacts simply because it was something happening, offering extraordinary sights in otherwise ordinary lives.

Schwieger's comment is illuminating – he 'did not really notice' the atmosphere in Berlin because, 'you know, those who had a job went to work and the unemployed had no money to go there'. Mind you, even though he had a job he'd go . . . .

And we might listen to Fritz Wandt, living so close to the Olympic Village. He collected autographs, as we shall see. The family talked about his collection as it grew. 'But my parents were not so much interested. They had other things to care about: their business. They worked on the farm from dawn til dusk – well, starting at 5.30 a.m. finishing at 7.30 in the evening. We youngsters tried to go to the Village as often as possible. For us it was a big thing. My parents, they took notice of it but weren't much interested.'

The stone-clad city dressed for the occasion with tall masts along Unter den Linden, through the Brandenburg Gate and all down the rod-like avenue to the stadium. Nazi banners fluttered everywhere. As the Opening Ceremony drew near, the number of foreign visitors rose.

MONDAY 20 JULY

The flickering flame and the padding feet moved across the rugged, difficult Greek terrain from the western side of the Peloponnese to the east. At some points the route threaded through narrow mountain passes cut into cliffs and rose, unprotected, to 1,500 metres.

Three hours were needed to cover the first 37 kilometres and a further six the 50 to Vytina, a historic mountain town with a small population – 2,988 runners to go. The flame kept coming across the Greek mainland and at midnight there were twelve days to the Opening Ceremony.

TUESDAY 21 JULY

By mid-morning the flame turned north for Corinth. At 7.20 in the evening it reached Athens and was run into the big stadium where King George of Greece waited. The Greek Olympic Committee had organised popular festivals at points along the route but this place, with the King taking part, became laden with symbolism. It was here, in 1896, that the modern Olympic Games had been born, growing ever stronger, through Paris, St Louis, London, Stockholm, Antwerp, Paris, Amsterdam and Los Angeles. Now, for an enchanted moment or two, what had become a sturdy adult returned to the cradle of its birth, as if completing a great historic loop of time and, in the completion, opening another, towards Berlin.

The German radio transmitting car got a connection but when the runner appeared and the speaker started to make his report the crowd stood so deep the cable was broken underfoot: a pity, because the commentator had a lot to describe – the white marble stadium, the crowd, the runner bringing the torch to the King who used it to light a flame on an altar, maidens in period dress and fifty-two guards holding the flags of the nations going to Berlin.

Still the *Manhattan* kept on coming from the New World to the Old – nearing the shore of Ireland on a chill day – and the flickering flame and the padding feet kept on coming, too, from the ancient world.

On board the *Manhattan* Owens captured the boredom in simple words in his diary: 'The day as a whole was very dreary & nothing exciting happened.' Stephens noted in hers how pretty yet bare Ireland looked and, later, with the *Manhattan* sailing mostly within sight of land, how 'picturesque' Plymouth looked.[2]

That was eleven days before the Opening Ceremony; towards midnight, the flame left Eleusis; 2,728 runners to go.

WEDNESDAY 22 JULY

On the Wednesday the torch left Thebes at 3.45 a.m. and by midday reached Delphi, to the ancient Greeks the centre of the universe. There, in an ancient stadium with stone tiers cut into the parched countryside, runners, some in traditional costume, some in athletes' singlets, ran with it in a ceremony lasting 70 minutes. From Delphi the narrow old road wound slowly down to the town of Lamia by the coast and another ceremony, this one lasting an hour.

The German broadcasters encountered problems at Delphi. Because of a 'misunderstanding only one cable had been laid, and under difficult conditions in tropical heat a second cable had to be laid in order to provide the necessary means of communication . . . after an hour this difficulty too was removed. The broadcast went off without further incident.'[3]

In Berlin, German journalists – already ordered 'to use Olympic Games and preparations for them for extensive propaganda in Germany' – received another directive from the Ministry of Propaganda, warning that if they published anything 'prior to the official press report' they did so 'at their own risk'. Nobody could mistake what that might mean. 'Reports about the *Rassenschande* [sex between Aryans and Jews] will be reduced to a minimum. The racial point of view should not be used in any way in reporting sports results. It is the duty of the press to remember that during the Olympic Games no attacks against foreign customs and habits should be reported. The Chinese in Berlin have already complained twice.'

At Le Havre the *Manhattan* prepared for her final leg to Hamburg. Customs officials came on board and did all their paperwork so that the Hamburg disembarkation could proceed with minimal inconvenience. Later the ship moved past Dover and out into the North Sea.

Holm followed the impetus of her own saga. The details are understandably scant and sometimes contradictory, but clearly between Cobh and Hamburg something happened. One source quotes her as saying she was 'free, white and 22' and intended to behave as she wanted, adding that during the French port stopover she was 'seen staggering with a young man along the deck and was later overheard shouting obscenities through her porthole'. Some sources suggest she told Brundage she trained on champagne and caviar, others that she said this loudly but before the trip. It seems likely that at a farewell party she got very drunk and, trying to get back to her cabin, met the chaperone of the women's team who, worried about the state she was in, called for medical assistance. She let loose a tirade against the team's officials and their rules, and passed out. When the doctors arrived they couldn't wake her.[4]

The Icelandic team arrived at the Olympic Village.

That night the flame reached Lamia, a sprawling hilltop town with a fort, some 200 kilometres north of Athens: leaving Lamia, 2,497 runners to go and, from midnight, ten days to the Opening Ceremony.

THURSDAY 23 JULY

The flame moved through Larisa and cut inland to the mountain town of Kozano, founded by Christians in Ottoman times, cut back towards the coast and Thessalonika. The roads were deep in the countryside, isolated, and wound through the thinly populated Thessalonian plain. That meant the runners had to be conveyed long distances to arrive at their posts. No trees grew along this stretch to protect them from the burning Greek sun which at times took temperatures as high as 122 degrees Fahrenheit.

The *Manhattan* moved along the Dutch coast, sometimes travelling at only a few knots, and Stephens found the glimpses of Holland picturesque, too, including of course the windmills. Evidently she went to bed early but couldn't sleep, took a stroll on deck and heard distinctive sounds coming from under the canvas of a lifeboat. Soon enough Owens emerged. Minutes later a girl emerged, too, and, passing Stephens, wished her good morning.[5]

Stephens subsequently recalled that the morning after the Holm incident all the female competitors were 'paraded' through Holm's cabin, presumably as a warning against the demons of drink because Holm had a very visible hangover.[6]

The *Manhattan* kept on coming, now towards Cuxhaven at the mouth of the River Elbe and Germany. At Cuxhaven a boat bearing the Olympic and Nazi flags came alongside to take off the horde of newsmen and photographers who had boarded at Le Havre. As the *Manhattan* moved down the Elbe, passing river traffic greeted her with waves. Then she rode at anchor for several hours waiting for the high tide. The team practised their march past for the Opening Ceremony.

China, Latvia and Yugoslavia arrived at the Olympic Village.

A single Chinese competitor had gone to Los Angeles in 1932 and this 'aroused worldwide attention as it had not been expected by the Chinese government'. It sparked even more worldwide interest that the most populous nation on the planet was being represented by a single individual. Since 1935 the Chinese had prepared very seriously, setting up special training camps for sixty-nine competitors – athletes, swimmers, basketball players, footballers, weightlifters, boxers and cyclists – as well as preparing thirty-nine observers and nine demonstrators of the traditional Chinese martial art of *wushu*. A party of 150 journalists and visitors accompanied the team and paid their own way.[7]

The *Manhattan* sailed into Hamburg that night, her Olympic flags illuminated by searchlights and whipping in the wind. The competitors were excited and so were the people on shore and in other boats nearby, those on board shouting enthusiastically up at the competitors, who responded with what sounded like Indian war whoops.[8] When the *Manhattan* docked the searchlights went off and the competitors were ushered to bed to get whatever sleep they could in the excitement. After breakfast at 6 a.m. they would have a long, long day in prospect.

The *Manhattan* ought to have docked that Thursday but because of

the reception of the City of Hamburg we arranged with the United States Lines officials . . . to have the arrival delayed so that the team could disembark on the morning of July 24. This . . . made it possible for the athletes to be received by the City of Hamburg in the morning and by the City of Berlin in the afternoon and reach the Olympic Village, be roomed and settled in their new quarters before nightfall. No extra charge was made by the United States Lines for the extra night on board ship or for the additional meal served.[9]

The flame continued to move across Greece; there were now nine days to the Opening Ceremony, 2,250 runners to go.

FRIDAY 24 JULY

Near Thessalonika, towards midday, a storm – rain and hail – pounded the relay run and a cloudburst transformed the route into a muddy morass. Still the flame came and it did reach Thessalonika, Greece's second city, modern and decorated by Byzantine churches. The rain beat down but the radio car reported everything ready. It broadcast that several thousand people lined the streets and the houses were decked with green and Olympic flags. At a ceremony in the St Dimitri Church Square the mayor received the torch and, in a speech, set out the virtues of bringing different people together. He handed his torch to a local runner and the flame headed north again, towards the Bulgarian border. The radio team packed their equipment and set off after it.

The American Olympic Committee met over Eleanor Holm and decided to dismiss her from the team. Brundage made the announcement that she 'has been dropped for violation of training rules and her entry in the Olympic Games cancelled'. After the 'cocktail party' episode she had received an official warning and now became the only competitor to be disciplined. She would be asked to return her uniform and housed apart from the team. The following day she would return to the United States on another ship, the *Bremen*.

This was front-page news, and big front-page news. Holm was famous, extremely good looking, expected to win a gold medal, married to a celebrity and the antithesis of a humble Olympic competitor ready to tug their forelock to anybody: a potent cocktail. Many things amused Holm – including men, parties and champagne, but Mr Avery Brundage did not amuse her and being dropped didn't, either. Through a mixture of tears, pleas for sympathy, begging forgiveness, kicking, screaming and threats she intended to let the world know exactly how she felt: another potent cocktail.

At Hamburg the Americans came down the gangway from the *Manhattan* in a great column, each man wearing boater, blue uniform bearing the Olympic emblem and white trousers. The way they carried themselves, so open and easy and confident, made a great impression on the people watching, as did their sheer numbers, emphasising that a boycott would have delivered a terrible blow to the whole Games – but they were here and, at this instant, they were on German soil.

The Americans attended a ceremony in the town hall and some expensive wine glasses went missing. Whoever had 'borrowed' them was ordered to return them or else. The team boarded two special trains for the three-hour journey to Berlin. The engines had large swastikas draped over their sides.

Coming as Holm did from a free country, sporting officials had the power to deselect her, but once they had done so they became powerless. Holm did not get on the *Bremen* or any other ship. She intended to continue pleading her case and raising hell.

Stephens remembered Holm out of her uniform and holding suitcases, preparing to board the train which the team wasn't on. Stephens found the situation 'pathetic'. Presumably the American officials boarded the second train because on the journey to Berlin Holm spent an hour talking to members of a special subcommittee, trying to persuade them to reinstate her. She told one of its members, 'I know I've been drinking too much and I'm all wrong.'

The two trains eased into the Lehrter station, one of those stone-clad buildings with heavy porticos. A band welcomed them, various dignitaries prepared to greet them and the crowd in the foreground held their arms rigid in the Nazi salute. Many in the crowd wore military uniform and that immediately set the tone. Men in uniform were so numerous they provided a constant backdrop to daily life and, thus, to the Olympics.

The American team engulfed the platform, and reporters and newsreel cameras moved in among them.

Velma Dunn says that, in general, 'every man, and every boy of military age, was in uniform. *Everyone*. That was very striking. When we got to Berlin about two-thirds of the people on the platform greeting us were military people. Definitely.'[10]

As Marty Glickman made his way slowly down the platform a stranger tapped him on the back. Glickman turned and saw a man smaller than himself. The man enquired in English with a perfect American accent, 'Are you Marty Glickman?' Glickman felt immediate apprehension and said he was an American. (Paradoxically, Glickman had some command of German and could probably have understood the question if it had been put to him in that language.)

The stranger: 'You're Jewish, aren't you?'

Glickman said he was.

The stranger said he was, too. He explained that he attended medical school in Berlin because he couldn't get to one in America because of the anti-Semitic regulations. They wished each other luck and the stranger melted into the throng.[11]

Outside the station an immense crowd waited and the American team stood in the open-top buses taking them to the town hall. They were happy and making a lot of noise. The traffic halted to let the buses through, causing congestion. Brundage said that the streets 'had been roped off and hundreds of thousands of spectators cheered and waved greetings to the American athletes from every sidewalk, window, balcony, roof and other point of vantage. It was a cordial and inspiring welcome.'[12]

Glickman likened it to a Broadway parade and even people with considerable Olympic experience confessed they'd never seen anything like this.

At the town hall, Reich Commissar for Berlin Julius Lippert made a speech – amazingly the only speech. He presented Brundage with a commemorative medal, in response to which Brundage said: 'No nation since ancient Greece has captured the true Olympic spirit as has Germany.' It was a breathtaking statement, even from Brundage's fixed position and even given the necessity to flatter.

Then the buses took the Americans out to the Olympic Village where, in those boaters and blue uniforms, they marched two and three abreast along the winding pathway to their cottages. German reporters, who had travelled from Hamburg with the team conducting interviews, were astonished at how little the Americans appeared to know about the performances of other athletes. One journalist sought out Owens and quizzed him over a rival long-jumper, Luz Long from Leipzig, who'd done 7.82 metres, enough to beat the Olympic record of 7.73 metres set in 1928. Owens professed ignorance.

However, he found the Village 'all "very interesting" and impressive, especially the little television screen – the first one he ever saw – set in one of the central buildings for the transmission of the Olympic events. For his first evening, however, he was most impressed with the cool night air, which afforded solid sleep at the end of a hectic day.'[13]

Years later Owens claimed he hadn't prayed in public on the *Manhattan* and there was even less question of doing that in Berlin, which he described as a 'godless city' although he felt there must have been some believers who rejected Hitler's theories of racial supremacy.[14]

Because the women's quarters were within the Olympic complex, after dinner Stephens and some of the other American athletes wandered over to have a look at the stadium.[15]

Glickman wrote a letter to his parents recording his impressions. He roomed with Eddie O'Brien, a Syracuse runner on the 4×400 metre relay squad, and some of the other sprinters – Owens, Wykoff, Stoller – occupied rooms nearby. Glickman set out the geographical location of the Village and found its layout and buildings perfect. He described the hundreds of cottages with their twelve rooms, each containing a couple of beds, a desk and wardrobes.

Zamperini bunked nearby, too, and claims that Owens – 'a prince of a guy, a sweet, humble man' – was delegated to act as his chaperone for two interrelated reasons: Zamperini was by his own admission 'frisky', and the athletes were allowed into Berlin at night.[16] Owens didn't prove much of a chaperone, and for two more interrelated reasons: Zamperini discovered that when you order beer in Germany they'll be big ones and the effects can lead a man to scale a flagpole near the Reichstag to get a Nazi flag as a souvenir. When armed guards gathered below him he shouted the only German word he knew: '*Bier!*'

Marshall Wayne found himself in with fellow diver Elbert Root, whom he described as a 'wild Indian'. Wayne was supposed to chaperone him, but Root regularly escaped by the window, went to Berlin, filled himself with *Wurst* (sausage), came back and threw up all over the room.[17]

Holm, booked into a Berlin hotel, shed her tears in copious amounts and pleaded for Brundage to give her one last chance. Many team members supported her reinstatement – more than two hundred signed a petition, but Brundage remained unmoved. 'We gave you every chance,' he was quoted as saying to her. 'You have only yourself to blame. Now you've got to take it [the consequences]. I appreciate how you feel but you forced our hand and we had no alternative. I can tell you the Committee's mind is definitely made up.' Back home in the United States, her husband Art Jarrett told the Associated Press news agency that obviously he was disappointed his wife had been dropped, but added that she 'wasn't a ten-year-old any more. She's been around long enough to know how to handle herself. They ought to give some more of those swimmers champagne. Maybe they would win a couple of races.'

The American women went to their own quarters where Stephens found a political manifesto sent through the post to her, as it had been to various other likely medallists. Originally in Dutch but now translated, it said hundreds of innocent Germans could not attend the Games because they were political prisoners. It expressed the hope that Hitler would be influenced by the Olympic spirit to free them, but appealed to women competitors to refuse to compete. Similarly, Australian Pat Norton remembered Argentina's Jeanette Campbell receiving a letter from Holland asking her to organise a women's boycott of the Opening Ceremony and demand the release of two Dutchmen who had disappeared on a trip to Germany.[18]

Dorothy Odam, the British high-jumper, remembers: 'I was given a letter from somebody in a concentration camp telling me of all the horrible things that were going on, what was happening to them, and asking me to show it to someone in England. But being rather young I showed it to my chaperone and they took it away from me.'[19]

Costa Rica, Haiti, Hungary and Switzerland arrived at the Village.

Fritz Wandt stood 'in front of the reception building trying to get autographs. I happened to be there when the Swiss team arrived. I saw that something was going on at the entrance to the reception building and there came all the dignitaries, the commandant, a band and also the boys of honour [in white shorts and white knee-length socks wearing white caps]. The Swiss team arrived in buses and were welcomed by the commandant, who made a speech. They lined up in formation and the national anthem was played while their flag was hoisted. What was especially interesting was the standard-bearer in front of the Swiss team – it must be a habit in Switzerland – but he brandished flags in the air to produce different patterns. That was so impressive I can still remember it. Then the band moved in front of them and they all marched into the Olympic Village.'[20]

At midnight, two hours after the torch had left the town of Sérrai near the Bulgarian frontier, there were 2,016 runners to go and seven days to the Opening Ceremony.

SATURDAY 25 JULY

The flame reached Kula on the Bulgarian frontier at 2 a.m., the rain still falling and the roads bad. The intrepid and dogged radio car crew broadcast the moment the torch crossed over from Greece into Bulgaria; it had covered

1,108 kilometres and, because of the allocation of one runner per kilometre, had so far been carried by 1,108 runners.

In Bulgaria 235 runners took the flame to the capital, Sofia. The whole route was marked by road signs bearing the five Olympic rings, and officials on horseback helped with problems and directions. Virtually every village it passed through celebrated and the big cathedral square in Sofia was packed for a ceremony. Some in the crowd, no doubt Germans, gave the Nazi salute and a banner hung nearby with a swastika on it. The intrepid radio crew were almost undone (the Official Report says they received a 'surprise') because no cables had been provided. The Bulgarian Radio Company stepped in and offered their facilities, and the broadcast went ahead.

Owens had woken to find himself gazing into a gloriously blue, unbroken sky. He needed to make the most of it because changeable weather returned and during his two weeks in Germany rain fell every day, including later this day. He noted in his diary: 'The weather in Germany is somewhat funny. In the morning the sun is shining beautiful and suddenly it will rain.' The food compensated – generous quantities of steak, bacon, eggs, ham, fruit and juices. He made friends, too, with 'people from strange lands & most of them could speak some English'. He liked the Australians and wrote, 'sitting around listening to a Victrola having a bull session with some of the boys. What liars they are.'[21]

Wayne was woken at 6 a.m. to take part in Leni Reifenstahl's film. 'I could hardly stand on the platform. I was still partly seasick. I did the worst diving in that film I have ever seen, and they've been running it for the last forty years, for God's sake. My legs were like lead. All of ours were. I mean, 6 a.m. in the morning and we had barely gotten any sleep and were still half seasick.'[22]

The American team began to train, although sporadic rain and cloud decorated the day. They had plenty to sustain them: an immense quantity of Philadelphia turkeys and Long Island ducks had been shipped over, clams for chowder, crab, 1,000 honeydew melons, 2,000 muskmelons. (Before the end of the Games, the team – plus the Canadians – would eat 36,000 grapefruits.)[23]

Some American competitors, especially the hockey players and swimmers, did some light training while others simply unpacked or took a look around. Stephens wrote that she got her competitor's badge and, perhaps subconsciously in writing that, reflected the quickening pace towards the beginning of the Games, because the photographers started arriving and so did the autograph hunters.[24]

Stephens carried an injury – the shin – because she limped. She was already the centre of some attention because of her bitter rivalry with Walsh, whose sprinting career blossomed in Cleveland, Ohio. (Mercifully, for every contemporary journalist – except the Poles, of course – she did not use her full name,

Stanislawa Walasiewicz. No doubt many subsequent authors share the relief.)
Stephens seemed relaxed and said she'd take care of Walsh even with the injury.
For her part, Walsh seemed relaxed and said she had vowed to herself that
Stephens wouldn't beat her again, here or anywhere else. Stephens said, 'Yes,
we'll see about that.'

Like Owens, Stephens appreciated the food and the generous American-style
helpings. Moreover her sexual predilections led her to a German waitress
called Ruth who gave her special food and generous helpings. There would be
accusations and counter-accusations of sexual impropriety between Stephens
and Walsh, however, culminating in the assertion by Walsh's supporters that
Stephens was in fact a man, and much more plausible assertions that Walsh –
known as 'Stella the Fella' – *was*.

Esther Myers, the student, remembers that

everyplace in the city there were always people completely armed but they
never molested us, never harmed us in any way – never stopped us, except
we were certainly aware that they were there and we'd better not try
anything. I was young and having fun – a wonderful time – and it didn't
bother me. Berlin itself was a perfectly beautiful place to be, magnificent
city, just magnificent. But you wondered what was going to happen
[afterwards] because you knew something would. It was bound to.

We got the impression that they wanted to do away with the Jewish people
and the black people and anybody else they didn't think were as good as they
were. There weren't many propaganda posters – no, it was all so wonderful,
they were the supreme people and they had accomplished so much.[25]

Holland and Norway arrived at the Village, and the Canadian team of 120
competitors and officials reached Le Havre on the liner *Duchess of Bedford*.

Holm gave vent to her grievances in a great outpouring of feeling, printed
in the *New York Times* on 26 July 1936:

Since the American Olympic Committee apparently has definitely decided
that my behavior during the trip to Germany was such they won't alter the
decision to keep me from competing in the event which I won at the last
Olympics and for which I qualified as the No. 1 American in the final
tryouts, I feel now that my friends as well as the Committee are entitled to
have a statement of the facts from me.

I've never made any secret of the fact that I like a good time, particularly
champagne. Everyone knows that, including the Committee. The newspapers
published my statements on that subject during the final tryouts at New York.

Why then, if they felt so strongly on the subject, didn't all the American Olympic Committee keep me off the team right away? Why did they have to wait until we were in the middle of the Atlantic Ocean before suddenly deciding that my conduct was too unbearable to permit my remaining on the team, or that I was such a bad influence on the rest of the boys and girls?

In the first place I wasn't the only athlete to break training rules or stay up after the curfew sounded. There were at least one hundred offenders one way or another.

I'm not attempting to condemn any athletes for so doing, nor do I wish to single out any one of them for mention. They are my friends. They are just as innocent of any real wrongdoing as I am. They've shown through their action in petitioning the Committee to reinstate me that they don't think I should be made an example of.

The Committee refused to reconsider this, believing they would be made ridiculous and that their laxity in maintaining discipline would be disclosed.

Brundage's statement that I was the sole serious offender and that I alone was responsible for any impression detrimental to the team as a whole is absolutely false. It is well known by all connected with the American team that Brundage not only warned me but specifically referred to members of two teams, namely, field hockey and fencing. Newspaper men assure me that Brundage's statement to that effect was dispatched from the *Manhattan*.

I've no feeling against Brundage nor any other member of the Committee personally. Dr. Raycroft [Dr Joseph E. Raycroft of Princeton, vice president of the American Olympic Committee] was particularly considerate in giving me an opportunity to be heard after I had been condemned without a hearing.

The fact remains that officers accompanying the team, who were presumed to be setting a good example for all on board, failed to do so. Cocktail parties were a nightly occurrence. Not only was the social activity such on the upper decks that the athletes as a whole received scant attention from committeemen, but officer-members of the Olympic party disgraced themselves during a performance given for the benefit of the athletes.

I refer to the mock marriage and mock trial ostensibly given as an entertainment feature but so shocking that many athletes walked out of the social hall.

The trial was presided over by Gustavus T. Kirby who so handled the dialogue having to do with marital situations that it was open to questionable interpretations and altogether unsuitable for youthful ears.

The reaction to the whole show was such that it was the talk of the boat for days afterward.

Furthermore, there was no general rule against drinking among the athletes. The bar was open daily and nightly in two of the sections in which the athletes were quartered. On at least one occasion the bar didn't close until well after midnight.

Under such conditions how did the American Olympic Committee think it could maintain such absolute discipline as it appeared to desire or condemn me because I was unwilling to make a secret of the fact that I like champagne?

They told me that if I wanted to take a drink I should be more careful. In effect they said it was all right as long as they didn't see me.

This is my third Olympics trip and I had my heart set on winning the back-stroke gold medal for the second time.

In spite of all these things they have said about me and all the criticism, the fact remains that I have been unbeaten for seven years in competition and that I am the only member of the swimming team, except the divers, to make the team for the third time.

I'm pulling for the American swimming team as well as all our athletes to win. I only wish I could be there to help them. I expect to be there as a spectator cheering for them.

Kirby, still in Hamburg, defended himself vigorously. 'All I have to say is that only an evil mind could see anything improper in the performance. There was nothing to offend anybody. I acted the part of the judge and prosecuting attorney; the bride carried a bouquet of vegetables. We were all merry and the whole thing was done in the spirit of fun without anything offensive whatsoever.'

Holm was by now being flooded with offers, including working for an American media syndicate during the Games. The American Olympic Committee told her they would pay her hotel bill and a ticket for home on the *Manhattan*, due to leave Hamburg on Wednesday.

Brundage said he was saying nothing more.

The ceremony at Sofia finished at eight in the evening. The flickering flame and the padding feet set off towards the Yugoslav frontier, the transfer regarded as a gesture of friendship between the two countries. As the torch left the last town in Bulgaria there were 1,772 runners to go and, at midnight, six days to the Opening Ceremony.

SUNDAY 26 JULY

The flame reached the Bulgarian–Yugoslav frontier at 1 a.m.

At 7 a.m., the United States 10,000 metres runner Don Lash from Indiana went out for a run which (although he took a break for lunch) lasted until early evening. A collegiate, he had been a leading distance runner for a couple of years. During the Games he'd celebrate his twenty-second birthday.

By 8.40 a.m. the flame had reached the town of Niš for the obligatory hour-long ceremony. One competitor, who evidently hadn't made the Yugoslav team for Berlin, mounted a bicycle and, reserve torch in hand, 'rode beside the runners hour after hour through the heat and dust, singing and encouraging them on their way'.[26]

The American team had a more concentrated training session at the Village's track but so did plenty of other countries because the New York Times said the track resembled Times Square 'in the theater hour'. The Japanese avoided this by setting off for a training ground near the stadium, although not before their high-jumper, Yoshiro Asakuma, impressed the Americans by doing 6 feet 4 inches (1.93 metres) in his tracksuit.

The Italian team, under an American coach, spoke English and their Luigi Beccali, who had won the 1,500 metres in Los Angeles, impressed the Americans by circling the track dressed in black – the rest of the Italians wore blue. Beccali, a Milanese who originally came to running through a love of cycling, had been the first athlete to give a Fascist salute when he won in Los Angeles.[27]

There was a lot to be impressed about, not least the Indian 10,000-metre runner Ronak Singh – bearded, a handkerchief knotted in his hair as if he were attempting to balance 'a white dove on the top of his head' – trying to get used to spikes because at home he ran barefoot.[28]

Evidently Owens trained at the stadium. Later he'd claim that Hitler had said Long would demonstrate Aryan superiority by beating him, and Owens professed himself 'shocked' that Hitler would be so specific or potentially unwise as to name anybody.[29] Owens, who now knew Long by reputation of course, was naturally curious about what he looked like.

About a quarter of an hour after reaching the stadium Owens found himself gazing at the other athletes; he knew immediately which one was Long: Aryan, blue eyes, sandy-coloured hair, taller than Owens. As Long practised Owens thought *he's good*. They ought to have been more than sporting rivals because politics decreed that. They ought, in the authentic meaning of the word, to be enemies. In effect, one of the great sporting friendships was about to be born.

At 3.10 that afternoon the flame reached a small town, Pojate. There the schoolmaster entered into the spirit of the run with wholehearted enthusiasm.

During the final 15 days before . . . he had his 12 runners cover the course each day in order that they should attain the correct speed. In addition, all of the stones had been removed from the 12-kilometre stretch; a large sign with the inscription 'Heartily Welcome' was set up, and a youth on a festively decorated bicycle was stationed at each lap to accompany the runner. The schoolmaster's preparations did not stop here. He posted youths at every crossing to indicate the correct route by waving flags, and he himself accompanied the runners, standing on the running-board of an automobile with a large placard containing a sketch of the route in one hand and a watch in the other for controlling the speed of the torch-bearer.[30]

The flame's third stage this Sunday, to a place called Jagodina, might have brought disaster and did bring official intervention. A torch failed – its material was faulty – and the runner was picked up by one of the accompanying vehicles and driven to the next relay point as fast as possible.

Torch after torch was ignited in this manner until, after 25 kilometres had been covered, the torches again proved to be in order. This incident, which gave rise to rumours that the Olympic Fire had gone out, meant that a considerable amount of time had been unintentionally gained, and in order to equalise this so that the runners could continue according to schedule, a bonfire was ignited in front of the gates to the town of Jagodina from which the next runner ignited his torch and departed promptly on the following lap.[31]

Stephens recorded how, visiting the city of Berlin, Berliners gawped at the coloured American athletes as if they were seeing such people for the first time.[32] Berliners came to the Unter den Linden to stroll and get a sense of proximity to the Olympics through the flags and symbols there. This seems to have been both a manifestation of communal feeling and an expression of mounting excitement. One estimate suggested that they came in their tens of thousands and by evening must have totalled several hundred thousand.

Close to the stadium a second Olympic Village called 'Strength through Joy' neared readiness. It consisted of several vast halls and the idea was to bring in 20,000 German workers a day by train to watch one of the Olympic events then go to the Village for food, beer, wine and cabaret. It could accommodate 24,000 people. The soup pot alone held the equivalent of 125 US gallons (460 litres). Foreign visitors were welcome.[33]

Canada, Czechoslovakia, Italy, Liechtenstein, Romania and Sweden arrived at the Village. The Canadians were awestruck, a feeling captured in their Official Report:

The Reception Building was long but comparatively narrow, and semi-circular in shape, with the concave side across the outer Front entrance to the Village. To the left of the main gate was a luggage room, in the charge of an Olympic Forwarding Agent, he alone authorised to be in complete charge of the transportation of all team luggage – from the depot to the Village, then to the living quarters, and later back to his central office, whence it was sent on its way to all parts of the world.

Here also was the customs office, where incoming parcels or baggage were inspected, eliminating formalities at the frontier, and the team leaders were advised of the hour they would be cleared. For the convenience of the athletes there were small shops for the sale of sporting goods, stationery, souvenirs, photographic supplies, fruit and confectionery, and a travel office with information on excursions, etc.

Next to the press quarters was the post office, which took care of both local and foreign mail. Mail was ready at 7 a.m., 12 noon and 7 p.m. for delivery to a representative appointed by each nation, who had to return the mail bag used to take away one delivery before he could get another. Card notice of registered mail was sent the athletes at their cottages, and they had to call in person for it. A branch of the Deutsche Bank was a great accommodation in buying marks and exchanging money. Here also were the Sports Department headquarters, where the team leaders upon arrival received the team badges and medals for distribution, training schedules and the names of the athletic fields which had been allotted them.

Over the main entrance, between the two wings of the Reception Building, were the administrative headquarters, or main business offices. As in large hotels, a registration card was kept for each inhabitant of the Village, and here you paid all accounts, and gave notice to the athlete for home after their events were over. The Village Police Office was next door. Officers and patrolmen were specially trained.

The safety system arranged for the welfare and benefit of the dwellers was perfect. The first room in the right wing of the Reception Building included offices and reception room of the Commandant. He was appointed by the German Army, which was host at the Village. He looked after the welfare of the teams and made their lives pleasant. Incidentally Sam Manson [chef de mission of the Canadian team] made a hit with him and the whole German staff the very afternoon we arrived. Spaced around the front of the Reception Building were flagpoles, on which each team as it arrived hoisted its colors. Then the band played the team to their housing quarters, and when Manson came to haul up our flag on the pole in front of the Canadian office, he insisted on the Commandant assisting him hand over hand. After that gesture Canada almost owned the place.

Next to the information desk was 'The Hall of Nations.' Prior to the Games each nation named an Attaché, who was the official means of communication between his team and the German Organising Committee. Canada named Arthur W. Treadsway, CPR [Canadian Pacific Railways] agent in Berlin, who talked English perfectly, and was at our service at all times, arranging transport and smoothing out difficulties that were inevitable because Canadians could not speak or read German.

The Hall and the large visitors' restaurant at the end of the wing afforded facilities for meetings between the team members and their friends who were not permitted to enter the Village. Permission for friends or those on business to enter could only be secured from a team leader, and women visitors could not get in at all. Entrance passes had to bear the name of the visitors, the team member to be visited, and the house he lived in. Then the visitor was conducted to the address and back to the gate by a member of the Honorary Youth Service.

About 170 university youths had been in special training for almost two years for this service. They were of wealthy parents, and assisted free of charge. In their attractive white uniforms they were on hand at every scene of activity in the Olympic Village to render assistance wherever needed. They were familiar with the scenes of competitions and places of interest in the city, and acted as messengers or guides. Best of all they talked the different languages of the nations represented, and one who talked English was always sent with a Canadian. . . . A similar corps of university girls, also dressed in white, performed a similar service for the girls' teams of all the nations.

The village, occupying 325 acres, was constructed by the National Army. Within the grounds were built 161 cottages, of permanent brick construction and stuccoed. Every cottage bore the name of a well-known German city. Canada occupied four. Manson . . . had his headquarters office in House 'Glatz.' The other three cottages the team occupied were 'Beuthen,' 'Breslau' and 'Oppeln.' The streets were named after the German provinces. Each cottage accommodated about 25 to 35 men. The rooms were double, each containing two single beds.[34]

The Canadians were also impressed by a host of other arrangements. For example, that 'each nation had its own separate entrance to its own private dining room' and once there you could eat as much as you wanted; the 'special refreshment room, the "bastion", located on a knoll' and 'affording a magnificeint view of the entire Village'; and although the Organising Committee had 'requested the participants not to take or use radio sets or gramophones in the Village, Berlin artists came out to entertain. There were also selected films'. The Canadians were grateful that each competitor was issued with an identity card, allowing free travel on all Berlin transport.

A journalist working for the French daily *Le Figaro* summarised all this beautifully. When you entered the Village, he wrote, you had the immediate impression of being on holiday.

Fritz Wandt says the Village was fenced in.

I have read somewhere that there were about 130 policemen guarding the place, among them twelve on horses, and four or eight detectives in plain clothes. There was a lot of security there. The Olympic Village was run like a hotel. There was a reception desk just like in a hotel. Every team had to declare how many sportsmen had arrived, and for every sportsman 6 Reichsmark had to be paid per day by the Olympic Committees of their respective countries as a contribution to the expenses it was [incurring].

I guess other boys started to collect autographs so I got myself a little book, too, and at that time we would use pencils. Maybe at that time you wouldn't really know the importance of it, you just wanted sportsmens' autographs. I walked. There was a tunnel at the entrance under the road and mostly we stood near there, that's where we were allowed to be. Sometimes I went there with friends, not after school but weekends. You would show them the book and say you would like to have an autograph. They knew what you meant and most of them would do it – in fact, I cannot remember anyone who refused. There was always something going on, always someone coming out and giving autographs.[35]

Leaving the Yugoslav town of Kragujevac there were now 1,543 runners to go and, at midnight, five days to the Opening Ceremony.

MONDAY 27 JULY

By 9.20 a.m. the flame had reached Belgrade where a fountain had been transformed into a high altar from which it burned while a ceremony was enacted around it.

In Yugoslavia some kilometre stretches were covered by peasants in the long-tongued shoes traditional to the area and when the flame passed through villages of the German minority (descendants of Swabians) the cheering was particularly enthusiastic. At one point, however, the flame went out after a couple of minutes and the runner covered the kilometre by car.

Holm, hired by an American news syndicate for the duration, filed her first story.

In Warsaw, Stella Walsh equalled two world records – the 50 and 100 metres – in her final competitive appearance before the Games. Word got back to Berlin because Stephens wrote she'd heard Walsh had done 11.6 seconds in the 100 metres.

In Berlin training was washed out by the rain, although the 4 × 100 United States team of Glickman, Stoller, Metcalfe and Wykoff did manage some runs. Intriguingly, the *New York Times* pondered whether in fact they would be the team. . . .

Word had it that when Leni Reifenstahl went to Greece to film the beginning of the torch run she saw a handsome young Greek and said he looked like a god. She promised to make him a film star and flew him back to Berlin in her plane. There was, she insisted, nothing else in it.

The Estonian team arrived at the Village, where a diplomatic incident with the Americans and the Germans had been resolved. The Germans were accustomed to giving the stiff-arm Nazi salute as a reflex action and did so every time they saw an American. The Americans had no idea how to respond and certainly weren't going to reply with Nazi salutes. In the true traditions of diplomacy a compromise was reached, with the Germans giving a more military kind of salute.

The flame reached the Yugoslav town of Bačka Topla, home of the royal family. On top of a nearby mountain, where the royal mausoleum stood, thirteen-year-old King Peter welcomed the flame.

Torch and runner left ten minutes before midnight; 1,258 runners to go and, at midnight, four days to the Opening Ceremony.

TUESDAY 28 JULY

The flame reached the Hungarian frontier at 6 a.m. The horizontal barrier was raised and the 'broad band of the Hungarian asphalt highway stretched undeviatingly ahead, cutting through the endless plain. To the right and left lay the interminable fields of corn and sunflowers above which the straw roofs of the peasant homes and high rigging of the wells projected.'[36]

The flags of the two countries were crossed in friendship and a local mayor lit the first Hungarian torch from the last Yugoslav torch. The tempo increased, not just because of the improved road surface but because of a need to gain time to allow for ceremonies at two towns, Szeged and Kecskemét, on the route to Budapest. In the second of these, famed for its fruit, the ceremony was held in the scenic market square where the Olympic rings had been fashioned out of apricots. A big crowd gathered in traditional costume.

Huge crowds met it at 8.30 p.m. at Budapest. Gypsies serenaded the runners with music and a gypsy chieftain performed during the ceremony while the flame burned at the tomb of the unknown soldier.

The *New York Times* reported rumours of both pro- and anti-German demonstrations when the flame reached Vienna: the Nazis demonstrating their antipathy for one of the runners, Vice Chancellor Prince Starhemberg, who was also in charge of home defence – hence the hostility. The Nazis had no wish for Austria to defend herself but felt she should be incorporated into the Reich. Other rumours spoke of the German national anthem *Deutschland über Alles* and the Nazis' *Horst Wessel* song being allowed.[37] For three years both had been expressly banned.

The Belgian and New Zealand teams arrived at the Village. The main body of the Finnish team came in, too, and watched the Americans training. They saw shot-putter Torrance but he was in poor form and 'when he stepped out of the ring he had a steam bath in an attempt to boil the kinks out of his muscles'.[38]

Holm went to a swimming pool in Berlin to practise, even though she had no chance of reinstatement. She paid to get in, something she'd never done in her life before. The German team recognised her and came across. She gave them tips on technique.

The Japanese attracted attention. Wayne and another diver went to watch them practising and locked eyes on to a Japanese diver who 'augured' (corkscrewed) his dives beautifully and consistently. Days later they watched him again, every dive as perfect as the one before. Then he'd surface, grinning. They decided to apply a little reverse psychology, got changed – didn't even take towels – and dived as perfectly as he had; they wandered round whistling casually between dives while he watched them. *Anything you can do . . . .*

The Japanese attracted attention in another way. Pat Norton, the Australian swimmer, remembered:

the Japanese uniforms were grey in colour and made the girls look drab, but when we met them at a concert one night we saw the ugly duckling turn into a swan! They came dressed in beautiful kimonos complete with obis [Japanese sashes] round their waist. What a difference dress can make – they looked delightful.

One day we were at the training pool when the Japanese male swimmers arrived to train. They immediately began to undress at the poolside which made us three modest Australian girls let out a yelp and dive for cover! We were only just getting used to men wearing topless costumes. When this was explained to the Japanese trainers they undressed in the rooms provided. They wore a costume with a cord through the legs tied at the back – they were beautifully built and did not cause any offence. We continued to happily share our times together.

Topless costumes caused a lot of talk in our newspapers back home, in fact our coach Harry was chosen in 1935 to model how men would look in the waist to thigh costume. One lady wrote in to the *Sunday Sun* and said if they all looked like Harry why there's no problem![39]

Stephens practised the discus. On the track, her coach wanted her to modify her running style but that concerned her, and at night she applied ice packs to her injured, still troublesome left shin.[40]

The American male athletes trained every day at the Village. Coach Snyder, who commuted from a Berlin hotel, arrived to supervise the preparations of Owens and high-jumper Albritton. Snyder found that one of the other coaches had tried to change Owens's arm action and the way he positioned himself for the start. Snyder quickly put a stop to that.

Snyder had several concerns. On the voyage over he learnt that Owens had taken three pairs of spikes to Randall's Island, two new and one old, and lost the new pairs. Now Owens faced the Games with only the old pair. Would they stand up to the 100 metres, 200 and long jump? He was using a German pair as back-up and didn't like them. Snyder 'urged' the American Olympic Committee to order a new pair from England but, as the Games approached, they hadn't arrived. Snyder found a sports shop in Berlin and bought a pair with his own money. That led to a further concern because not enough time remained to break them in properly and Snyder feared they could give Owens blisters. Owens remarked laconically that if they hurt he'd jump further.

Snyder was also unhappy that a mass of photographers and autograph hunters milled about during the practice sessions, all seemingly drawn to Owens. He said 'it seemed to me that Jesse spent most of his time in Berlin smiling at the birdie, with a dozen or so foreign athletes clustered around him or hanging on him, so that they might have a souvenir to take back home'. Synder wanted both athletes, Owens and Albritton, to concentrate on their preparations and tried to have the intruders banished. How far Snyder succeeded is not clear, but each day when he commuted back to Berlin in late afternoon people *were* drawn to Owens.

Women slipped notes under his door at night, often with marriage proposals. Several times Jesse was awakened in the early morning by people

shoving autograph books through his open window. One night he closed
the window even though the room was too stuffy to sleep soundly, but
awoke to early morning sounds of clicking camera shutters as people took
pictures through the windowpane. When Jesse stepped outside the Olympic
Village, he was immediately recognized, lionized. Once he and Dave
Albritton went out for a night to Shebini's Bar in Berlin to hear a black
trombonist. There Albritton drank his first champagne, which tasted to
him like ginger ale. According to his recollections, neither he nor Owens
had difficulty finding dance partners. Men came up asking them to dance
with their wives.[41]

The adulation reached such a pitch that, Glickman claimed, the only way
Owens could get in and out of the stadium without being mobbed was by
using the tunnel.

Max Schmeling, one eye still swollen from his victory over Louis, came to
visit the Village. Naturally he and Owens fell into conversation but, much
later, Owens reflected that 'he and his black team-mates were incensed at the
proud manner in which Nazis paraded Schmeling around the Village'. It may
be that, inwardly riled, Owens and some of the other black athletes intended
to atone for the defeat of Joe Louis.[42]

The Stephens affair with Ruth the waitress grew more intense, with Ruth
offering her culinary delicacies which she left in her room.[43] But girls met
boys as well. The German boyfriends of two of them evidently caused a scene
trying to get into the Friesenhaus.

In Berlin, services during the Games by the Evangelical churches were
banned, and printed advertisements for daily services at a church in the
district of Schoneburg seized.

The flame left Budapest at ten that evening and would be out in the
Hungarian countryside at midnight. That was four days to the Opening
Ceremony, 1,009 runners to go.

WEDNESDAY 29 JULY

By that Tuesday night, as it left Budapest, 2,058 runners had borne the
flame. On the Wednesday, with four days to the Opening Ceremony and on
the way from Budapest to the Austrian frontier, the route passed through the
Hungarian mining district, the runners moving 'past high mining shafts and
through workers' settlements in order to bring an Olympic greeting to the
miners'.[44] At the frontier, officials could not control a huge crowd as the
flame passed to the first Austrian runner, Dr Theodore Schmidt, President of

the Austrian Olympic Committee. A great cheer went up and some gave the Nazi salute. Schmidt struggled through the crowd and padded off.

In Berlin, as the IOC met in formal session Baillet-Latour proclaimed that politics and religion had not been permitted to infiltrate these Games. His assertion represented another statement from a fixed position, and by now those such as Baillet-Latour and Brundage were either in denial or trapped within the reality that in these last moments soothing words, however surreal, were required. No practical alternative offered itself. Ernest Lee Jahncke would discover within the week that IOC politics was very much alive.

Other Americans were about to make painful discoveries. Two boxers, featherweight Joe Church and welterweight Howell King – their team's best in each category – had been spirited out of the Village under cover of darkness, taken to Hamburg and put on board the *Manhattan* for the return journey to New York. The man in charge of the boxing said they were 'homesick', an explanation greeted with some derision in the press. What had they done? Brundage confessed all, but only when he no longer felt trapped by the proximity of the Games. He would wait until they were over.

In training shot-putter Torrance (a.k.a. Baby Elephant), who held the world record, found himself hemmed in by too many spectators and it niggled him. Someone said he'd move these people away but Torrance, fingering his 16lb shot, said 'Leave them be. I'll clear them with this.'

The flame flickering through Austria was the shortest stretch of all and, covered on good roads, the day's total (292 kilometres) was easily the furthest so far. Outriders on motorbikes parted the crowds for the runners and a swarm of cyclists followed in their wake. The flame reached Vienna at 7.30 that evening.

The last runner into the city was silhouetted against the evening sky as he padded along to and through the Heldentor, the heroes' gate separating the inner ring road and a big square, to light the Olympic Fire at the high altar there. As he came a great cry went up: 'Hitler!' The streets teemed, sporting flags fluttered from a tower and spotlights played across them.

One report suggests that local people noticed a mob which looked 'poor, ragged and half starved', but they sang the *Horst Wessel Lied*.[45] With darkness coming on, a 'Heil Hitler!' chant began and the police made no effort to stop it. Schmidt tried to make a speech of welcome but was drowned out by jeering that grew into a great swell of abuse when he mentioned the President, Wilhelm Miklas. Vice Chancellor Starhemberg followed but, even with the volume on the loudspeakers at maximum, the jeering drowned his voice out, too. When Starhemberg set off with the flame thousands of Nazi sympathisers heaped abuse on him.

It made nonsense of what Baillet-Latour had said.

The Official German Report, written from its fixed position – don't touch anything unpleasant – recorded disingenuously that neither 'through the Burgen district to Vienna nor the richly wooded highlands of Lower Austria [were the runners] offered difficulties.'

The tempo sharpened in Berlin, the railway stations and airports busy as they disgorged more and more arrivals. The German railways braced themselves for a total of 4 million movements during the Games: 2 million arrivals and departures. Cars from out of Berlin filled the streets. The Lodgings Bureau struggled to find accommodation for the growing army of visitors (1.2 million by the end of the Games, 150,000 of them foreigners).

The information office at the Reich Sports Field opened. Personnel required a working knowledge of languages and stamina because their task proved 'extraordinarily strenuous. Women assistants were also employed . . . but they proved to be incapable of standing the strain of constant service during the rush hours. Before the competitions began, this office was often crowded with thousands of applicants, but the personnel proved to be extraordinarily capable in every respect even under the most difficult conditions.'[46]

Six interpreters, recognisable by armbands, manned the stadium's entrances dealing with whatever came along. 'A foreign lady visitor, for example, wished to be introduced to the Führer, and after her reasons for making this unusual request had been considered, the interpreter established connections with the proper officials and was actually successful in arranging an audience with the German Chancellor.'[47]

The competitors from Denmark, Malta and Poland – including Stella Walsh – arrived at the Village.

Fritz Wandt remembers 'a problem with the Polish team. Each house was named after a German city and, since these houses were named after Upper Silesian cities like Oppeln, Gleiwitz and so on [Silesia was once part of Poland] the Poles said "This is a provocation, we won't move into these houses." The Canadians and the Afghans I think, did. This is why the Poles were the only team that had to be divided, one part in the Village and the other part in the barracks to the north.'[48]

The British men's team left Liverpool Street Station, London, at 8.30 p.m. for Harwich, the ferry to the Hook of Holland and the train to Berlin. The British said: 'The London & North Eastern Railway Company made excellent arrangements for the transport of the team. The food on the journey proved expensive, especially as many meals were taken in Holland, and the rate of exchange to Dutch florins was very unfavourable.' This despite the fact that 'every competitor and team official received a return ticket from London to

Berlin and vouchers for meals on the journey. Sleeping berths were reserved on the boats.'[49]

For some reason the British women went by train to Dover, taking the Ostend ferry and resuming their journey by train again. Dorothy Odam recalls how she clutched 'a lion which was our mascot. At sixteen I was very excited. I had very old spikes with my toe hanging out because I couldn't afford new ones, a pair of shorts and a top that I had to make myself. They gave me some red and blue bands to put round my top and some red, white and blue stripes to put down my shorts. We were given a cravat, dress, jacket and beret, but the rest we had to provide ourselves.'[50]

As the torch emerged from the Austrian town of Stockerau at 11 p.m., 2,350 runners had borne the flame. Out in the Austrian countryside, that was three days to the Opening Ceremony and 717 runners to go.

THURSDAY 30 JULY

The flame moved north from Vienna towards the Czechoslovak frontier which it reached at 9.45 a.m. Two policemen kept a path open through the crowds at the frontier while the flame was transferred to the first of the Czech runners.

In the Friesenhaus the American women complained about the monotony of the food – presumably they were not receiving any of the feast shipped over for the men – and found it not particularly well cooked. Initially they'd been given green apples and typical German heavy black bread for breakfast, which they had never eaten before. The Americans hollered and got cereals, bacon and egg.

Velma Dunn remembered that the 'women's quarters were in a brand new building. It wasn't decorated, let us say, with pictures and things of that sort because as soon as the Olympics were over the Army moved in – it had been built as Army barracks – so it was very spartan but otherwise very adequate. We were two to a room and I shared with Iris Cummings [200 metres breaststroke], a Californian girl. I couldn't complain about the accommodation at all. The food was adequate although not what I might have got at home. We just weren't used to so much boiled potatoes, boiled vegetables.

'We walked to the diving every day for practice or competition. It was not very far, I don't think even half a mile.'[51]

There had also been complaints because the rooms were damp and cold, the plaster not yet properly dry. Stephens also described the conditions as 'spartan' with a bed although not a real mattress, communal baths and showers, and a well-furnished lounge to welcome guests.[52]

Ruth told Stephens that among the 150 German youngsters acting as gofers some might have been spying on the athletes, so she hid her diary and made sure her luggage was always locked.[53]

The French team left from Platform 1 at the Gare du Nord, Paris, on a special train. Those of Monaco and Portugal arrived at the Village and the British contingent reached Berlin at 4.30 p.m. that afternoon.

The flame arrived in Prague at 11 p.m. that night for a ceremony in Wenceslas Square attended by the country's president.

The French team's train experienced mechanical problems and only pulled into Berlin shortly before midnight.

That Thursday 2,628 runners had borne the flame, 439 to go. At midnight, two days remained before the Opening Ceremony – the Friday and the Saturday itself.

At 1 a.m. on the Friday the flame resumed its journey from Prague towards the German border.

It kept on coming.

Chapter 6

WAR GAMES

The famous thoroughfare was afire with flags and banners, some
flying from four lines of poles running the whole length of the route,
others waving from windows or from the top of houses. The red of
the Nazi banner predominated.

Canada at the XI Olympiad 1936 Germany

At 11.45 a.m. that Friday the last Czechoslovak runner approached
the frontier, just south of a hamlet called Bahratal in deepest rural
wooded Saxony. The excitement was now palpable and it brought an
estimated 50,000, many travelling long distances, to witness the handover.
The frontier lay in the countryside midway between Bahratal and Petrovice
on the Czech side.

At the frontier a middle-aged customs official in white, armless singlet –
only his surname, Goldhammer, is recorded – shook hands with the last
Czechoslovak runner through a dense press of people, some in traditional
costume. Goldhammer accepted the transfer of the flame and padded off
along the open road, lined with trees, which dipped in a long undulation
towards Bahratal. He could see, to his right, meadowland falling away and
beyond that hillsides dark with taller trees.

The route reflected the Games themselves because they belonged just as
much to the rural folk here – isolated farming communities lost in the
woodland, small clusters of solid old houses, roads little more than tracks – as
they did to the inhabitants of Berlin. From Olympia in Greece to this German
frontier, the route had come to prove and would now prove within Germany
itself, that the Games belonged to everybody. Moreover, between here and
Berlin, as it wended its way north, the torch would pass through only one big
city, Dresden, and one town everybody had heard of – Meissen of the
exquisite china. The rest was heartland Germany and the places were places
nobody had heard of.

When Goldhammer came into sight the crowd in the little square at Bahratal roared 'Heil Hitler!' and collectively froze into the Nazi salute. In the square the flame lit up a temporary altar, the band played, the choir sang and the governor predictably gave a speech proclaiming that the Olympic Games should serve as a unifying force in the world.

A great flock of carrier pigeons fluttered into the sky and headed north towards Berlin. Their arrival there meant *the flame is now in Germany.*

When word reached the market square in Pirna, a town on the Elbe and the next staging post, groups of Hitler Youth sounded fanfares and as they melted away church bells pealed out.

Berlin, ready, waited impatiently. Trevor Wignall wrote in the London *Daily Express*:

Almost every street is deliriously decorated and be-flagged but gem of them all, if not indeed of the world, is the famous boulevard that leads to the Brandenburg Gate. Gone are the trees that for so many long years were its principal glory. They have been uprooted and their places taken by red clothed poles that seem to reach nearly to the skies. From each pole flies a banner. They bear two emblems only – the intertwined five rings of the Olympic Games and the Swastica of the Nazis. The organising ability of the German nation has never been so palpably in evidence. Years of preliminary work have resulted in the vast machine operating in the manner of a newly oiled clock.[1]

The *New York Times* reflected that mood, writing about the decorations from the Brandenburg Gate to the stadium: loudspeakers at regular intervals to relay not just Olympic news but official announcements and music such as Viennese waltzes and quick-steps. The squares and *platz* along the avenue out to the stadium sported big Olympic banners and tall flagpoles. A million people were expected to line it to watch Hitler and the flame go by to open the Games.

The luxurious, meticulously run Adlon Hotel beside the Brandenburg Gate provided sanctuary for the 'royalty and nobility' who 'thronged to Berlin'. They included the King of Bulgaria, the Crown Prince and Princess of Italy, the heir to the Swedish throne, the Crown Prince of Greece, Mussolini's sons, the Duke of Hamilton, and Lord and Lady Londonderry. The hotel owner, Hedda Adlon, remembered that 'it was at this time that I again met Prince Philip of Hesse and his wife, Princess Mafalda, the second daughter of the King of Italy. I have often thought of the Princess's large, dark, ardent eyes and of the appalling fate that awaited her eight years later.'[2]

Bermuda and Luxembourg arrived at the Village, making fifty-one countries and, at their maximum, 4,202 competitors. Village life offered fertile ground for the German love of statistics: by the end of the Games each competitor had 'spent an average of 19 days and 17 hours in the Olympic Village'.[3] By contrast, the Canadian swimming team were very angry about an astonishing failure to allocate them proper training time at a pool and scoured Berlin trying to find out at which they ought to be, eventually getting an hour at 6 a.m. in the main pool.

Jesse Owens moved easily around the American quarters with a big smile and a polite refusal to discuss any possibilities of gold. In the Village the American men's team staged a march past rehearsal for the Opening Ceremony but reports called it unimpressive and said that however many medals the Americans – and Owens – might win, one for marching would not be among them. It begged a much bigger question, the twin themes of politics and sport drawn tight together. As the athletes paraded past Hitler country by country – the tradition at every Opening Ceremony – should they give the Nazi salute? If they did, would they be publicly regarded as recognising the Nazi creed and, by extension, endorsing it? Worse, the Olympic salute resembled the Nazi salute and might be mistaken for it.

The Americans had to make a decision on this delicate matter, not least because some of the athletes felt so strongly that they refused to take part in the parade if they were ordered to give the salute. Some insisted they would not give it in any circumstances, others expressed indifference. Originally the men were to remove their straw hats and hold them out with the brims at arm's length but that had been moderated to holding them against their bodies below the left shoulder and keeping their eyes to the right. During the afternoon two American officials went to the women's quarters to tell them what they should do but neither the officials nor the athletes spoke publicly about it.

The IOC met in secret session and awarded the 1940 Summer Games to Tokyo rather than Helsinki – Britain had withdrawn her bid the night before.

From Hellendorf a chain of twenty runners bore the flame up towards Pirna, the entire route 'lined by phalanxes of the members of National Socialist Party organisations, school children and sportsmen'.[4]

Dresden, itself a stone-clad city but of cathedrals, churches, opera houses and museums of almost fragile beauty, lay a further 20 kilometres up the Elbe. The flame arrived there in the evening. A truly immense crowd, including members of the Reich Association for Physical Training and different Party organisations, watched as Hitler Youth trumpeters sounded a fanfare announcing that the twentieth runner was near.

Inevitably pomp and spectacle attached themselves once more to the flame during a ceremony on the Königsufer, the big open space on the north bank of the Elbe commanding a view of the city's spires: a programme of music, a speech from the Regional Leader of Physical Training, a gymnastics display and more music before it left on the 28-kilometre leg to Meissen – 227 runners to go. There, more pomp and circumstance surrounded the third ceremony since the run entered Germany: fanfares sounded from towers, an altar was lit in front of the town hall, the district leader of the National Socialist Party and the mayor made speeches, then the mayor lit a torch and padded off into the first of the 19 kilometres north to Grossenhain – 200 to run.

At Grossenhain, floodlights and thousands of candles turned the main square into an enchanted place filled with a crowd of more than 20,000. Floodlights played too on the town's 1,000-year landmark, a tower, now decorated by the Olympic rings. At 10 p.m. three canon, fired from the tower, signalled the start of festivities although the flame was still a couple of hours away. The flags of the seven nations through which the torch passed fluttered from flagpoles

At midnight, 1 August – the Opening Ceremony only sixteen hours away – Grossenhain's church bells rang out to announce the flame's approach. The crowds cheered and the Regional Governor gave a short address of welcome before the next runner padded off for Herzberg – 123 to go. The flame wended its way north through a string of anonymous little communities and reached Herzberg at around 2 a.m.; between Herzberg and Jütebog it passed from Saxony to the *Land* (the province) of Brandenburg, where the stone-clad city sat.

In the Olympic Village preparations for breakfast began, as they did each day, at 5 a.m. Vans from the Spandau Dairy Company arrived bringing fresh milk; biscuits, rolls and bread soon followed. Service was from 7 a.m., with menus in English, French, Spanish and German for the various dining rooms. The choice:

> Apples, bananas
> Porridge with milk
> Cornflakes, puffed wheat
> Grapenuts
> Orange marmalade, raspberry jelly
> Eggs prepared as desired
> Scrambled eggs with ham
> Coffee, tea, 'Sanka' coffee
> Malt coffee, cocoa, milk
> Breakfast biscuits, toast[5]

At 7 a.m., too, controllers and policemen moved to their positions at the stadium's entrances while others patrolled the area. At 7.30 a roll call ensured they were all present.

The flame reached Jütebog towards dawn and then at 8 a.m. a tiny place called Trebbin, the last staging post before Berlin – 40 to go.

Berlin seethed under an overcast sky and suddenly, at 8 a.m., two military bands struck up along Unter den Linden. The Canadian team noted that 'the opening ceremonies began with the thudding of drums and the blare of brass bands. Berlin troops poured through the Brandenburg Gate to the Armory [down] the Unter den Linden for a great parade, performing the ceremony of "The Great Awakening" by marching round the central streets of the city – with colors flying and stirring music.'[6]

Would the weather ruin the day? A south-easterly wind dragged cloud over and brought showers which might develop into more persistent rain or a downpour.

At 9 a.m. entry to the Reich Sports Field was forbidden.

Between 9.15 and 10.30 a hundred vans brought 20,000 carrier pigeons in cages to the stadium.

At 9.30 – the flame still out in the country, the runner jogging steadily towards Berlin's outskirts – a column of cars drew up outside the Adlon Hotel to take the IOC members to church: Catholics to St Hedwig's for mass, Protestants to the Evangelical Cathedral for a sermon.

Werner Schwieger, the gymnast, had received his Olympic pass a few days earlier.

I can't remember where it was issued but I do remember I had to deliver a passport photograph. It was a picture of me wearing my sports club's badge at my jacket's lapel. At first sight it looked like a party badge with a Nazi symbol or a swastika on it and a woman there said 'You know, we are not allowed to use pictures with swastikas as passport photographs', but it was not because I wasn't a member of the Party. First of all I got the participants' pass and then came the torch run, the dates given to us for the performances, the badge and so on.

For the torch run we were taken into the country outside Berlin by lorry and dropped off one at a time. You stood there until the torch was handed over to you, and you ran to the next man – great to be given a chance to take part. It was a country road lined with trees and there weren't many people watching. I took the torch – it wasn't heavy – and handed it over. Then the lorry brought us home. Was I allowed to keep the torch? Of course not.[7]

All approaches to Unter den Linden and the *Via Triumphalis* were closed to traffic. Spectators, some of whom had camped out all night to secure their vantage point, stood ten deep in places.

The famous thoroughfare was afire with flags and banners, some flying from four lines of poles running the whole length of the route, others waving from windows or from the top of houses. The red of the Nazi banner predominated. The huge crowd – there must have been half a million in Unter den Linden alone – were good humoured and comparatively quiet, but there were cheers for various prominent personalities. When the members of the International Physical Education Students' Camp marched down the Linden from the Lehrter station, the biggest cheer went to the Indians in their pink and grey turbans.[8]

At 9.45 a.m. three overland trains and three underground ones brought 28,000 members of the Hitler Youth to six stations. They marched in columns four abreast for their rendezvous at the Lustgarten beside the Armoury.

At 10.45 a.m. a guard of honour – infantry, navy and air force detachments – marched from the Brandenburg Gate to the Lustgarten.

Few police were present to control the crowd. The authorities had, apparently, forgotten that they were not dealing solely with the highly disciplined people of Berlin, but with hundreds of thousands of less disciplined foreigners. Gen. Goering's appearance, for instance, caused the crowd to sweep away the containing police and practically block Unter den Linden. . . . The General, dressed in an air force uniform, waved gaily to the crowd as he drove by. The cheers he received were by far the loudest accorded to any of the Nazi leaders. Then came Dr. Goebbels in brown storm trooper's uniform, with his arm held rigidly in the 'Old Party Members' version of the Nazi salute – bent back at the elbow. Herr Rudolf Hess, Herr Hitler's deputy, and Herr Baldur von Schirach were also loudly cheered.[9]

The flame arrived at the outskirts of the city at 10.38 a.m. It had 1 hour and 52 minutes to reach the Lustgarten.

After the church services, Baillet-Latour, Lewald, Tschammer und Osten and other dignitaries went to the low stone war memorial on Unter den Linden – a brief walk from the Lustgarten – and laid wreaths to commemorate the dead of the First World War. The assembly stood in an arc round them, the Germans giving the Nazi salute as an infantry batallion marched past. The dignitaries were cheered as they walked back towards the

Lustgarten: the Old Museum, a heavy building fronted by pillars, faced it, the Lustgarten actually the long, broad paved area in front of it stretching down to Unter den Linden. They went to the oval room where Goering and other government ministers welcomed them. Baillet-Latour made the formal reply.

Meanwhile at 11.55 a.m., the 28,000 members of the Hitler Youth moved into position on the Lustgarten. For some reason the German Organising Committee – or more likely Nazi politicians – had wanted the Lustgarten to be deserted when the dignitaries entered and full of men in formation when they came out. It *had* to be impressive, perhaps genuinely breathtaking – planning, organisation, discipline, speed; and, for those who thought about these things, ominous.

Within six years Germany would control all the countries the flickering flame of international peace had passed through except Austria, which it swallowed whole.

At noon every controller, supervisor, fire inspector and post office official had taken up their places at the Reich Sports Field and the stadium. The booths and stands sold only programmes, guide books and Hitler memorabilia no Olympic merchandise on this opening day.

Kansas student Esther Myers found the stadium 'Oh, magnificent. They had spared no amount of money to make it into the most beautiful spot you could imagine. By the time we got there the Games were just opening and I remember banners from the countries. They wanted you to know they were welcoming you. They were so gracious to us, oh my, yes. There were guns constantly but we never felt threatened.'[10]

'Halfway down from the top was an area where they had the places to eat. . . . There were souvenir shops — pictures of Berlin, pictures of Hitler, pictures of the German countryside, that sort of thing.'[11]

In the Lustgarten, von Schirach gave an address of welcome, seemingly oblivious to the ranks of uniformed men in front of him and saying German youth had been wrongly described as militaristic. 'We serve no warlike aims but only those of peace. My comrades, consider the Olympic Games a safeguard of peace. In this spirit I bid you welcome in a peaceful, honourable Germany.' Tschammer und Osten spoke and so did Goebbels.

The last runner – a strong young German – brought the flame up the Wilhelmstrasse, the long, straight avenue lined by many embassies and ministries as well as the Reich Chancellory. As Goebbels finished speaking the runner reached the intersection with Unter den Linden and turned right. 'The flame could be seen approaching over the countless heads of the assembled Hitler Youths, and cheers rang out as it came closer.'[12] 'The final transfer of the torch took place half way down, and the runner, preceded by the cars of film operators, bore it on through the now wildly cheering crowds.'[13] When the runner reached the Lustgarten he went to a temporary altar beside the Old Museum and the IOC members watched him light it. A band played *Deutschland über Alles* and the *Horst Wessel Lied*. The runner ran back across Unter den Linden to the Royal Palace where another altar stood and he lit a second flame there. It would burn throughout the Games.

At 1 p.m. the artillery regiment deputed to fire the salute at the Opening Ceremony arrived at the stadium and spectators with tickets were allowed in.

The IOC members and the other dignitaries walked to the area in front of the Palace where a motorcade waited to take them to Wilhelmstrasse, the Chancellory and lunch with Hitler. They looked, as someone observed, 'strangely civilian in their morning dress among so many uniforms'.

At the Olympic Village a vast fleet of military buses – 170 of them: the Indians were on number 150 – took the competitors to the stadium. Each bus bore the national flag of the team it carried. The Indians boarded at 1.15 and, all along the route, would find crowds cheering and waving.

At the Chancellory, Baillet-Latour made a diplomatic and effusive speech to Hitler who stood before him in light jacket, dark trousers and wearing a black swastika armband. Then the 150 guests sat down to lunch in the new state dining room.

That was 1.30. At that moment the first buses pulled up at the stadium. 'Male athletes of all the nations, led by their officials, came in by bus from the Olympic Village and from Grunau, and the women athletes from their living quarters at *Friesenhaus*. They formed up in columns facing from both sides a wide central laneway, their ranks extending back horizontally to right and left'[14] – twenty-six nations on the north side, twenty-seven on the south. The women began arriving from the Friesenhaus at 2.30.

The last athletes from the Village were due at 3 p.m. By then, their lunch with Hitler over, the dignitaries would be taking their places in the stadium.

American diver Velma Dunn remembers, 'we had to wait outside the stadium for a long time but that's true of every Olympics.'[15]

The Zeppelin *Hindenburg* circling low over Berlin, headed towards the stadium.

By now the stadium was full. From 3 p.m. the Olympic Symphony Orchestra – formed by members of the Berlin Philharmonic, the National and other orchestras – gave a concert. At 3.18, while they played, Hitler's motorcade left the Chancellory, moved up Wilhelmstrasse, passed through the Brandenburg Gate and onto the *Via Triumphalis*. Hitler stood stiff and upright. His Mercedes was followed by four others with guards in them. Those Mercedes ran at either side of the avenue close to the kerb. The motorcade travelled fast.

At 3.30, the loudspeakers along the way announced excitedly that Hitler was on his way and the concert ended.

'Punctually at 4 o'clock the two German national anthems – *Deutschland über Alles* and the *Horst Wessel* song – came through the loudspeakers and stilled the crowds, with their arms outstretched in the Nazi salute. While the last notes of the *Horst Wessel* song still rang on the air, the sacred flame was seen once more coming from the Lustgarten. There was one change of relay, and then it passed through the Brandenburg Gate towards the stadium followed all along the route with deafening cheers.'[16]

Once the flame had passed, the crowds dispersed to find something to eat and drink, but they came back to see the *Hindenburg* 'nosing its way low over the city'.

A little rain fell.

The layout of the area from road to stadium was impressive. Hitler would walk through the tall Bell Tower – so sheer and tall it loomed – and find, spread before him, the vast May Field where the athletes were now assembled country by country. He would walk along the passage left between them to the stadium, entering by the Marathon Gate and ascending tiers of stone steps. He would pass the crucible that would cradle the Olympic flame and then descend more tiers of stone steps to the centre of the stadium.

At 3.52 p.m., Hitler came through the Bell Tower and passed four field guns ready to fire the salute. A loudspeaker bayed '*We await the Führer every moment. Never would this great field have been built except for the Führer. It was created by his will.*' He reached the May Field.

Pat Norton and the other three Australian swimmers 'stood without rest for two hours before entering the stadium but the air of excitement and noise among the teams drove our tiredness away. While we were making friends with the only girl in the Argentinian team of ninety men [Campbell], who were standing next to us, the teams suddenly became quiet at the sight of Hitler and his entourage striding down between the teams. He looked neither to the left nor right and gave no sign of greeting or welcome. It was my first direct look at the man who was the talk of the world, and a more uninspiring-looking person would be hard to find.'[17]

Hitler walked down the passage accompanied by a group of dignitaries. Riefenstahl had laid track down one side of the passage so a camera could stay abreast of Hitler as he walked.

'We had to wait for Hitler to enter – the teams were lined up either side,' British competitor Violet Webb recalled. 'The diplomats came through and some countries gave the salute but we were told not to.'

Hitler reached the steps.

The loudspeaker bayed: 'We can see the Olympic Stadium where 100,000 persons wait feverishly for the moment when the Führer will appear. We can well understand the expectancy of the 100,000 awaiting the moment when the Führer will enter the stadium. Attention! The Führer now enters the stadium!' Then thousand upon thousand voices raised the Sieg Heil! and drowned out the loudspeaker while the orchestra played Wagner's 'Hymn of Praise'. Violet Webb remarked that as Hitler 'went into the stadium you would have thought that God had come down from heaven'.[18]

Hitler descended the first set of steps, crossed the running track, walked briskly for some distance, recrossed it and ascended to his box in prime position in the grandstand.

Back on the Via Triumphalis a lone cyclist, evidently unaware that the avenue had been cleared, cycled home between the astonished ranks of police and storm troopers – the whole route double- and triple-lined with uniformed men standing elbow to elbow – and got a bigger ovation than the runner with the torch. The Berliners had not lost their sardonic wit or their sense of irony.

Esther Myers found herself 'ten, fifteen feet maybe from Hitler. We had wonderful seats. They passed out our tickets and it just happened that I got an awfully good one. First he came and then following him was the stodgy little, fat mayor of Berlin a few steps behind, never level with him. They paused on the steps so that people could take their pictures. Things happened so fast that he wasn't there very long. Hitler happened to turn, strictly controlled but he knew how to turn! He stood there and people were taking pictures like crazy and going "Heil Hitler." He was an average sized man and he made quite an imposing looking figure there on the steps. He wasn't a particularly good looking man but a uniform makes most people look pretty good. And it did.'[19] (Her father thought she had lost her senses when she told him that.)

'Before the Opening Ceremony,' Dorothy Odam said, 'there was mass hysteria when Hitler arrived in the stadium, but we had to wait for an hour before we could enter. It was so hot that they had to bring us refreshments.'[20]

The Canadian Official Report noted that the teams 'assembled in line at the mouth of the tunnel ready to enter the stadium. A German carrying a banner was allotted to each nation, the cards bearing the names of the countries in German. The nations marched in alphabetical order, according to German spelling, with Greece at their head. . . . It was fortunate for us that they spelled our name "Kanada" because alphabetically it brought us in the centre of the line that eventually stretched across the full length of the field facing Hitler, where we could see and hear the ceremony perfectly. The marching order for each national group was banner bearer, flag bearer, officials, women athletes and men athletes. Many dipped their flags, they all gave their particular national salute before the tribune of honor at the top of the first tier of the stadium, where Hitler and his guests stood, with Hitler saluting each team in turn.'

The space between the successive countries was regulated at the mouth of the tunnel. The banner with the national name on it went first with a gap of 15 feet to the athlete who carried the national flag and another 15 feet to the team itself. The distance between the teams measured exactly 20 yards – military precision.

When each team emerged from the tunnel it followed the procession along the track past the boxes where Hitler and the dignitaries stood, went around the end of the track and back along the far side, turned left to the infield and crossed that, maintaining the column formation, to a position facing the boxes. By the end, competitors covered the entire infield and formed a vivid, living landscape of national colours. From start to finish the procession took 45 minutes.

At 4.14 p.m., when the Olympic bell had been rung, Spyridon Louis, who won the first modern Games marathon, led the Greek team in. He faltered 'a little now and then but was still stepping out bravely'. The Greeks wore modern blue coats and white flannel trousers. They did give a stiff arm salute but was that the Olympic or Nazi version?[21]

The Afghans wore turbans and did give the Nazi salute.

The Argentinians wore naval caps.

The Australian team, wearing cricket caps emblazoned with kangaroos, heard the French were not going to give the salute, so they didn't.

The Belgians looked picturesque in grey flannels.

Bermuda, carrying their flag with the British Union Jack on it, wore white sun hats and did give the Nazi salute.

Bolivia did give the Nazi salute.

Bulgaria's team of twenty-seven goose-stepped by to loud applause and did give the Nazi salute.

The Chinese, surprisingly tall, wore American-style straw hats. Rather than give the salute they placed these hats over their hearts.

The Colombians wore blue blazers and grey trousers, and did give a kind of Nazi salute.

The lone Costa Rican had to carry the flag himself and got a huge cheer although, holding the flag, he could not give any salute at all.

The Czechoslovaks were received in almost total silence.

The *Daily Express* noted that 'the entry of the gladiators would have been more impressive if it had not turned into a rather amusing game of lottery.

After the sixth delegation had passed the saluting point, ninety per cent of the crowd were principally concerned with how the remainder would salute.'

The Danes wore rose and white.

The Egyptians wore red fezzes.

The Estonians did give the Nazi salute.

The French team came in. Patricia Down, a member of the Australian team, remembered the French did give the Nazi salute to a tremendous reception but later claimed it had in fact been the Olympic salute. Nobody, Down added, had heard of that before.

The *New York Times* described how the French *intended* to give the Olympic salute and did 'as they understood it', but the Germans simply didn't know the difference and later, delighted, said that 'even the French heiled Hitler'.

The *Daily Express* described how 'the loudest ovation went to France and Austria, both of whom out-Nazied the Nazis in the way they flung out their right arms. The officials of the many competing countries are still arguing about what they should have done, but the pity is that an arrangement was not come to long before the processions were started.'

The Canadian Official Report admitted that 'while Canada was given a great reception, France perhaps stole the cheers of the day. The French in blue berets, nearly two hundred and fifty strong, did something that none had expected from them. The flag bearer dipped the Tricolor to Hitler, and the entire French section raised their outstretched arms in the Nazi salute. For one moment there was silence as the French marched past the reviewing stand – the next moment the two-tiered stand rocked with an ovation that continued in rippling volume all around the track as they proceeded to their place on the field. How the German folk love that gesture of admiration.'[22]

The Great Britain team was criticised by the *Daily Express* because it 'contented itself with a turn of the head, or eyes right as soldiers would describe it, but it is to be stated that these men and women were received with little more than a whisper. It would not have done the British any harm if they had made a gesture to the country housing the Games by following the unexpected example of France.'

Even the British Official Report said: 'It was a little unfortunate that no uniformity of saluting was agreed upon by the International Olympic Committee. The French team giving the Olympic salute, so similar to the Nazi form of salutation, received a tumultuous welcome. The British contingent with their "eyes right" met with almost complete silence.'

The single athlete from Haiti had to carry his flag and was given as big a cheer as the Costa Rican although he, too, could not give any salute.

The Icelanders, bare-headed, did give the Nazi salute.

The Indian team wore flowing turbans and reportedly one of them ignored the instruction for 'eyes right' as they went past the boxes but waved a 'How are you, Hitler?' salute of his own.[23]

The Italians did give the Nazi salute, and the *New York Times* noted cryptically that they ought to have done: they invented it. They wore black shirts over white trousers.

The Japanese did not give the salute but the man at the end of their front rank held an orthodox military salute as they went by, the rest all looking to the right.

Canada – 'Kanada' to the Germans – were delighted when the London *Times* reported that they 'made a brilliant spectacle in bright red blazers'. The Canadians also wore 'red and white ties for the men, our team were dressed all in white, with white shoes, and they certainly looked spick and span. They were drilled . . . in marching and in giving the Olympic salute, and they did both well in unison. The majority of the 800 Press men voted Canada the place of honor as the smartest and most colorful unit in the parade. We had an imposing array of 160 in line.'[24]

Ab Conway, a runner from the University of Toronto, remembered the dilemma. To give the Nazi or Olympic salute? 'But the Nazis had taken it over. We decided that we were not going to let them do it, that the Olympic salute was the Olympic salute and we were going to give the Olympic salute.' The crowd went wild because they imagined the Canadians were giving the Nazi salute. The flag bearer, hurdler Jim Worrall, has said: 'We took a lot of backlash criticism for that. The kindest thing you might say is it was done in naivety.'[25]

The *Daily Express* reporter thought the Canadians gave the Nazi salute . . .

The Latvians, in white jumpers, white shirts and dark ties, marched solemnly by.

Liechtenstein, wearing jackets, marched solemnly by followed by Luxembourg, Malta – all in white, including caps – and Mexico in tops with single dark hoops on them.

The little Monaco contingent did give an indistinct salute.

The Netherlands marched solemnly by led by their women in pretty skirts.

The New Zealanders evidently mistook an erect German official for Hitler and doffed their hats to him, putting them on again when they reached Hitler himself. Jack Lovelock, their leading runner, carried their flag. The *Daily Express* noted that during the wait at the May Field 'Lovelock was forced to stand about for more than two hours and I observed that when he was not hopping from one foot to the other he was leaning very heavily on his flagpole.' He carried the flag high.

The Norwegians marched solemnly by.

Austria – Österreich – received almost as much applause as the French, but a curious thing happened reflecting, no doubt, the political divisions of that troubled land. Some made an ostentatious show of holding their arms sideways so everyone could see they were giving the Olympic salute, while the majority, and the whole women's team, gave the Nazi salute.

The Peruvians, wearing buttoned-up blazers, did give a salute, some stiff arm, some slightly crooked.

The team from the Philippines, like the Chinese, placed their white sunhats over their hearts.

The Poles marched solemnly by and so did the Portuguese, Romanians, the Swedes and the South Africans.

A merry Swiss carried their flag, whirling the pole round his head, casting it into the air and catching it. Was it perhaps the self-same Swiss who had done something similar when the team reached the Village?

Turkey did give a salute throughout but waving their hats.

The Americans were pleased, too. Their 400-strong team – fifteen athletes were excused the parade because they were competing the next day, including Owens – felt they

> made a splendid showing. . . . The men were outfitted in a double-breasted blue serge coat with emblem on left breast and six Olympic buttons, white trousers, white shirt with red, white and blue striped necktie, straw hat with blue band and emblem, white sleeveless V-necked sweater trimmed in red and blue with shield in center, white sport shoes and white sox. Blue leather belts bearing the team insignia were worn. The women wore a blue serge jacket with emblem on left breast and two Olympic buttons, white skirt, white blouse, white shoes and stockings and white sport hat.
>
> The men's uniforms were tailored by Smith-Gray Corporation of New York who furnished well-fitting and neat looking clothes. This concern sent two tailors at their expense on the SS *Manhattan* to make the necessary alterations in the uniforms. The women's suits were made by Long Mark of New York and were well fitted and most satisfactory.[26]

Glickman remembered marching into the stadium although, as he subsequently confessed, marching was not perhaps quite the right word. They shambled forward amid fears they'd disgrace themselves. They were extremely curious to see exactly what Hitler looked like. As they passed they turned their gaze to where he stood and, Glickman sensed, they all had the same thought: *Yep, he really does look like Charlie Chaplin.*[27]

Hitler meets Spyridon Louis, winner of the 1896 marathon, at the Opening Ceremony and accepts an olive branch. *(Fox Photos/ Getty Images)*

But Jesse Owens stole the Games with four gold medals, which Hitler didn't like at all. *(Keystone/Getty Images)*

Central figures in the organisation of the 1936 Olympic Games. Clockwise from above left: Hans von Tschammer und Osten, Theodore Lewald, Avary Brundage and Carl Diem. (*Cigaretten-Bilderdienst Altona-Bahrenfeld*)

The Jewish sports club, Stuttgart, 1934, showing the shocking training conditions. Gretel Bergmann is on the far left. *(Courtesy of Margaret Lambert)*

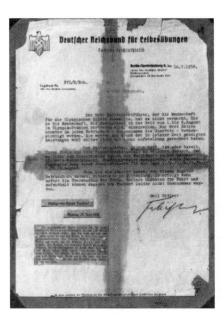

The letter from Tschammer und Osten telling Bergmann that she'd failed to make the team. *(Courtesy of Margaret Lambert)*

Gisela Mauermayer, the Aryan ideal. *(Cigaretten-Bilderdienst Altona-Bahrenfeld)*

The bell on its journey to the stadium . . . *(Cigaretten-Bilderdienst Altona-Bahrenfeld*

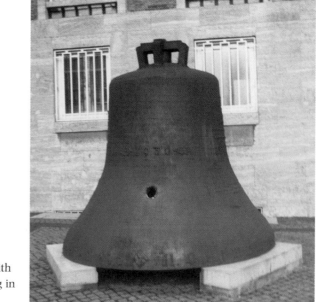

. . . and today, complete with shell hole from the fighting in 1945. *(Author's Collection)*

An Olympic torch, showing how sturdy it was. It is enscribed with the five Olympic rings and the route from Olympia. *(Cigaretten-Bilderdienst Altona-Bahrenfeld)*

The belle who meant trouble, Eleanor Holm. *(Fox Photos/ Getty Images)*

Bahratal, the first hamlet in Germany where the flame was officially welcomed, as it looks today. *(Author's Collection)*

A. A. U. BACKS TEAM IN BERLIN OLYMPIC; REJECTS BOYCOTT

MAHONEY FORCES LOSE

Withdraw Motion for Ban as Five-Hour Debate Shows Defeat Sure.

INQUIRY IS VOTED DOWN

Resolution Adopted Calling on Game Committees to See No Injustice Is Done.

BRUNDAGE NEW PRESIDENT

Mahoney Refuses to Run Again —Calls Result Moral Victory and Plans to Fight On.

The general convention of the Amateur Athletic Union of the United States closed at the Hotel Commodore yesterday with a rejection of all attempts to keep American athletes out of the Olympic Games in Germany.

After five hours of speeches indicated there was no chance of success, the anti-Olympic forces, led by Jeremiah T. Mahoney, president of the union, withdrew the following proposed amendment to the resolution stating the union's policy:

"It is the sense of this convention that the Amateur Athletic Union of the United States is opposed to participation in the 1936 Olympic Games."

They took their last stand on a proposal by Supreme Court Justice Aron Steuer that a three-man investigating commission be appointed to visit Germany immediately. Justice Steuer said: "Forget the expense; I know people who will find the funds." On that they were defeated by a vote of 58.25 to 55.25

Sister of American Held As Spy Suspect in Spain

By The Associated Press

MADRID, Dec. 8.—Sarah Alcunovitch, 28 years old, sister of Benjamin Alcon of Peoria, Ill., was arrested and held incommunicado today pending hearing on a warrant for her deportation issued by the Department of Public Safety.

The warrant did not specify the charges against her, but jail attendants at the women's prison said she was suspected of espionage.

The girl, a White Russian, has been employed in various parts of Spain for thirty months, translating books and teaching languages. She is understood to have two other brothers who are naturalized Americans living in the United States.

200-INCH 'EYE' BORN WITHOUT A DEFECT

Mirror for World's Largest Telescope Is Removed From Oven at Corning Plant.

GRINDING TO TAKE 3 YEARS

Astronomers Hold That Great Glass Will Enrich Man's Knowledge of Universe.

By WILLIAM L. LAURENCE.

Special to The New York Times.

CORNING, N. Y., Dec. 8.—The success of man's most ambitious effort to build a "tower to infinity" was assured here today, after more than a year of anxious waiting, when the giant mirror-disk for the 200-inch telescope was

The Yanks were coming: High jumper Alice Arden and diver Marjorie Gestring on the *Manhattan. (Alice Hodge, courtesy of Daniels & Tedder)*

The decisive moment, *New York Times,* Monday 9 December 1935.

The opening ceremony. The countries march past and assemble across the infield as the crowd gives the Nazi salute. *(All courtesy of Esther Wenzel/ I, Witness to History)*

Among the other heroes . . . 1,500-metre victor Jack Lovelock . . .
(Cigaretten-Bilderdienst Altona-Bahrenfeld)

. . . magical hockey player Dhyan Chand
. . . (M.N. Masood, courtesy E. Masud)

Above: Owens destroys the rest of the world in the 100 metres, and moments later the controversy with Hitler was born. *(Keystone/Getty Images)*

. . . and four true Brits, winning the 4 × 400-metre relay. From the left: Godfrey Brown, Frederick Wolff, Godfrey Rampling and Williams Roberts. *(Central Press/Getty Images)*

The 108-metre high terraces of the amphitheatre of the Olympic Stadium under construction. *(Cigaretten-Bilderdienst Altona-Bahrenfeld)*

The 'Haus des deutschen Sports' within the Reichssportfeld. The indoor events were held here. *(Cigaretten-Bilderdienst Altona-Bahrenfeld)*

The Olympic Village assumed more than symbolic importance, as it disproved Hitler's racist and nationalistic outpourings.

The Kansas connection: Harold Manning says cheerio to his visitors. Esther Wenzel is on his right. *(Courtesy of Esther Wenzel/ I, Witness to History)*

The tranquillity of the Village is demonstrated by the lakeside sauna. *(Cigaretten-Bilderdienst Altona-Bahrenfeld)*

United nations sing-song in, it seems, the *Friesenhaus.* *(Alice Hodge, courtesy of Daniels & Tedder)*

Dora Ratjen, the man who claimed he'd been forced to compete as a woman. The photograph itself is enigmatic. *(© Südwestrundfunk)*

Ladies and gentleman . . . Helen Stephens wields her 9ft stride to storm the 100 metres. *(Allsport/Getty Images)*

Helen Stephens and bitter rival Stella Walsh shake hands. The gender of both was questioned. *(Fox Photos/ Getty Images)*

Dorothy Odam, the Briton who would be second in the high jump. *(Dorothy Tyler, courtesy of Daniels & Tedder)*

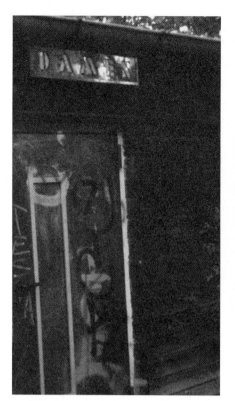

Within sight of the stadium, these derelict toilets and their signs still stand from 1936. *(Author's Collection)*

The hockey stadium gates. *(Author's Collection)*

Gymnast Werner Schwieger's Olympic pass and him today. *(Birgit Kubisch)*

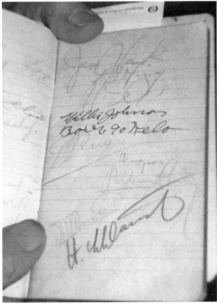

Fritz Wandt and his autograph collection. *(Birgit Kubisch)*

The Olympic Village seventy years on, sadly overgrown. (*Verlag B. Neddermayer*)

Then and now. The wall of honour at the stadium with the Olympic winners. (*Birgit Kubisch*)

The Mayfield today, looking from the stadium to the Bell Tower. The fence is keeping people out during renovations for the 2006 football World Cup. (*Birgit Kubisch*)

'When the march into the stadium was arranged we were a total disgrace,' fencer Joanna de Tuscan said. 'First about thirty or forty non-members of the team, fat, with cigarette ashes on their clothes, marched at the head of the team. Then came the chaperones. I had to produce my passport. I was 29 years of age and too old to march with the athletes. They made me march with the chaperones.'[28]

Velma Dunn 'saw Hitler go by' as he came across the May Field. 'The march past? We weren't used to military styles and all the rest of the countries were pretty well in order. It may be the American character that doesn't like being told what to do!'[29]

The American team was the only one that did not lower its flag when they passed Hitler and later an official explained that 'army regulations' – whatever that meant – prevented them from doing so.

They were given a cordial reception, no more and no less.[30]

The Yugoslavs marched solemnly by.

The 400-strong German team, all in white, went last as hosts and they appeared while the Americans went round the track. Their appearance created such a surge of emotion among the spectators that the band abandoned what they were playing and moved into *Deutschland über Alles* and the *Horst Wessel Lied*. The Americans found themselves marching to the music of those.[31]

For the first time an Olympic Games could be listened to on the radio and the German Broadcasting Company set up facilities so the world could hear. Conditions proved perfect for transoceanic transmission and listeners in America heard the speeches with great clarity. Shortly before midday Eastern Standard Time two networks with over a hundred stations coast-to-coast prepared to broadcast the arrival of the flame and the inevitable speeches when the athletes were in place across the infield. In Japan listeners to the NHK (Japan Broadcasting Corporation) who wanted to hear events as they unfolded had to be up at dawn because of the time difference. This broadcast, and the subsequent radio coverage of the Games, provoked a 'previously unheard-of national sport frenzy' in Japan, fuelled by the fact that Tokyo had just been given the 1940 Games and the Japanese competitive successes. Huge numbers of people prepared to follow the Games in 'real time' – the dawn watch or late at night – and NHK claimed 'storms of excitement for about half of August'.[32]

The British took it in their stride. The broadcast came, as one newspaper put it, from Berlin to the national transmitter and the commentary, by a Mr T. Woodruffe, covered the runner lighting the Olympic flame in the stadium. It culminated in 'Handel's Hallelujah by the band of 450 instrumentalists and chorus of 1,000 voices'. Programmes then returned to normal: in the evening the first act of *Orpheus and Eurydice* went out while the Western Brothers and Miss Phyllis Robbins 'contribute[d] to the variety entertainment'. [33]

Gretel Bergmann was not among the listeners. 'There was no television at Laupheim and very little radio – and we weren't allowed to have a shortwave radio. Jews weren't. There was a little newspaper and whether there was something in it about the Games I do not remember – I do not remember one thing about the Olympics. Maybe psychologically I just shut everything out because I was so traumatised by the whole thing. I would love to tell you "I did this, I did that", but I have no recollection whatsoever.'

In fact there was television, albeit limited. Two German companies provided the first live television coverage of any sporting event anywhere. Three cameras would transmit 72 hours during the Games and they could be watched at special booths in Berlin and Potsdam.[34] Werner Schwieger says he appeared in close up in film transmitted by one of the companies, Wochenschau. 'The camera was right in front of me and I could be seen in the middle of the picture. This was the first time that there were television cameras and so the first time I ever saw them. One day, when there was a little less going on in the stadium – around noon – I just strolled around and I saw the cameras. They were huge.'

In the stadium, Lewald spoke from a small rostrum, thanking Hitler for being the protector of these Games, 'built according to your will and purpose'. Lewald invited Hitler to declare the Games open. Hitler said only: 'I proclaim open the Olympic Games of Berlin, celebrating the XIth Olympiad of the modern era.' Olympic flags were raised, trumpets sounded and the four-gun salute exploded into the air. The great flock of pigeons took to the sky and a chorus in virginal white sang the Olympic Hymn.

At this moment – 5.20 p.m. – the runner appeared at the top of the steps on the East Gate. He was tall, slender and he hesitated, brandishing his torch above his head. He was a champion student athlete, Fritz Schilgen, and 'with his fair hair and blue eyes' represented the 'image of an "Aryan youth"'.[35] He ran down the track and ascended the steps at the Marathon Gate.

The stadium fell silent.

He thrust the torch deep into the bowl and the flame leapt up.[36]

A few minutes later Louis, the old marathon runner – moved to tears – presented Hitler with a gift from Greece.

It was an olive branch.

Chapter 7

THE FÜHRER AND THE RUNNER

Do you really think that I will allow myself to be photographed
shaking hands with a Negro?

Hitler to Baldur von Schirach

C loud covered Berlin on that humid Sunday morning of 2 August as
the thousands trekked towards the stadium, the gymnast Werner
Schwieger among them. The sun tried to break through but never
quite managed it.

A track and field competition is quite unlike anything else in sport because
so many different events are contested, sometimes simultaneously. An
Olympics is even more different because other sports are going on, inevitably
scattered over a wide area, as well as the track and field. In the case of Berlin,
that made the enormous results board at one end of the stadium invaluable.

Schwieger intended to savour as much as he could, coming every day. He
travelled on the S-Bahn to the Reich Sports Field station. His competitor's
badge permitted free travel and entry to the various events, including the
stadium, and he decided to take the week off work and studied the
programme so he would know what was on each day. 'I even smuggled in a
workmate who had no pass. He was from my company and I managed to get
him in. Section E [Block E] was especially reserved for participants so
everyone who had an Olympic pass was allowed to sit there.'[1]

This Sunday, the fencers began their probing, reflexive art form; the
modern pentathlon – the event that made perhaps the greatest demands on
the athlete – the wrestling and the weightlifting began, too, although the
yachting at Kiel did not get under way until the Monday, a flame being taken
there in an extension to the relay run.

In scale and variety this profusion can be slightly disconcerting, somewhat
overwhelming, but centre stage, the heart, is always the Olympic stadium,
that loop of track for the runners, that level infield enclosed within it for the
throwers and jumpers. Almost every event is so simple that spectators barely

need to know the rules, a simplicity that makes all the drama instantly accessible to every spectator. It generates a special sense of anticipation and those who trekked in, coming from the Reich Sports Field station and walking towards the stadium so large it seemed to fill the horizon, must have felt that. They were familiar with the full variety of what they were to witness from the morning's newspapers and the incessant radio coverage.

10.30 a.m.	100 metres round 1
	high jump eliminators
11 a.m.	shot-put eliminators
3 p.m.	100 metres round 2
	high jump semi-finals
	women's javelin eliminators, final
4 p.m.	800 metres round 1
5.30 p.m.	10,000 metres final
	high jump final
	shot-put semi-finals, final

Velma Dunn could get a taste of this diversity because 'in fact our badge let us into the Olympic stadium every day when we were not practising or competing. We sat within fifteen, twenty feet of Hitler every day. He used the same *Heil Hitler!* that all of them did.'[2]

Neither Dunn nor the trekkers could have known that, almost immediately, the central story of the whole Games would unfold before them in the shape of the strong, lean frame of the athlete son of the poor Alabama sharecropper. (The other sports will be examined later but with exceptions – the fencing, swimming and the football – because amazing things happened in all three. The football match between Austria and Peru shattered the harmony of the Games and led to a mob stoning the Germany Embassy in Lima.)

As the trek to the stadium got under way, twelve telephone information desks came under siege in what would be a daily occurrence. Thousands of requests flowed in for information as well as for tickets.

When the first main number was dialled, the call went over one of the 20 exchange lines to one of the 12 information desks. The person dialling was automatically connected with an information operator who was disengaged at the moment. When all desks were busy, a special control light burned above each of the 12 desks. This warned the operators to deal quickly with the conversations in order to take the waiting calls. When an operator had finished giving information, the call light went out and by pressing a key the desk was made free for a new call.[3]

Like so much else, the efficiency of the information system acted as a microcosm of the whole Games, with every eventuality anticipated, explored, covered, rehearsed.

If one of the operators could not give information in a required foreign language, she pressed a key. This turned on lights on all the other desks, indicating the desired language. At the same time, the call was disconnected from the desk of the first operator and was automatically held. The first operator who had received the call was now free to answer other inquiries. Any other operator could take over the waiting call by pressing a key. When this happened, the lights on all the desks went out. In difficult cases, the operator could obtain further information through calling other offices in the building.[4]

The Summer Games had not been broadcast on the radio before, and transmitting the Winter Games showed what demands

would be likely be made on the resources of the broadcasting system – artistic, technical, and economic. The squeezing of the sporting and artistic events into the sixteen days of the Olympiad made it essential to work out a broadcasting scheme capable of transmitting the most exact Olympic programme ever drawn up. Only by this minute division was it possible to broadcast directly to the listeners of the world all the final contests of the Olympic Games in spite of the fact that the different groups of events were sometimes taking place simultaneously.[5]

Sometimes between fifteen and twenty German commentators, extensively trained for months by covering national and international sports events, sat poised and ready to speak in order that coverage could be switched between sports. They worked from a centre dubbed the '40-Countries Exchange' – broadcasting to forty countries – and during the Games 3,000 transmissions came from it. The switchboard alone extended a distance of 21 metres.

The broadcasters had a lot to talk about. The 100 metres, like so many other Olympic events, operated on escalating stages of sudden death: initially twelve heats, the fastest two sprinters in each going forward to four second-round heats in mid-afternoon; the fastest three from each of these going to the semi-finals the next day with, an hour and a half after that, the six fastest competing in the final. Like every other individual Olympic event, it produced only one survivor, the one with the gold medal.

While the sprinters prepared, the high-jumpers limbered up. The positioning of the actual jump, near the stands, helped shield the jumpers from a wind recorded at 1.6 metres per second. The high jump worked to an even more brutal formula: in the initial round anyone who did not reach 1.85 metres faced immediate elimination.

The Olympic organisers had addressed the problem of timing, so crucial in track events but particularly the sprinting. Each day stopwatches, bought in Switzerland and 'of the same Omega quality that had been used at the Games of 1928 and 1932', were handed out to officials for 'all the contests in which timing by the hand is prescribed'. A watchmaker from the factory and a technical institute checked them daily for accuracy.[6] A timing camera, on a 40-foot tower to cover the full width of the track, provided back-up. It recorded the positions at the finishing line by taking a hundred photographs a second and slow-motion film could be used for reference in cases of disagreement.

> A sensitive contact is attached to the pistol and through the starting shot an impulse of current is released, setting the time-recording mechanism in action. This mechanism is coupled with the slow-motion camera at the finishing line. The camera taking the photos remains out of action until the runners are approaching the finish. The camera then takes the photographs at the finish and records the time which has elapsed from the beginning of the contest. In order to deliver the photos in the shortest possible time to enable the judges to arrive at a decision, a special quick-development film was manufactured permitting cinematographic photographs to be thrown on the screen in the judges' lodge ten to twelve minutes after the runners had passed the finishing line.[7]

In Berlin, very suddenly and very deliberately, the full force of current technological innovation replaced everything that had gone before. Many competitors, awestruck by the fact and scale of these advances, sensed that nothing would be the same again because there could be no going back.

Owens ran in the twelfth heat although the crowd, naturally, watched for Erich Borchmeyer, a versatile sprinter from Stuttgart who had been to Los Angeles, in the eighth as well. Cyril Holmes (inevitably known as C.B.) from Bolton, Lancashire was versatile, too, because he played rugby for England. In Berlin he is reputed to have worn shoes so light they were designed to last only a single race. He once said 'the faster a sprinter moves his arms, the faster his legs will move'. How fast would he move in heat eleven? Not fast enough. He would come second.

Inevitably the fact that Owens went last meant each of the first eleven heats became a ratchet heightening the anticipation of the 100,000 in the stadium notch by notch. They would all know what Owens had to do.

First heat: Lennart Strandberg (Sweden)	10.7 seconds
Second heat: Chris Berger (Holland)	10.8 seconds
Third heat: Wijnand van Beveren (Holland)	10.8 seconds
Fourth heat: Gyula Gyenes (Hungary)	10.7 seconds
Fifth heat: McPhee (Canada)	10.8 seconds
Sixth heat: Martinus Theunissen (South Africa)	10.7 seconds
Seventh heat: Metcalfe (USA)	10.8 seconds
Eighth heat: Borchmeyer (Germany)	10.7 seconds
Ninth heat: Wykoff (USA)	10.6 seconds
Tenth heat: Martinus 'Tinnus' Osendarp (Holland)	10.5 seconds
Eleventh heat: Paul Haenni (Switzerland)	10.7 seconds

The Olympic record, 10.3 seconds set by Eddie Tolan (USA) in the Los Angeles Games, had comfortably survived this first round of assaults. The sprinters for the twelfth heat came out and, as all the others had done, dug small holes to give their feet purchase as they burst forward from the gun. Owens was inevitably of his time: a running vest, shorts, running shoes and no socks, strong but in no sense muscle-bound. He had short hair and the easy, loose movements of a natural athlete as he took up the starting position. A Japanese, a Brazilian, a Belgian and a Maltese took up their positions, too. A millisecond after the gun fired he moved in his compulsive, clockwork lope, the legs pumping faster and faster and faster. The others melted back from him.

10.3 seconds – the record equalled.

He beat the Japanese Sasaki by seven-tenths of a second – an eternity in the world of tenths.

In the background nine high-jumpers went out with the bar at 1 metre 70, including the Briton Stanley West who, in his second jump, 'employed the "Western roll" and strained himself badly. He had to be carried off.'[8] A further nine went at 1 metre 80.

The shot-putters were out, facing their own brutal elimination if they did not reach the statutory 14.5 metres.

Events, names, times and distances came at speed and with bewildering profusion, the authentic Olympic experience.

The high-jumpers locked into their semi-finals, wind from the west increasing in strength.

The women's javelin began, into the wind.

Helen Stephens came across Stella Walsh in the treatment centre. They gazed at each other but did not speak.

The anticipation heightened at the second round of the men's 100 metres: four heats of six runners and the fastest three in each going forward to the semi-finals. Owens went in the second heat.

The first:	Strandberg	10.5 seconds
	Osendarp	10.6 seconds
	Wykoff	10.6 seconds

A light shower lowered the temperature as the runners in the second heat prepared. Owens moved around the area behind the starting line, hitching his shorts up – an unconscious, instinctive gesture. Hands on hips, he took a couple of deep breaths and rocked his torso, keeping it in constant motion. He looked around but his body language suggested he wasn't seeing anything.

They assumed their places, Owens in the second lane from the inside, Haenni next to him. As Owens bent into the crouch he rocked his body gently as if moulding it to the moment. He raised his head so that, eyes wide open, he could see the whole of the track spread before him – and, perhaps, his life, too. He took a breath so deep it was almost a gulp, opened his mouth, tongue scouring it for moisture. His calf muscles seemed to be so taut they vibrated.

The starter bellowed '*Auf die Plätze!*' – on your marks.

The stadium of 100,000 fell absolutely silent.

'*Fertig!*' – ready.

He exploded as he rose, those taut calf muscles freed. His thigh muscles gave him a tremendous locomotion so that his legs were visibly pumping faster than any of the other five's. In a great, sustained surge of power he accelerated away from them and for one astonishing moment a camera panning across to capture the finish had *only* Owens in shot.

He distilled it into a single word: *flying*.

The crowd made the stadium a tremendous, reverberating bowl of sound.

10.2 seconds.

He had dismissed the Olympic record from his presence.

Haenni finished in 10.6 seconds but he might as well have been in another race and, in a sense, he had been.

Metcalfe won the third heat in 10.5 seconds.

The crowd concentrated on Borchmeyer as the runners dug their holes and took their tracksuits off for the fourth heat. Much to the disgust of the starter somebody went off too early just after the starter's deep, commanding voice called 'Fertig'. He swivelled his head in mock admonishment: *What can you do with these boys?* They settled again, were launched. Borchmeyer wasn't away fast but his strength carried him past the others, British runner Arthur Sweeney going with him and finishing a stride behind. McPhee and the Japanese sprinter Suzuki were so close that the automatic camera photograph was needed to separate them.

In the background, Tilly Fleischer beat another German, Luise Krüger, to win the javelin, 45.18 metres against 43.29, setting a new Olympic record. Fleisher, nervous, began badly in the early stage but her second throw – 44.69 – set a new record which the 45.18 surpassed in the final. 'There was a tremendous outburst of enthusiasm when this finely-built young woman was conducted to the winner's stand, where for some minutes she stood stiffly at attention giving the Nazi salute. During this period *Deutschland über Alles* was sung fervently.'[9] Hitler had not been present but he was there for the shot-put.

In the foreground John Woodruff, an American who stood 6 feet 3 inches ('I was tall for a runner') and had a 9-foot stride, finished third in an 800 metres heat. He was a lean freshman from the University of Pittsburgh, weighing 'around 180lb [12st 8oz]' with an awkward running style. One of twelve children, his grandparents had been slaves. Hard times. His mother did laundry. She would remind him that he had 'chores to do around our home and I was getting home from football practice too late to get them done. I had to cut wood and bring in coal. So, football would have to go, period. My chores came first.'[10] No one in his family had ever been to college before and he arrived at university with 25 cents. His athletics coach lent him $5 so he could feed himself for the first week.

He was, it seemed, in no hurry in his heat. He soon would be.

At 5.30 p.m. three events went on simultaneously: the semi-finals of the shot-put, the final of the high jump and the 10,000 metres – a stand-alone event, no eliminations or qualifying rounds, just this single chance for twenty-nine men.

The Americans were not to be held in the high jump: Cornelius Cooper Johnson ('the kangaroo-legged Negro from California'),[11] Albritton and Delos Thurber took the first three places and all three broke the Olympic record. Both Johnson and Albritton were black, a fact which Hitler hardly neglected to notice.

The shot-put developed into an intense struggle. Hans Wöllke and Gerhard Stöck represented Germany against Torrance and the Finn Sulo Bärlund. In the semi-finals Torrance, a man so muscular that he looked almost square, held the shot in his enormous hand and made it look puny. He took two staccato steps and pitched it – but only 15.38 metres, an indication of his form. Bärlund, the only man to reach beyond 16 metres, broke the Olympic record but in the final Wöllke faced his great moment. He had a chiselled face full of character and the white singlet he wore emphasised his strength. He tucked the shot under his chin, feeling it into a comfortable position. He launched it.

16.20 metres.

When that was announced as a new Olympic record the crowd made so much noise they drowned out the loudspeakers. Hitler, grinning broadly, beat the programme he held in his right hand on his left hand while Wöllke, so far away down there, turned and gave the Nazi salute before hauling his tracksuit top back on. Bärlund had one last put. A strong, swarthy-looking man with a shock of hair he pivoted his body and flung the shot.

16.12 metres.

The swastikas flew over the results' tower for Wöllke and Stöck, third, with the Finnish flag for Bärlund's second place. Hitler invited Wöllke up to his box to congratulate him personally, and did the same with Fleisher for her javelin victory. 'There was another demonstration [of enthusiasm] when she was led by a guard of officers to the box where Herr Hitler and General Goering were seated.'[12] Goering, in a light coat and homburg hat, stood beside Hitler beaming. It all seemed so natural, so ordinary and so understandable.

The 10,000 metres began hesitantly, two Britons – William Eaton and John Potts – treading with trepidation into the lead while the fearsome Finns Ilmari Salminen, Arvo Askola and Volmari Iso-Hollo bided their time. They had plenty of that. A neat, urgent little Japanese runner, Kohei Murakoso, struck early and took the lead. Salminen moved up behind him, tracking and covering, the other two Finns poised. They cast long shadows across the track as they pumped their way round.

When the Finns were ready they struck and went through in a phalanx, Murakoso clinging on, settling in fourth, counter-attacking and taking third, but the Finns – lean, long-striding – increased the pace and with 200 metres to go they shed Murakoso. They surged past lapped runners and now Salminen and Askola duelled, Iso-Hollo falling away. Round the final bend Salminen, taller and with the longer stride, 'kicked' but Askola clung like a terrier. Salminen half-glanced over his shoulder to try and gauge where

Askola was, ran on, half-glanced again as Askola tried to mount a final attack. Salminen had it by a stride, 30 minutes 15.4 seconds against 30 minutes 15.6 seconds, Iso-Hollo third, Murakoso a brave fourth.

Hitler invited them up so he could greet them, too. That, too, seemed entirely normal, although the *New York Times* reporter pointed out Hitler had been a spectator, along with Nazi leaders like Streicher, during the afternoon. To greet the medal winners in each event he held a little ceremony of his own, giving them a warm handshake and patting them on the back in the most amicable way to enormous cheering. The reporter noted, however, that some five minutes before the three men's high jump winners went to the podium to receive their medals Hitler vanished from his box. The reporter pointed out that none of the winners up until then had been black – but Johnson and Albritton were. The reporter did not read anything definitively sinister into this but suggested that before the Games had ended there would be enough black winners to know if his suspicions were unfounded or not.[13]

At some point late that afternoon or evening Baillet-Latour conveyed to Hitler the rule that 'only IOC-designated people performed such duties in an Olympic stadium'.[14] No doubt this was couched as a point of information rather than a rebuke but Hitler, consummate exploiter of the moment, must have seen it as an escape route from the prying eyes of the *New York Times* and the rest of the world. Publicly from this moment he would not greet any of the winners. Those who delight in irony will find a rich seam of it in the thought that Adolf Hitler, slayer of millions and reshaper of worlds, found refuge behind a 60-year-old Belgian count who devoted his life to promoting non-violence through sport.

Woodruff gives a slightly different reading of these events when he says that 'our coaches, the American coaches, protested against Hitler and said if he couldn't invite everybody to his box then he shouldn't invite anybody. So they stopped that. I guess if he had invited me at that time I would have gone and shook his hand.' On the strength of these words, it may well be that the American coaches approached Baillet-Latour and prompted him into action.

Wöllke, an ordinary policeman, so impressed Goering that he promoted him to lieutenant, just like that.

And that was the first day of competition.

The weather on the Monday would be changeable, cloudy, a sprinkling of rain heralding a heavy shower at midday, then the temperature rose despite sporadic showers. None of it was going to dampen Jesse Owens.

9 a.m.	hammer eliminators
3 p.m.	400 metres hurdles eliminators
	hammer semi-finals then final
3.30 p.m.	100 metres semi-finals
4 p.m.	100 metres eliminators (women)
5 p.m.	100 metres final
5.15 p.m.	800 metres second round
5.30 p.m.	100 metres semi-finals (women)
6 p.m.	3,000 metres steeplechase eliminators

An astonishing 30,000 spectators came to watch the hammer eliminators though the prospect of subsequent medals for Germany's Karl Hein and Erwin Blask might have had something to do with it, and so may the fact that only Americans and an Irishman had ever won it before. Blask went well in the morning but Hein beat him to the gold by 1.45 metres, a new Olympic record.

Owens learnt that his 10.2 metres had been wind assisted and could not be ratified as a new record. He ran in the first semi-final, at 3.30 p.m., the sky slightly cloudy, a diagonal following wind pushing gently at the sprinters. He jogged, loosening his legs, then walked deep in concentration. He faced Wykoff and Strandberg of the very fast men. The starter – an imposing, portly presence by now familiar to all – positioned himself on the rim of the curving athletics track behind the runners, the gun with its trailing wire for the timing in his right hand. He was able to see them all clearly.

'Auf die Plätze!'

The six sprinters moved to the crouch position, Strandberg in Lane 2, Wykoff next to him, Owens three lanes away on the outside. When they had settled, the afternoon sun cast symmetrical shadows from them and lay these shadows, in all their distortions, up the lanes ahead.

'Fertig!'

The starter held the gun theatrically high and fired. The wind plucked a plume of smoke from it, but even before that the runners were in motion. For the first three or four strides Owens was just one of the six, Wykoff – at least – clearly ahead. After 25 metres Wykoff drew the men inside – Strandberg and van Bevern – with him so that they ran shoulder to shoulder, all three clearly ahead of Owens. It did not matter. Owens went deep into his compulsive, clockwork lope, the legs pumping so fast that within three strides he drew level with Strandberg and van Beyeren. Six more strides and he caught Wykoff. An instant later he was quite alone and moving *faster*. . . .

10.4 seconds.

In one of the world's great understatements, the German official record of the Games noted that 'Owens did not exert himself'.

Wykoff and Strandberg did 10.5 seconds.

The crowd were on their feet and Owens smiled broadly. He had the toothy, slightly self-conscious grin of a schoolboy and it conveyed delight quite naturally. He came off with Wykoff, shorter, also smiling, and as they went Owens tapped him on the back: *Well done.*

Moments later, Stephens and Walsh ran in different heats of the women's 100 metres eliminators. The waiting during the day tormented Stephens and she finally left for the stadium an hour before the event with a couple of other girls. It was not of course a long walk from the Friesenhaus.[15] The sudden death here: six heats of five athletes, fastest two in each progressing to the semi-finals. The first great confrontation of the Games was at hand.

When Stephens got there the sky was overcast, the conditions damp. Emmi Albus, from the Berlin sports club in Charlottenburg, the same district as the stadium, won the first in 12.4 seconds with Stephens's room-mate Harriet Bland fourth.

Stephens beat the Canadian Mildred Dolson decisively in 11.4 seconds, 0.2 seconds faster than the new world record set by Walsh in Warsaw but, as for Owens, the wind was too strong for ratification. Stephens remembered the reason being given as crosswind and, as she said, a crosswind never hurt anybody. The officials were, she ruminated, not yet ready for that sort of time.[16] Dolson did 12.3 seconds.

Walsh, running tactically, did 12.5 seconds to take her heat.

Audrey Brown (Great Britain) went in the fifth.

I was always nervous at the start of a race because of my considerable deafness and fear of not hearing starters orders. My hearing difficulty was not a severe one – just an inconvenience – but I found I could not relax sufficiently to be assured of a good start. In those days very little was available in the way of help for the deaf and one did not speak about it but just adapted as best one could. People are more positive about disabilities now, I am thankful to say.

My effort in the 100 metres was ruined by the fact that at the last moment I was moved out of my lane where I had already 'dug' my starting holes to fit my small feet and into the next inner one, which was empty, where I found enormous 'pits' dug by the very large and mannish ******, and was given insufficient time to fill in and re-dig my own! Our feelings that women athletes, particularly non-German ones, were a lesser breed were well borne out![17]

Brown finished third – Krauss won.

The semi-finals were not until 30 minutes after Owens's 100 metres final. Stephens, a blanket round her, sat and watched. Under a sky still cloudy the big stadium clock ticked towards 5 p.m. and Owens got lucky. He'd drawn the outside lane, the one also used by runners in the distance events and, naturally, they had churned the surface up. The track, however, spanned seven lanes and officials decided to move everyone across one lane, the outside becoming 6, not 7, and smoother. The six finalists – Owens, Strandberg, Borchmeyer, Osendarp, Wykoff and Metcalfe – wielded their trowels and scooped out their footholds.

Borchmeyer tugged off his dark tracksuit top and so did Wykoff, kicking his legs as he did so to keep the muscles supple. Owens patrolled again staying loose and at the command '*Auf die Plätze!*' he acknowledged a great roar from the crowd by raising his hands and clasping them.

Some in the crowd kept getting up and sitting down again as if to dissipate a great restless energy of their own.

Owens breathed deeply. A camera fastened on to him in close-up and you could see his Adam's apple bob, his eyes and face like those of a panther poised for a kill. He'd remember thinking purely like an athlete, concentrating on the finishing line, not Hitler, and – in a brief vista – how long the journey from childhood to here had been, how many people had helped.[18] He saw, too, the great truth: eight years' work would be vindicated or destroyed in the next 10 seconds.

'*Fertig!*'

He rose, poised, his eyes still locked on to the track.

The starting gun fired, the smoke billowed. Owens moved instantly into the lope and by ten strides he forced himself *two* strides ahead of Strandberg, three ahead of Borchmeyer. By twenty strides Strandberg and Borchmeyer had gone from him, broken and discarded, but on the far side Metcalfe came up and as Owens lunged at the line Metcalfe almost caught him.

Owens 10.3 seconds.

Metcalfe 10.4 seconds.

And there was the toothy grin again. This time it could last forever. He had a gold medal, which confers immortality in any Olympic event but a higher degree of it in a basic, bedrock event like the 100 metres. And he had only just begun. By the end of the week the clockwork lope and some leaping would make him the greatest athlete who ever lived.

Stephens went over to Owens in the area where the athletes congregated and congratulated him. They sat on the ground, talked and Owens wished her the best of luck for her semi-final, now only a few minutes away.

Stephens wondered about Riefenstahl, the woman directing the filming of the men's final, and Owens said she was Hitler's favourite film-maker. Stephens said she hoped she could meet her and Owens said she would – if she won.[19]

The *Daily Express* noted, somewhat enigmatically, that 'Owens and Metcalfe were boisterously honoured and were conducted towards Hitler's box so that they could salute him from a distance. It was noticed that when Owens and Metcalfe walked to the victor's stand they acknowledged the hoisting of their own flag and the playing of the American national anthem with a correct military salute, although they were not wearing hats.' On the podium, Owens shed tears at the playing of the Star-Spangled Banner and judged this the happiest moment in his whole career. (The *Express* added: 'Hitler was again present, but his welcome was no warmer than that accorded Max Schmeling, the German fighter, who will shortly journey to New York to meet Jimmy Braddock for the world's heavy-weight title.' The Louis re-match would have to wait.)

The moments after the finish of the 100 metres have become arguably the most celebrated myth and misunderstanding in the history of sport. The terrain is so delicate that even fleeting gestures made during those moments *still* carry an enormous potency. What is certain is that Hitler did not invite Owens up to congratulate him: he turned and left the stadium.

Esther Myers, sitting within clear sight of it all, remembered 'when Hitler and his entourage walked out it was so tense you could hardly breathe. Would it get violent? With him you never could tell. He certainly let us know he didn't approve of that black man having a gold medal.' The journalists, it seems, did not know of Baillet-Latour's stricture to Hitler of the day before and, without knowing it, drew the obvious conclusion: Hitler was delighted to bask in the success of white people but not of blacks.

The *New York Times* reporter kept his steady eye on movements and nuances. He found something disagreeable in the German nationalism 'and the prejudice that seems to go with it' when Hitler did not receive any of the winners but, he added, journalists investigating what happened yesterday – Hitler's departure, no handshakes for the black high-jumpers – discovered he did greet the German hammer throwers Hein and Blask privately out of sight inside his box.

The *Daily Express* came closer to understanding. 'Herr Hitler, it was officially stated in Berlin this evening, received none of the victors in today's events . . . . People in close touch with the Chancellor explain that this is due to his desire to avoid any appearance of discrimination, since it is impossible for him to be at the stadium to receive all the victors. Thus it was that not only the American negro, Jesse Owens, but also the German winners of the hammer throw were not received by Herr Hitler this afternoon.' Not in public, anyway.

As if to endorse this positive gloss on events, in *Jesse Owens, an American Life* William J. Baker writes that Owens thought he saw Hitler smiling and waving at him. 'Jesse waved back.'

John Woodruff said in a 1987 interview that 'I do recall seeing Jesse while still on the track waving and exchanging salutes with Hitler in his box.' I asked Woodruff in 2005 to confirm this and he said 'That's true.'

However, von Schirach, who happened to be in Hitler's box, remembers him saying 'the Americans should be ashamed of themselves, letting Negroes win their medals for them. I shall not shake hands with this Negro.' Tschammer und Osten, present, evidently pleaded with Hitler to do it if only for the sake of sport.[20]

Violet Webb said that at Owens's events 'we would automatically turn up to the box and look at Hitler to see the expression on his face.'[21]

Speer recorded how Hitler followed the athletics with 'great excitement. Each of the German victories – and there were a surprising number of these – made him happy, but he was highly annoyed by the series of triumphs by the marvellous colored American runner, Jesse Owens. People whose antecedents came from the jungle were primitive, Hitler said with a shrug; their physiques were stronger than those of civilized whites. They represented unfair competition and hence must be excluded from future Games.'[22]

Somehow the incident – whether truth, myth or a mosaic of both – caught the true atmosphere of the Games and captures it still. Hitler's shadow fell across the Games and Owens ran clean out of it.

However, Werner Schwieger – who was present – provides a different perspective. 'The press really messed things up a lot. The next day's newspapers would only report where the German runner finished. Five days passed before they would finally talk of Jesse Owens. Recently I went to look it up in the old newspapers in an archive in Unter den Linden, where all the newspapers from that time are stored, and it is true.'[23]

And the shadow? Hitler saw as much of the Games as he reasonably could. If he came to the stadium his arrival was signalled by the raising of his own standard at one end of his box and the Olympic flag at the other. Australian high-jumper Doris Carter felt 'it was very obvious Hitler was preparing for war. We heard that Hitler could travel from the Reich Chancellory to the stadium via a tunnel – we walked through tunnels from the dressing rooms to the arena. All these were prepared for air raid shelters for the Berliners if needed.'[24]

American basketball player Francis Johnson remembered that Hitler's visits to the stadium were surrounded by 'tremendous secrecy. They had ten big, black

Mercedes seven-passenger touring cars, and you never knew which one he would be in. He'd be in a different one each day. They had a tunnel under the stadium, and all of these cars went into the tunnel, and from it Hitler could go right up to his box, which had a glass shield built around it. When he left the stadium, people packed both sides of the street just to watch him pass by.'[25]

> Hitler came to the stadium most days, flashing through the streets in his great Mercedes, and his arrival and departure always dislocated the traffic arrangements for some time. From [the Chancellory] to the stadium the enthusiasm of the crowd was amazing. They lined the streets ten deep to watch him go by. Every afternoon a hundred thousand people who couldn't get inside assembled on the plaza outside the stadium just to get a fleeting glimpse of Hitler as he emerged from the stadium and left in his car.[26]

At his appearance the crowd acclaimed him even if, as sometimes happened, he arrived when an event was going on. One reporter noted that he immediately concentrated on the events rather than the crowd and was the first to get to his feet when the flags of the victorious nations were raised on the three huge poles at the far end of the stadium.[27] Naturally he delighted in any German victories and his pleasure was visible then but, overall, it seems a very simple thing. He was enjoying himself.

The second round of the men's 800 metres moved into its preliminary stage, twenty-four runners contesting three heats. The strength of the American team asserted itself. They won all three heats and in the first Woodruff destroyed a competitive field from Poland, Argentina, Hungary, Germany and Austria, even 'loafing' into the home straight to win by some 20 metres.

A following wind meant records could not be recognised – a pity since in the first women's 100 metres semi-final Stephens did 11.5 seconds, Kathe Krauss of Germany was second in 11.9 seconds, with Albus third. An impression seemed to be growing that Stephens would take the gold or, as the *Daily Express* predicted, 'is expected to run off with the final'. The 'clash' between Stephens and Walsh 'should be one of the outstanding features of the Games'.

Walsh came second in the other semi-final to Marie Dollinger, both at 12.0 seconds. Was Walsh holding back? Was she, as some rumours suggested, carrying an injury?

Football hadn't been included in the Los Angeles Games 'because of the growing professional influence', making the definition of an amateur elusive and, from 1930, the sport had its own World Cup. In fact, after the 1928

Games the 'tournament gradually became an outdated concept for the nations of South America and Western Europe'.[28] It returned in Berlin 'because organisers needed the money' it generated.[29]

Eight matches comprised the first round, beginning on Tuesday with Italy v. America and Norway v. Turkey. A crowd of 7,000 watched Italy lead 1–0 and the German referee send off an Italian, Achille Piccini, for a deliberate foul. The player wouldn't go, the Italians jostled the referee and, intimidated, he let the game continue. The Associated Press said one American 'suffered torn ligaments in his knee when pushed roughly by Piccini'. Three times the referee ordered Piccini off and three times he stayed. 'A half dozen Italian players swarmed over the referee, pinning his hands to his sides and clamping hands over his mouth.' Italy won 1–0.

Norway beat Turkey 4–0.

And that was the second day.

It was Black Tuesday, for many obvious reasons, as the changeable weather continued, cloud bringing cool conditions and brief, inconsequential showers.

10.30 a.m.	long jump elimination
	200 metres first round
3 p.m.	400 metres hurdles semi-finals
3.15 p.m.	women's discus elimination and final
3.30 p.m.	200 metres second round
4 p.m.	women's 100 metres final
4.30 p.m.	long jump semi-finals
5.30 p.m.	400 metres hurdles final
5.45 p.m.	long jump final
	800 metres final
6 p.m.	5,000 metres elimination

At 9 a.m., before the track and field programme began in the stadium, six pools of women fencers embarked on their long struggle for the foil medals in the Cupola Hall at the end of the House of German Sport. Helene Mayer, the German *Mischling* lured back from America and proud to be German, was trying to regain the title she'd won at Amsterdam in 1928. She faced Ilona Elek-Schacherer (Hungary), a Jew who at twenty-nine had not competed in a Games before, and Preis (Austria), defending champion from Los Angeles. These three were at the peak of their form, arguably three of the best fencers of modern times, and the competition seethed with undercurrents, not least Mayer's relationship with her team-mates. According to one report the relationship was normal and many of the Olympic team went to her bouts to support her.[30] Certainly 'some were surprised' to note that Mayer looked so Germanic, 'with her flaxen hair braided and pulled around her head'.[31] Elek-Schacherer, Mayer and Preis won their pools but in the second round that afternoon, while Mayer and Preis won their pools again, Elek-Schacherer came third.

In the stadium Owens, wearing his pullover, wandered across to the runway, ran down it and through the pit following his usual preparations. The red flag went up: *No jump!* – warm-up jumps were not done in Europe. One of his three allowed jumps had gone. His second, over 7.6 metres, looked to have qualified him but the red flag went up again: he had overstepped the board. According to Owens, Luz Long advised him to make a mark 6 inches in front of the board to be safe.

If Long did, in fact, make a helpful suggestion, no-one but Owens heard it. No-one else even observed the two men in conversation at that time. The doyen of American sportswriters, Grantland Rice, was in the press box with binoculars trained on Owens, between his second and third attempts to qualify. Rice was 'searching for some telltale sign of emotion' in Owens but saw only a calm mask of a face as Jesse walked down the sprint path to the take-off board, retraced his steps, then 'anteloped' down the path to make his final jump.[32]

Owens did jump from well back and qualified with another 7.6 metres. The first round of the men's 200 metres was going on concurrently and, breaking away from the long jump for the third heat, Owens broke the Olympic record with 21.2 seconds.

That was the last event before lunch and foreign visitors discovered that in Germany rules meant rules. During the daily lunch breaks (competition resuming at 3 p.m.), these visitors thought it would be a nice idea to sit on the May Field grass and have their lunches like picnics. *Verboten!* The police enforced that very firmly: the grass, recently planted, had not had time to thicken.

Owens faced a taut afternoon. The sun out, the 200-metre runners prepared for their second round. Immediately, Canadian Lee Orr ran 21.2 seconds, equalling the Olympic record. Owens, in the third heat, did 21.1.

He could relax for a few minutes before the long jump semi-finals.

Stephens faced a taut afternoon, too, because the women's discus and 100 metres final overlapped. The *Daily Express*, describing her as 'a strapping girl who in appearance is more masculine than feminine', noted that the women's discus took the whole afternoon and the Olympic record was 'beaten so often that even the officials lost count'.

Preparing for one throw, Stephens saw Walsh digging starting holes for the 100 and suddenly felt very nervous, unable to concentrate properly on the throw. Then she walked over to the 100.[33] A shower peppered the stadium but a cold, strong wind dropped as she dug her holes. From the inside: Marie Dollinger, Rogers of the USA, Albus, Stephens, Krauss, Walsh. Stephens made a poor start but her fearsome strength and powerful striding overwhelmed the others by half distance. The *Volkischer Beobachter* newspaper wrote breathlessly, 'these legs are developed like no other runners. Against her speed our German women Krauss and Dollinger are powerless.' Stephens hammered the world and Olympic records with 11.5 seconds – Walsh at 11.7, Krauss 11.9 – but what time had she actually run?

She would remember 'some people there timing it by hand, and they claimed that I ran that thing in anywhere from 11.1 [seconds] up. Some said 11.3. There was quite a debate. My Olympic coach was there when they decided to set that record . . . afterward. They just didn't feel it was possible for anyone to run that fast and cut the record down that much. Stella Walsh's time had been 11.9 in 1932. My time probably should have been better than 11.5. You got to realise that I was strong! I was really strong, and I had a nine-foot stride.'[34]

Stephens and Walsh shook hands. Stephens, on the podium, felt pride but nerves as well and they were so bad she thought her feet were moving convulsively.[35] The *New York Times* reported that Hitler received and congratulated her, which would be unremarkable except that after the delicate problems of the first day Hitler wasn't supposed to be meeting or congratulating any gold medal winners. The meeting was in private. According to her biographer, who has re-created the episode in detail, Hitler sent an aide to bring her to him.[36] The aide, complete with Hitler-style moustache, spoke broken English. He indicated that she had to follow him. She explained that apart from anything else she had a radio interview to do with CBS. The aide seems to have been aghast that anyone would not obey a direct summons from the Führer.

She and her coach went to the broadcast room and when they emerged the aide hovered urgently. He took them to Hitler's room, situated behind his box. Hitler came with bodyguards and she had her photograph taken with him. She asked for his autograph and he signed her book. (There is a suggestion that he made a pass at her, which is amusing in view of her sexual preferences and, as it would seem, his lifelong lack of any sexual activity.)

Stephens returned to the discus and elimination.

Gisela Mauermayer threw 47.63 metres for the gold, comfortably a new Olympic record.

The men's long jump semi-finals beckoned to Owens. The ground was dry, the wind in their faces, and Owens and Long went head to head. Of their six jumps only Long's first did not beat the Olympic record of 7.73 metres set by the American Edward Hamm at Amsterdam in 1928 and all three by Owens did, the second becoming the new record.

| Owens | 7.74 | 7.87 | 7.75 |
| Long | 7.54 | 7.74 | 7.84 |

The Japanese Naoto Tajima broke the old record, too (7.74) and the Italian Arturo Maffei equalled it. The wind plagued them all, preventing ratification – this wind which pursued Owens so relentlessly. He rested again before the final at 5.45 p.m.

Glenn Hardin and Joe Patterson, both Americans, had won the 400-metre hurdle semi-finals and now Hardin won the final from John Loaring of Windsor, Ontario, Patterson coming a disappointing fourth.

Of the five long jump finalists only Owens and Long were in serious contention. Hitler, in uniform and cap, watched intently from his box.

| Long | 7.73 |
| Owens | No jump |

Long waited at the end of his run, concentrated, launched himself, hair lapping and flapping. He had lengthening strides and he compressed all his urgency into them. His legs made three rotating motions as if to force him further and he landed so violently he dug up a sandstorm from the pit.

7.87, equalling Owens in the semi-final

As the result boomed over the tannoys the whole stadium erupted and a member of the German team lifted Long bodily off the ground. Reports speak of frenzy and ecstacy, of Hitler smiling as if to say, 'Now beat that, black man'.

The greatest champions know, when their moment has come, what to do. Owens, fluid, languid, loose, could make his body a catapult as he faced the runway stretching to the pit; could force it into a stride pattern that swallowed the runway in a gathering momentum which, after the last stride, pitched him far, far into the air.

7.94 metres

It brought a terrible pressure to bear on Long, who faced his third jump and his great moment – and he got a red flag. That gave the gold to Owens, who still had his third and final jump. He moved loosely to his mark, stooped and made a short sequence of unconscious gestures, touching his hips, touching his nose, rubbing his hands lightly down his flanks. He lowered his arms, rocked easily to and fro until he had created an impetus for motion. Then he exploded down the runway and, rather than rotate his legs in mid-air, made his body into a dart. Someone said it was as if he was trying to jump clean out of Germany. He landed with such impact that the force pitched him into the air again, causing him to dive forward.

8.06 metres

His record would stand unbeaten until the Rome Olympics, 1960; more than a quarter of a century later.

Long was the first to congratulate him and there can be no doubt of his spontaneity or sincerity. They walked along the track arm in arm in full view of Hitler who would congratulate Long, but in private.[37]

The 800 metres produced a wondrous race. Woodruff had won the Randall's Island trials and was now told to go out and break the field. Instead, with sunshine leaking through the cloud, the pack swallowed him. Phil Edwards, a Montreal doctor born in Guyana (British Guiana), led but ran slowly, conserving his energy. Woodruff was, he'd confess, 'just a young, novice runner and pretty soon they had me boxed in. I couldn't get out.' Because of the length of his stride, breaking out would almost certainly involve fouling somebody and disqualification.

After some 300 metres he found himself ejected through the back of the pack or, as he put it, slowed down so much he almost stopped.[38] He loped along alone and last, almost disorientated, until like a great windmill he got his long legs pumping – the 9-foot stride – and came round the outside in a great arc. Edwards still led but suddenly Woodruff appeared at his shoulder, kept on coming and went past. Edwards reacted, overtook him again but Woodruff's lope looked unforced. He tracked Edwards and they ran abreast, Woodruff on the outside again.

Emerging from the final bend, their feet digging cinders, Woodruff lengthened his stride and won it from Italian Mario Lanzi, with Edwards third. Woodruff wondered how far he had actually run by going the long way round at least twice.

The podium reflected the politics. Woodruff stood immobile, Lanza to his left giving the Nazi salute, Edwards giving something like the Nazi salute.

In the 5,000 metres heats Finland's Gunnar Höckert and Lauri Lehtinen won nicely enough, suggesting Friday's final would be that shape, too.

It was a long day for the women fencers contesting the semi-finals because they began at 8 p.m. that evening, Preis in one, Mayer and Elek-Schacherer meeting for the first time in the other. Preis finished in second place in hers before all eyes turned towards the tall, classical Mayer and the strategist Elek-Schacherer.[39] Mayer managed only 1 hit, Elek-Schacherer 5, although after all their bouts both were easily through to the final the following day.

Owens went to Long's room to thank him for what he'd done and they had a two-hour conversation, or rather as much of a conversation as could be sustained by Long's English. They found they were both the same age, had similar backgrounds and faced problematical futures when they stopped competing.

Many years later Owens reached for a handful of words to explain this most improbable of friendships. He and Long were 'simply two uncertain young men in an uncertain world'.[40]

In the football, Japan beat Sweden 3–2 and Germany beat Luxembourg 9–0.

And that was the third day.

Chapter 8

BITTER TASTE

When I got to the window, I could see young people with shovels held like rifles over their shoulders. I learned that they were Hitler Youth. When we went shopping we were greeted with '*Guten Morgen, Heil Hitler.*' We replied '*Guten Morgen, King George!*'

British high-jumper Dorothy Odam

On the Wednesday the Olympic gaze turned briefly from Berlin to New Orleans. In July the IOC had voted to drop Lee Jahncke, the leading campaigner for the American boycott – officially because he missed two consecutive IOC meetings – and voted Brundage in to replace him. Now Jahncke responded publicly. He derided the reason and said that a strong letter he wrote to Baillet-Latour, explaining why he pressed for a boycott, had never been published although Baillet-Latour had responded, 'ripping me up the back'.

Brundage liked power.

In Berlin, rumours – it's not clear who started them, maybe the Polish press, Walsh's coach or even Polish Olympic Committee members – insinuated that Helen Stephens was a man. Shown translations of stories in the Polish press, she responded by saying anyone in doubt should go talk to the physician who had carried out sex tests on the whole team before they sailed.

Stereotypes that female athletes had masculine and less attractive qualities occasionally permeated reporting. A journalist in *Berliner Illustrierte Zeitung*, for instance, observed that 'Amazons' entered the stadium just before the start of the women's 100m. In particular, the press scrutinised . . . Stephens . . . for signs of masculinity. The *Völkischer Beobachter* related that some people said Stephens ran like a man. The reporter concurred with the opinion, writing, 'they were not incorrect making this claim.' The article noted that Stephens' time . . . was faster than any German man's time in the same event for a stretch of twenty-five years. Moreover,

Stephens' appearance left an impression on the reporter. He wrote how she towered over her competitors and had very developed muscles. Likewise, a female journalist from Die Frau argued that although most of the sportswomen did not show signs of masculinity, Stephens was an exception. She asserted that Stephens must carry stronger 'masculine hereditary factors' than most women.[1]

'In those days,' Dorothy Odam recalled, 'men were more important than women in every walk of life. The women took second place and therefore you toddled along behind. There was a special village for the men but we were in a women's PT [physical training] college and never allowed in the men's Village. The only time we met them was at the communal training area, but I quite often thought I heard a man's voice behind me, only to find it was a woman! We didn't have sex tests in those days.'[2] By that she meant sex tests were not universal although any country could, as the Americans had done, carry them out and anyway the very strange Stephens–Walsh story had another whole chapter waiting to be written.

Holm remained very unhappy. Husband Jarrett had planned to come to Berlin and arrived. He said that when he returned to New York he intended to instigate legal action against the American Olympic Committee. He stated plaintively that he had asked for, and been refused, a meeting with Brundage. He wanted to 'obtain the facts about the case, which the American Olympic Committee apparently tried to conceal, and secondly to get redress for damages to my wife's reputation'.[3]

The newpaper Der Angriff carried an astonishing and revealing comment condemning the American team for bringing 'black auxiliaries' to Berlin. How this inflammatory statement got through the Goebbels safety machine is not clear because his Propaganda Ministry published the paper. Der Angriff suggested the Americans had been 'compelled' to pick these 'auxiliaries' to combat the might of German athletics.[4] This drew lofty responses from the American press on the grounds of gratuitous offence – and, anyone could have added, it demonstrated that for all the money, preparations and events contested so far, some people in Germany still did not understand the ethos of the Olympic Games. At one stage the German Foreign Minister, Joachim von Ribbentrop, actually made a complaint to Martha Dodds, daughter of the US Ambassador, that America virtually cheated by bringing black athletes like Owens – 'non-humans'.[5]

Owens would say 'we knew all about the racial thing but we couldn't read German so we couldn't read what was being written about us, being animals and all that. But the German people were tremendous. Every day we got a standing ovation from the multitude of people. They were looking at you not as a black man but in terms of the ability you displayed. This was the Olympics and there was spillover into your own country. You made headlines here [in America] and people saw them and they had second thoughts about you and about blacks, instead of making just a categorisation.'[6]

One is prompted to ask: how did, how could and how should competitors reconcile themselves to a political climate? They were perfectly entitled to ignore it because they had travelled to Berlin only for the non-political Olympic Games and, as we have seen, no doubt a majority did ignore it.

John Woodruff recounted how in the city they saw a lot of soldiers 'moving about. Of course we didn't pay any attention to that activity.'[7] He heard about the anti-Semitism but he was not a political man and it didn't interest him. He thought many other athletes were like that, too. 'This is true: most athletes went to Berlin to compete and were *not* interested in the politics. It was certainly true of the American team. Very definitely. We just had no interest in politics. What we were interested in was going to the Games and trying to win gold medals.'

'Spec' Towns said 'Of course, I did not participate in the politics of it. I went there to run and do my thing, and that's what I did. I don't think any athlete got involved in the political side of things.'[8]

Australian swimmer Pat Norton, however, went to Berlin 'very conscious' the Games were 'politically-motivated'. She wrote in her diary that 'the sports fields were guarded by [storm troopers]. Their uniforms were very forbidding to see for the first time. The tunics and trousers are black, with black boots and leggings. The tunics are belted with red armbands with the Nazi swastika emblazoned on them, but it is the black helmets that add a sombre picture to this. They come low down on the forehead, level with the eyebrows, giving the wearer a sinister look. I became used to them after a while, but I did not like them.'[9]

Another Australian, Doris Carter, felt 'it was very obvious Hitler was preparing for war – more than every second person wore a uniform of some sort'. She 'did not hear any mention of concentration camps but several of the charming girls who worked in the Friesenhaus whispered to us that they were afraid – they were quarter Jewish and they had heard several of their Jewish friends had disappeared.'

Dorothy Odam remembered that 'we woke every morning to the sound of marching feet. When I got to the window, I could see young people with shovels held like rifles over their shoulders. I learned that they were Hitler Youth. When we went shopping we were greeted with 'Guten Morgen, Heil Hitler.' We replied 'Guten Morgen, King George!' On one shopping expedition the chaperone told her group not to go into a Jewish shop 'so we all just walked in'.[10]

American diver Velma Dunn says 'You've got to remember that being seventeen I didn't look at the Games at that time as so controversial, I looked at it as a swimming competition. If I had been older I might have thought more about the politics but we had gone for sport, not politics. That was the way I went, purely to dive.'[11]

A member of the American basketball team, Francis Johnson, remembered the 'unusual' sight of what must have been Hitler Youth out marching and training.[12] He was told they were the equivalent of the boy scouts and concluded they were much better provided for than the older generation. Young, healthy, fit, strong, obedient, unquestioning, they were to be Hitler's instrument of conquest.

The words of Owens, Woodruff, Towns, Norton, Carter, Odam and Johnson require a context. During those August days in 1936 nobody knew there would be a war never mind that it would be the most destructive ever fought, spreading death throughout Europe as far as Moscow, across North Africa, across the Pacific and whole tracts of Asia. Most people could not conceive of evil on the scale of the Holocaust, that atomic bombs would devastate entire cities and a thousand other unimaginable horrors. Perhaps the full realisation of the true character of the Berlin Olympics only revealed itself long afterwards, even to the people who attended it.

Esther Myers, visiting Berlin, caught the mood. She found

uniformed troops marching here and there in the streets. Often officers strolled into hotels or business places. Museums and public buildings would often remain closed so that the visitors could watch a parade of young boys and girls in uniform. There was one question on everyone's mind: 'What do you think about Hitler?' That was the question we asked our German friends at the balls, dinners, and entertainments. 'Please don't talk about him,' we were told. 'Are you a member of the Nazi Party?' we often asked someone. If the answer was negative, the reply was always a hushed 'no' and 'I don't want to talk about it.' However, if we went to the public cabarets to dance and eat the young Germans would more readily talk. I received a letter from my father sent by airmail all the way from Wichita, Kansas, to Berlin, Germany. He pleaded for me to return home as soon as the games were over. 'War is imminent, I fear,' my father wrote.[13]

Cool air currents brought cloud, sometimes heavy, that Wednesday and a shower fell in the morning with more rain later. The day's timetable inevitably ran against a backdrop of mounting tension as the time drew towards 6 p.m. in the evening and the climax, Owens and the men's 200 metres final.

10.30 a.m.	pole vault elimination
	discus elimination
11 a.m.	1,500 metres elimination
1.30 p.m.	50-kilometre walk
3 p.m.	200 metres semi-finals
	discus final
3.30 p.m.	women's 80 metres hurdles heats
4 p.m.	pole vault semi-finals, final
4.30 p.m.	110 metres hurdles heats
5 p.m.	1,500 metres heats
5.30 p.m.	women's 80 metres hurdles semi-finals
6 p.m.	200 metres final

The pole vault attracted an entry of thirty-six from twenty-three countries. From the 10.30 a.m. eliminators it stretched across the day and into the night, the final vaults taking place in a surreal dimension under floodlighting.

The discus sudden death was set at 44.0 metres and eighteen contestants failed to meet that.

The background, far beyond the stadium, teemed with activity.

The 50-kilometre walkers prepared to take on a course through the wooded Grünewald area with, mercifully, 42 of those kilometres in the shade of tall trees. The nine refreshment stations each had 5 litres of warm tea sweetened with grape juice, cold tea sweetened with grape juice, warm tea unsweetened, cold tea unsweetened, malt coffee, orange juice, cold lemonade sweetened with grape-sugar, warm oatmeal porridge; half a litre of sugar in cubes and thirty cubes of grape-sugar tablets, as well as copious quantities of bananas, oranges and whole lemons.

At the British trials, in July at Derby, a motor mechanic called Harold Whitlock broke the world record with 4 hours 30 minutes 38 seconds. Around the Grünewald, on a course damp from a shower, he intended to show what he could do but initially didn't feel well. He would wait and watch. The Swede Evald Segerström led from Germany's Friedrich Prehn.

In the foreground, as the twelve 200 metres sprinters prepared for the semi-finals, the walkers had covered 17.5 kilometres, Jaroslav Štork-Žofka of Czechoslovakia leading now and Whitlock ninth.

Owens watched Mack Robinson from Pasadena win the first semi-final in 21.1 seconds, a new Olympic record, from Orr (Canada). Owens was so relaxed he kept his sweatshirt on and did 21.3 seconds, enough to win from Osendarp.

The discus throwers moved into a long, unbroken session, the final following the semi-finals. Willi Schröder (Germany) held the world record and the crowd chanted 'Take your discus in your hand and throw it for the Fatherland.' It didn't help. He threw 47.22 metres and faced sudden death elimination but won a throw-off.

At 3.30 p.m., ten minutes before the walkers reached half distance, the women 80 metres hurdlers contested four heats. Two girls from Bologna had been rivals since their school championships: Claudia Testoni, taciturn and twenty-one, took the first heat, Trebisonda Valla, twenty, came second in the last heat. Her father called her Trebisonda after the Turkish town he judged one of the world's most beautiful. She was also known as Onida – 'little wave'.[14] She'd make a big wave the next day.

At 3.40 p.m. the walkers reached half distance, Jnis Dalnisch of Latvia leading from Štork-Žofka, Whitlock moving up to third.

The 110 metres hurdles seemed relatively open after the six heats though Americans won three of them and Towns looked in prime form: he did 14.5 seconds, the fastest. Towns was a character. A National Guardsman, he wore GI boots and sometimes before a race he'd place a cigar beside his starting position, return and get it after the race, but there were questions about whether he ever lit the cigars.[15] The others hurdlers through were Fritz Pollard Jnr of North Dakota and Don Finlay, Britain's best, on 14.7 seconds, Häkan Lidman (Sweden) on 14.9, and Californian Roy Staly and Tom Lavery (South Africa) on 15.0 seconds.

As the walkers reached 38.5 kilometres – Whitlock easing into the lead from Arthur Schwab (Switzerland), Štork-Žofka third – the 1,500 metre men lined up for the metric equivalent of the mile, a lean, strong New Zealander named Lovelock among them. He had been preparing for three years. Educated at South Canterbury, he was good early and in his last year won the school's senior 440 yards, 880 and mile. He went to Otago University studying medicine but playing rugby broke a leg. That led him towards athletics, where runners don't break their legs. At Princetown, USA, in 1933 he became the first New Zealander to hold a recognised world record when he ran the mile in 4 minutes 7.6 seconds. A year later he won the mile in the Empire Games in London.[16] Now he finished third in a slow second heat. Eighteen runners went faster than him, but that didn't concern him at all. He had a secret and he knew that when he revealed it every one of them would be vulnerable.

In the first women's 80 metres semi-final Valla broke the Olympic record. In the second semi-final the first three finished on 11.8 seconds, Testoni the third of them.

Ken Carpenter of the University of Southern California took the discus.

As the walkers moved beyond 48 kilometres – Whitlock leading from Schwab – Owens prepared for the 200 metres. Hitler arrived, as was his custom, in mid-afternoon and theatrically. He was just in time.

The six runners dug their holes when Harold Whitlock came into the stadium and moved on to the track to complete the 50 kilometres – and the six sprinters had to move off it. The wind raked the stadium, dragging rain which fell heavier and heavier. It stabbed at Owens, who shivered.

They went to their marks. A great, almost superhuman pressure bore down on Owens and he responded to it with a great, almost superhuman performance from the gun. He lined up in the third lane, the tall, angular Robinson – an impoverished college freshman and virtually unknown before Randall's Island – next to him. His only pair of running shoes disintegrated and he had no coach to seek out and pay for another pair, but here he was.

Coming out of the stagger on the bend that compulsive, clockwork lope took Owens ahead, Robinson clinging. The lope looked so natural that one seasoned observer felt Owens wasn't actually running in the way other human beings do;[17] *Der Angriff* coined a lovely phrase: *His feet didn't seem to touch the ground.* Towards the line he went faster still, crossing it in 20.7 seconds and scattering the Olympic record to the wind. No one had ever finished below 21.0 at a Games before.

Robinson, clinging on to the end, also beat the old Olympic record.

Hitler beat it, too – out of the stadium. A downpour forced him indoors from his box and, while the whole stadium roared their delight for Owens, Hitler chose not to return to see the presentation of the third Owens gold medal.

Owens could relax, his Games over, safe in the knowledge they would always be his.

The women's fencing final began at 5 p.m., the Cupola Hall filled by 2,000 spectators. The eight finalists fought each other but the three great fencers, Elek-Schacherer, Mayer the *Mischling* and Preis the Viennese Jew faced many pressures on many different levels. Reflecting that, an announcement warned the crowd to remain silent.

Elek-Schacherer beat Mayer by 5 hits to 4 and Preis by 5 hits to 3.

Elek-Schacherer, strong and sure, looked certain to take the gold because she won six of her seven bouts and then seemed to have thrown it away – or as *Der Angriff* put it, 'left everything hanging by a silken thread' – when she lost by 5 hits to 3 to the second German girl, Hedwig Hass from Offenbach. Elek-Schacherer finished on 12 points.

Preis beat Mayer 5 hits to 4 so, with these two defeats, Mayer could only total 10 points.

It turned on the Hass–Preis bout which Haas won by 5 hits to 4. That left Mayer, Preis and Haas on 10 points but the tie breaker resolved it: Mayer (19 hits received) had the silver, Preis (20) the bronze and Haas (23) nothing at all. *Der Angriff* carried a headline 'HELENE MAYER ANOTHER SILVER MEDAL'. 'These final stages will certainly be recorded in the history of the sport because, on one side, superb fencing was provided by all eight participants and, on the other, the result from first to last hit, was absolutely uncertain. According to the pre-Games form, it was pretty sure that the German Helene Mayer would get the gold medal because her fencing was so consistent and yet wonderful, and it seemed impossible to fence any better than that. Then, in this final round, everything went differently.'

In the football Poland beat Hungary 3–0 and Austria beat Egypt 3–1.

The pole vaulters vaulted into the darkness but fully half the crowd in the stadium stayed, despite the cold, and prepared to make a lot of noise.[18] Americans Earle Meadows, William Sefton and William Graber took on two Japanese, Shuhei Nishida and Sueo Oe. Officials loomed in the arc lamps as if they themselves were phosphorescent. An American cheerleader with a mini-megaphone orchestrated *their* noise. The Japanese in the crowd chanted. And it was cold: once a competitor had vaulted he buried himself in blankets as he waited to vault again.

Meadows, Nishida and Oe cleared the bar at 4.15 metres first time, Graber needing two vaults and Sefton three. At 4.25 Nishida and Sefton cleared it first time, Meadows and Sefton needing two. Graber faced his third jump and sudden death. A team-mate had a word as he concentrated at the end of the runway, limbs no doubt tired. He nodded thanks, came from the darkness and smashed the bar from the underside. He was out.

On the first vault at 4.35, a record height for an Olympics, the remaining four all failed. On the second Meadows sailed high, jack-knifed cleanly over and snapped his fingers – *yes!* He did a little dance: he had transferred all the pressure onto the other three but, enduring an agony of suspense, would have to wait for them to complete their vaults to know whether he had gold or would have to go again, the bar up to 4.45.

All three failed on their second vault.

Sefton just disturbed the bar on his third. He was out.

Oe seemed to be over but his chest brushed against the bar, disturbing it, and it tumbled down. He was out. The Japanese cheerleader drew the chant

'*Nish – I – da! Nish – i – da!*' from the Japanese spectators, sitting in a phalanx. Nishida, an earnest face under a shock of dark hair, stood at the end of the runway rocking gently to and fro to create rhythm. He came down the runway past ghostly white officials and launched himself. He must have been utterly exhausted. As his body arched over the bar his knees seemed to strike it and, as it began to fall, his body fell onto it. He landed heavily, his body casting a prism of shadows.

Meadows had the gold medal.

Nor was this all. Even after some twelve hours of combat he signalled the bar to be ratcheted to the 4.45, a world record. He made three attempts and they failed.

It's easy to be mesmerised by these public faces, even when they loom out of the dark, and any Games is that. But the private faces are there, too, if rarely even glimpsed. One of these August nights, perhaps this one, Williams found an American coach, Bob Kiesel, so homesick that he broke down and cried which reduced Williams to tears, too.[19]

And that was the fourth day.

The weather on the Thursday remained unseasonably cold with cloud lingering into the early afternoon and wind until evening.

The American 4 × 100 relay team – Stoller, Glickman, Draper, Wykoff – were training daily but, the heats looming on the Saturday, tension began to set in. Glickman estimated all four of them were so evenly matched that if they were racing each other they'd have different winners each time – except for Draper, who wouldn't win. Glickman would admit Owens and Metcalfe were faster but it did not disturb the conventions of selection.[20] Owens, bedecked with three gold medals, and Metcalfe had had their events. They would be watching to see what the other four could do.

The two coaches, Lawson Robertson and Dean Cromwell, organised a 100-metre race for Glickman, Stoller and Draper at the training ground at the Olympic Village; Wykoff, considered 'race sharp', was omitted. Stoller made a strong start, Glickman couldn't quite catch him, Draper came third and Glickman thought no more of it.

10.30 a.m.	400 metres heats
	triple jump heats
	javelin heats
3 p.m.	110 metres hurdles semi-finals
	javelin final
4.15 p.m.	1,500 metres final

4.30 p.m.   triple jump final
5.30 p.m.   80 metres hurdles final (women)
5.45 p.m.   110 metres hurdles final

The day centred round the men's 1,500 metres final and what Lovelock might do.

In the afternoon Towns, who had an energetic, balletic style, as if diving forward to clear each hurdle, did 14.1 seconds in his 110 metres semi-final, breaking the Olympic and world records. Häkan Lidman (Sweden), Finlay and fellow Briton Frederick Pollard would be the opposition in the final but none had bettered 14.5.

The javelin throwers were into their semi-finals and by the end of them eleven had been eliminated. Gerhard Stöck won the final with 71.84 metres.

At 4.15 p.m. twelve men came to the 1,500 metres. Lovelock, all in black, estimated Glenn Cunningham (America) and Luigi Beccali (Italy) posed the main threats; and still he guarded his secret.

Hitler made sure he was there for the start.

Jerry Cornes (Great Britain) led into the second lap, Beccali behind him, Lovelock lost in the pack but across 1,500 metres tactics unfold, moves and counter-moves are made; and still Lovelock guarded his secret. On the back straight Cunningham made a move, Lovelock covering it by flowing easily along in third place. Now Eric Ny, a 27-year-old from Stockholm, made his move, coming up the outside into lap 3. On the bend after the start–finish line Ny drew up to Cunningham's shoulder; on the back straight Cunningham held the lead, Ny at him, then Lovelock and Beccali. On the far bend Ny – still outside – forged past so tightly that Cunningham, squeezed, put a foot off the track.

Into the straight towards the fourth and final lap Ny moved fractionally ahead and Lovelock ducked out, ready to reveal the secret. On the first bend he accelerated at fierce pace: in twelve strides he went past Ny and in another twelve was completely clear. Ny melted, Cunningham seeing the danger – *Lovelock thinks he can sprint a whole lap* – lengthened his stride. They moved equidistant and into the final bend Cunningham held the gap at some 3 metres, but Lovelock sprinted on. Arms and legs working like a machine, he even had time to glance back. He didn't need to.

Harold Abrahams,[21] commentating on the BBC, bayed 'My God, he's done it! Jack! Come on! Lovelock wins! Five yards, six yards. He wins! He's won! Hooray!'[22] At 3 minutes 47.8 seconds he'd broken the Olympic and world records. Cunningham (silver), Beccali (bronze) *and* the next two to finish also broke the Olympic record.

Afterwards Lovelock, curly haired and beaming, explained that Cunningham and Beccali had been 'fooled' because they thought he could only sprint for the final 70 metres or so and were 'not prepared when I started my run. I think I could have sustained it for another hundred metres if necessary.' *That* was the secret.

Lovelock had a good friend, a surgeon, who said 'Jack was a great worrier. He ran on nervous energy. Physically he was very fit, but mentally he was very fragile, jumpy even . . . after the race in Berlin, Jack was absolutely delighted. I'd never seen him like that before and never again. He was human. He was overjoyed, and grateful.'[23] Cunningham sportingly accepted that, having given his all, he just wasn't good enough. Lovelock, he felt, must be the greatest runner – as distinct from sprinter, of course – ever. Cunningham drew pride from the fact that Lovelock had had to set this new world record to beat him.

When he had his breath fully back Lovelock said, 'This running is wrecking both my health and my work. It isn't the fun it used to be. I think it's about time to hang up my running shoes.'[24]

Something about the triple jump (then known as the hop, step and jump) attracted the Japanese because Naoto Tajima won it with 16.00 metres, which beat the Olympic and world records, and Masao Harada took the silver.

The electric recording device for settling close finishes proved invaluable in the women's 80 metres hurdles final where the first four – Valla, Steuer, Elizabeth Taylor (Canada) and Testoni – all did 11.7 seconds, equalling the Olympic record. They waited for the film to be developed and when it was, Valla had it from Taylor and Steuer.

Towns duly delivered the 100 metres hurdles final.

In the football Peru beat Finland 7–3 and Great Britain beat China 2–0.

And that was the fifth day.

Belated sunshine brought a rise in the temperature on the Friday but heavy cloud gathered by noon. After brief rain the wind dropped, leaving a fine day.

9 a.m.	decathlon 100 metres/long jump/shot-put/high jump/ 400 metres
3 p.m.	400 metres semi finals
3.15 p.m.	5,000 metres final
5.30 p.m.	400 metres final

At the stadium, coach Robertson made a point of telling Stoller that he had run 'a very fine race' the day before at the Village track and confirmed him for the 4 × 100 relay team. Robertson added that, had Stoller finished third 'as Draper did', he would not have been in. It meant Draper was out and he, Robertson, would have to break the news to him. Something serious was going to happen.[25]

Robertson told Alan Gould, covering the Games for the news agency Associated Press and therefore a conduit to the whole American media, that Owens would be in. Robertson must have already informed Owens of this because Owens gave Stoller the team: Owens, Metcalfe, Stoller, Wykoff. Evidently Draper got word of this because he went to Cromwell and, via him, to Robertson.

Glickman heard rumours but discounted them.

A crowd of 30,000 came to watch the decathlon, that ultimate all-round examination of an athlete. On this day they'd do the 100 metres, long jump, shot-put, high jump and 400 metres (with each event carrying points). Soon enough three Americans emerged: Robert Clark, Glenn Morris and Jack Parker.

The stadium filled for the afternoon heats.

English-speakers dominated the 400 metres heats. Williams, who had cunningly spent a long time before the Olympics telling Owens how tough the 400 metres was and how it would 'kill him' in order to discourage him from thinking of running in it, won the first heat despite the weight he had gained on board the *Manhattan*, from Bill Roberts (Great Britain).[26] The son of a furniture shop owner in Salford, near Manchester, Roberts left school at thirteen, led a dance band, managed a timber yard and would become the only working-class member of the British 4 × 400 relay team.

John Loaring (Canada) came third.

LuValle won the second from Arthur Brown (Great Britain), a 21-year-old student at Cambridge University, and William Fritz (Canada).

The 5,000 metres might have been explosive. Lauri Lehtinen had blatantly blocked Ralph Hill, an American, at the Los Angeles Games, zig-zagging from lane to lane – one report suggests he even tripped him – and here was Lehtinen again along with two other Finns, Gunnar Höckert and Ilmari Salminen. Early on, these three ran together at the front with Kohei Murakaso (Japan) and Don Lash (America) staying with them. The lead changed several times and Lash was over-extending himself: he'd fall back, sprint up again, fall back again and at 3,000 metres faded altogether. With two laps to go Höckert led from Murakaso and Salminen but as the pace hotted up Salminen tripped and fell. Höckert led from Lehtinen at the bell and unleashed a ferocious assault, drawing further and further ahead. Höckert broke the Olympic record, and so did the next two.

Louis Zamperini, who had eaten his way out of the Depression on the *Manhattan*, came in eighth but endeared himself to the crowd by sprinting the whole of the final lap, which he did in 56 seconds: fast. Lovelock would have appreciated that. Hitler did appreciate it, sent word he would like to meet him and when Zamperini arrived Hitler said through an interpreter 'Aha! The boy with the fast finish!'[27]

Williams approached the 400 metres final with a specific concern. When the runners came off the final bend their white-painted lanes crossed into the straight lanes for the 100-metre events, almost like railway points. At the crossing point the runner, tired, could find them confusing and unwittingly step out of his lane to disqualification.[28] Williams needn't have worried. He commanded the race from Lane 5 and when the stagger unwound Brown, outside, struggled to stay with him. Williams drew away, LuValle closing, Brown responding. Brown closed, Williams slowed – feet heavy – and in the lunge at the line Brown was half a stride behind. They had run themselves almost literally to a standstill.

Williams, only twenty, never would be sure if he'd stayed in his lane but always would be sure he hadn't been disqualified. He accepted the moment of victory with a particular philosophy: he had proved to himself that he could do something. When the American flag went up he regarded that philosophically, too, keeping his emotion under control. He thought of Brown and wondered what would have happened if that half stride at the end had been different. He fended off all suggestions that he was the best in the world by pointing out that all he had done was beat the opposition present. There might be, he added, somebody down in Abyssinia chasing or being chased by lions who could 'kick my ass without even taking a deep breath'.[29]

The football moved into its second round, Italy beating Japan 8–0 and Norway beating Germany 2–0. Werner Schwieger remembers Hitler attending the match, the first time he had done so. 'The German coach said, "Well, Norway are not that strong" and he left the best German players out. And the Germans lost. Everyone was annoyed that the coach had done this.'[30]

And that was the sixth day.

A cloudy Saturday with just a little wind as the first week neared its end. In the early afternoon rain fell and heavy thunder showers loomed.

Coach Robertson, a track coach at the University of Pennsylvania whom Glickman described as old, ill, grey and in need of a walking stick, called a meeting of the seven American sprinters at 9 a.m. in the Village. Controversy still surrounds that meeting even all these decades later.

Glickman, savouring the realisation of his life's ambition when the 4 × 100 heats would begin in six hours, knew nothing of what Gould had written or that Gould's copy appeared in the *New York Times* with Owens describing his own inclusion as 'swell news'.

Glickman remembered the meeting took place in a small room with a couple of beds: he perched on the edge of one, Draper and Wykoff on the other, Stoller to Glickman's left and coach Cromwell – a strong, no-nonsense figure from the University of Southern California – in an armchair. Owens sat opposite Glickman, 200-metre man Mack Robinson to Glickman's right, Metcalfe beside Robinson. Robertson remained standing beside the door.[31] What Robinson was doing there is not at all clear.

Robertson began to pace nervously.[32] His face solemn, he said he understood the Germans were playing a devious game by concealing their best sprinters so that they would come from nowhere to win. That necessitated a change in the team which would now be Owens, Metcalfe, Draper and Wykoff. Draper, third in the Village 'race' two days before, was included because of his greater experience.

Glickman was out. Sam Stoller was out.

What was unstated was that Draper was a 'product' of Cromwell's 'ambitious programme' at Southern California and Wykoff came from there, too.[33]

The small room fell silent.

Glickman, thunderstruck, blurted out that the Germans were no kind of a threat at all. Their best, Erich Borchmeyer, had finished a distant fifth in the men's 100 metres. Glickman knew that all seven Americans could beat him, no question, and never mind any other Germans; and he insisted that *any* American combination would win by 15 metres. They could lose, Glickman concluded, *but only if they dropped the baton*. Robertson refused to budge, insisting that his information about the German tactics was sound, although he refused to divulge his source. Glickman remembered Owens pleading for him – Glickman – and Stoller to be reinstated. 'Let Marty and Sam run. I've already won three gold medals. I'm tired. They haven't had the chance to run. Let them. They deserve it.'

Cromwell jabbed a finger towards Owens and said 'You'll do as you're told.'

Owens fell silent.

Glickman pointed out that he and Stoller were the only two Jews in the track team and to drop both would create great controversy at home.

'We'll take our chances,' Cromwell responded.

They filed out of the room, not speaking. Glickman, only eighteen, felt anger and confusion although he never did discuss the matter with Stoller who, he felt, was 'shattered'. They weren't particularly close and in those days athletes did do what they were told. Glickman reflected that the original team had been perfecting the vital matter of passing the baton, which Owens and Metcalfe hadn't practised at all. A mistake there could lead to defeat, namely, *that's how they could be beaten.*

Glickman believed they were dropped because of anti-Semitism. He 'suspected collusion between Dean Cromwell and . . . Brundage, both of whom were members of a pro-Nazi organisation, the America First Committee'.[34] Glickman reasoned the move prevented causing Hitler the embarrassment of having Jews win gold.

The obverse must equally be true, that including two black men was hardly the route to Hitler's affections either. A judgement can be risked, however: Hitler genuinely hated Jews to the point where the Nazis tried to exterminate them throughout Europe. He did not hate blacks; he merely thought they should still be in the jungle.

Did the American coaches – and Brundage – take Hitler's sentiments on race, and on Jews in particular, into consideration? Why should they? Was any pressure from anywhere brought to bear on them, even by themselves? Did the coaches not consider the most obvious compromise – picking Owens and either Glickman or Stoller? Nobody knows. The people who could answer these questions are all dead now, some long dead.

10 a.m.	decathlon 110 metres hurdles/discus/pole vault/javelin/ 1,500 metres
3 p.m.	4 × 100 relay heats
3.30 p.m.	4 × 100 relay heats (women)
4 p.m.	3,000 metres steeplechase final
4.30 p.m.	4 × 400 relay heats

From 10 a.m., and forming the backdrop to the day, the decathletes completed their event, climaxing with the 1,500 metres in darkness.

For the first 4 × 100 heat against Italy, South Africa, Finland and Japan the Americans lined up Owens, Metcalfe, Draper and Wykoff. It was sound tactically because Owens, going first, would only have to hand the baton over, not receive it – which of course he hadn't practised doing. It did, however, put real pressure on Metcalfe, receiving from Owens and handing to Draper, because he hadn't been practising either. Glickman watched from the area reserved for the athletes. Before the race the American press wanted to speak to him and he went to them, although he doesn't record what he said. Eleanor Holm was there in her guise as journalist and Glickman met her husband.

The *New York Times* amplified Robertson's claim that the Germans were holding back by adding that the Dutch were supposed to be doing the same thing. Both countries had evidently been recording times of 40.5 seconds. The reality was exactly 40.0 seconds in coming. Although the baton handling proved less than perfect that was the time the Americans did, equalling the world and Olympic records. Holland won their heat but in 41.3 and Germany theirs in 41.4, making nonsense of Robertson's theory.

Helen Stephens spent the day hanging about before the women's 4 × 100, her first relay. She'd run the anchor leg in Heat 1 which America won (47.1 seconds). Stephens recorded how, on this day of changeable weather, the crowd 'roared' and she completed the relay pulling away from the Canadian anchor, Holland third, Austria fourth. In Heat 2 the Germans faced Britain, Italy and Finland. Audrey Brown, running the third leg, remembered 'Leni Riefenstahl was a bit of a nuisance. She removed me from my chosen position before the start because it was just by her [filming] "pit" on the last bend and I was blocking her view!'[35] Germany won (46.4 seconds, beating the world and Olympic records) from Britain (47.5), Italy came third.

The Finns showed their stamina again in the 3,000 metres steeplechase, Volmari Iso-Hollo leading from Kaarlo Tuominen but Alfred Dompert of Germany made a spirited charge towards the end, inflaming the crowd to a great boiling passion. He caught and pushed Tuominen so hard that in the final straight he forced him up towards Iso-Hollo.

In the pool next to the stadium a seventeen-year-old Dutch girl, Hendrika Wilhelmina 'Rie' Mastenbroek, set off on a strenuous, almost inhuman, campaign towards the plateau created by Owens. Born in Rotterdam to parents who lived together for forty-six years but never married, she learnt to swim early and at eleven a leading Dutch coach noticed her. She began the campaign in 100 metres freestyle by winning her heat in a new Olympic record, dragging her great rival, the German Gisela Arendt, with her.[36]

In the stadium the 4 × 400 heats were tight and there wasn't much to choose between America, Great Britain, Sweden, Germany and Canada.

In the gathering gloom, that left the 1,500 metres to decide the decathlon. As the stadium announcer said in several languages, Glenn Morris needed to run 4 minutes 32 seconds for overall victory. He'd never done anything approaching that before and 4 minutes 49 seconds was his usual time. A strong, rugged man, he felt plain tired. Lengthening stride, his body went forward in great plodding movements. Maurice Boulanger (Belgium), red running shorts so visible in the dark, overtook him along the back straight. Morris responded as best he could, plodding on. The last 44 metres tormented him and at the line his 4 minutes 33.2 seconds was too slow.

The announcer had been wrong.

Morris hadn't needed to get below 4 minutes 32 seconds and at that moment, blanket draped around him against another cold night, he could justifiably claim to be the greatest athlete in the world.

Helen Stephens's leg felt 'tight' but that didn't stop her going dancing.

In the football Poland beat Great Britain 5–4 but the Peru v. Austria match descended into chaos. Peru went two goals down with 15 minutes left in a rough match handled by a weak referee. Peru equalised, taking the match into extra time and releasing dangerous emotions. Some reports say Peruvian supporters invaded the pitch, others that it was the Peruvian bench. Whoever they were they set about one of the Austrian players, Adolf Laudon, kicking him. In the ensuing bedlam Peru scored twice more to win 4–2.

If the Nazis were determined to wring every drop of respectability out of the Games, Goering intended to wring every drop of personal pomp and circumstance out of them, too. He was perfectly placed to do just that. He held positions in the national and Prussian governments and was a member of the Reichstag as well. This enabled him to throw three official parties. Following his dinner for the IOC, he now hosted a dinner for 2,000 in the State Opera House on Unter den Linden. It 'rivalled Friedrich the Great's victory celebrations held there in December 1742'. Goering picked red and white as the colours for the occasion. 'Over 100 periwigged footmen in pink livery and knee-breeches lined the stairs, holding glass lanterns on long poles.' Goering wore white. 'Berlin had known nothing like it since the start of the First World War.'[37]

And that was the seventh day.

The weather changed, it was now cloudy but warm on the Sunday, the final day of the track and field events. Some 160,000 people arrived in Berlin by train, the highest number so far.

In Vienna the *Neue Freie Presse* carried extremely restrained coverage of the Austria v. Peru match. The report, two paragraphs long, said

The Austrian team had to play against Peru and after a hard struggle the match went into extra time.

The Austrians had the better of the beginning and by half time they had two goals. Everything changed after the interval until, later on, Laudon was injured and taken off. With ten men our team was forced onto the defensive. An own goal by the Austrian defenders made it possible for the Peruvians to get their first goal and very soon after that they scored a further goal through Fernandez. In the later stages Austria were back to eleven men but the Peruvians showed that they had more stamina and by two further goals they won eventually. There were 20,000 spectators.

The Austrians protested to the International Football Federation, who ruled the match had to be replayed in an empty stadium on the Monday. When news of this reached the Peruvian capital, Lima, big crowds gathered round newspaper offices to follow developments. Their Olympic Committee met the country's President, Oscar Benavides, who ordered a complete withdrawal from Berlin.

Part of the crowd moved towards Benavides's palace and on the way tore down an Olympic flag at a business premises which had a German manager who was also acting Austrian Consul. The police intervened and the crowd surged towards the main square, where another part of the crowd arrived, too. They bayed their anger for Benavides and he came out onto the balcony flanked by senior politicians and the military. Speeches were made and he said he had just had cables from Argentina, Chile, Uruguay and Mexico proclaiming solidarity. He appealed for the crowd to show the restraint and sportsmanship which had not been shown to Peru in Berlin.

The crowd, noisy and growing all the time, marched five blocks to another square singing the national anthem. There they heard more speeches and marched on the German Consulate. The windows were stoned before police arrived in trucks and broke the crowd up in to 'noisy but otherwise harmless groups'.[38]

3 p.m.	marathon
	women's high jump semi-finals, final
3.15 p.m.	4 × 100 final
3.30 p.m.	4 × 100 women's final
3.45 p.m.	4 × 400 final

Helen Stephens spent the morning writing cards. Glickman decided to go to the stadium to watch the relays, whatever that might do to him.

The marathon followed a similar route to the 50-kilometre walk, meandering through the Grünewald forest beside the River Havel, turning inland to the gun-barrel straight motor racing circuit called the Avus, to turn at the end of that and return. As someone pointed out, although the course was proper road, the route subjected the runners to a particular kind of torture: as they got hotter and hotter under the sun they'd be going past bathers cooling themselves in the Havel or drinkers refreshing themselves in vast open-air beer gardens.[39] The race started in the stadium and an estimated million spectators lined the route, which was where most of the 160,000 who'd come by train were headed.

The Japanese team featured Sohn Kee-chung, a fiercely nationalistic Korean who had set a new world record the year before. He trained by filling the pockets of his shorts with sand and carrying a rucksack full of stones on his back. Japan had annexed Korea in 1910 and if he wanted to run in Berlin it would have to be in the Japanese team. He and another Korean, Nam Seung-yong, were 'forced to endure the further insult of adopting Japanese names (his participation is recorded under the Japanese name Son Kitei). Sohn, a fervent nationalist, always signed his Korean name in Berlin and whenever he was asked where he was from, he made it a point to explain that Korea was a separate nation.'[40]

The runners waited in a great group for the start. Here was defending champion Juan-Carlos Zabala who had not run a marathon since Los Angeles but had beaten the world 20-kilometre record and trained hard for six months. Here were the inevitable Finns, Erkki Tamila, Vaino Muinonen and Mauno Tarkianen who ran as a team taking turns to lead – and to demoralise their opponents. Here was 34-year-old Ernest Harper (Great Britain) and Johannes Coleman (South Africa). Here, too, were the troubled French trio of Khaled Nouba, Emile Duval and Fernand Leheurteur – Duval, who had a reputation for liking a drink, suffering from a boil, Leheurteur into the eighth day of an abscess (the tooth wasn't taken out in case of complications). The trainer gave all three runners cloth bracelets on which he'd written the times he wanted from them and posted people at the control points to monitor how accurately they were meeting them – a mistake. The times proved too conservative. Here was the Portuguese Manuel Dias who had made the fundamental error of wearing new running shoes.[41]

They moved en masse at the gun and strung out like beads on a necklace round the stadium, each seeking his own pace. Zabala in a white hat – like a silken balaclava – led out of the stadium and fully intended to break his own Olympic record, aiming at 2 hours 30 minutes. The order: Zabala, Dias, Harper and Sohn as they moved down a narrow lane between the trees, spectators standing deep on either side, the trees spreading shadows. At 4 kilometres Zabala led Dias by half a minute. He was going for broke.

The women's high jump moved into the elimination stages. Gretel Bergmann ought to have been in the German team and excluding her on anti-Semitic grounds subsequently became an even more grotesque travesty when the truth emerged about Dora Ratjen. Born in Bremen nine days after the First World War ended, he had joined the little club Comet in that city as a sprinter and shot-putter as well as high-jumper. In 1933 he competed in the German high jump championships, finishing sixth. Many years later he claimed the Nazis had threatened to harm his family if he did not compete as a woman in Berlin. Presumably they reasoned that, as a man, he would have to win (and who would care about Bergmann then?). The irony, if one can use such a word, is that Ratjen finished fourth. After a jump-off, Ibolya Csák (Hungary) won from Odam and Elfriede Kaun of Germany. Most people, Odam judged,

> have nerves and get in a state in competition. The women's high jump wasn't until the last day. I was getting fed up not getting out there. I wanted to get out and perform. I didn't fail at all until the final jump which we all failed, but I got over the one before on my first jump, which today would have given me the gold medal. In those days, they lowered the bar a quarter of an inch and you all tried. We all jumped it. They raised it, we all jumped, then lower, then higher, and the Hungarian girl cleared it. The German girl dropped out before then. During the actual competition, which lasted for three hours, there was an awful lot of cheering for the German girl and she was allowed a drink during the competition, which we weren't. The only people cheering for me were a crowd of British scouts! In the end, I won silver, though I jumped the same height as the winner. Lord Aberdare presented the medal in a box in the stadium.[42]

Ratjen reportedly concealed his private parts by binding them, tight, but even so Odam felt 'sure he was a man'.

At 10 kilometres in the marathon Ellison Brown (United States) moved up among the leaders. When they reached half distance Zabala led from Harper and Sohn, who had a compact, rolling motion as he ran. He and Harper were abreast and at one point Harper angled his head and said something to him. Sohn nodded back.

On the Avus, at the point where they turned, Zabala led in 1 hour 11 minutes 29 seconds but Sohn and Harper lay within 50 seconds, Sohn relaxed and comfortable. Behind, the Finns tried their tactic on Nam but he didn't crack, he kept on coming. Sohn felt a little tired at 25 kilometres but ran easily through that. At 31 kilometres Zabala took his hat off and was in trouble. At the refreshment stations runners dipped their heads into bowls of cool water. At one Zabala collapsed, instinctively rose, limped forward for another 100 metres only to collapse again. Sohn moved into the lead.

In the foreground, as the American 4 × 100 team prepared for the final Glickman sat alone. He had no idea where Stoller was, or even if he was there.

Hitler, in uniform, sat about 30 yards away. As Glickman watched the four down there warming up he had only one thought: *that ought to have been me.* Now his gaze locked on to Metcalfe, who would run the second leg – *his* leg. He thought Metcalfe looked in good form.

Then Marty Glickman felt very, very angry.

Before the start Owens blew Italian relay runner Fernanda Bullano a kiss.

He moved into the mechanical lope and it was so beautiful to watch that Glickman forgot his bitterness and gloried in being a witness to it. The lope was so fluid and so light, Glickman thought, Owens's spikes hardly seemed to bite the track surface. Owens led by 4 metres when he handed – slightly hesitantly – the baton to Metcalfe; and Metcalfe stormed away, 7 metres up when he handed over to Draper. Metcalfe almost went out of the change-over zone and in that instant Glickman might have been vindicated: *the only people who can beat us are ourselves.*

Draper, alone, maintained the lead and that gave Wykoff a solitary run for home. The Americans did 39.8 seconds, the Olympic and world records beaten. Italy came second (41.1) and Germany third (41.2).

Owens had his fourth gold medal.

Australian swimmer Evelyn de Lacy reflected what Glickman and so many others felt when, half a century later, she said that her Berlin memory was 'of watching Jesse Owens. I never missed any of his races, he ran with such beauty and grace, he was so beautiful to watch.'[43]

Hitler did not leave the stadium.

In the changing rooms immediately after the race, however, Secretary-Treasurer of the AAU Daniel Ferris reminded Owens he was expected to run in a meeting at Cologne on the Tuesday. Money could be made from the organisers of such meetings (the Cologne people said the AAU could have 15 per cent of the gate if Owens competed, only 10 per cent if he did not),[44] although by definition as amateurs Owens and the other athletes would not see a penny of it. Coach Draper reacted strongly. Owens had given everything over the week and you couldn't ask a man to run the day after this relay, but because Cologne lay two days away Draper's case fell.

As it would seem, no thought had been given to whether Owens would want to go to Cologne, never mind the further meetings being arranged. He felt deeply tired, homesick and, preying on his mind, an orchestra in California had just telegrammed offering $25,000 – a fortune – for a two-week appearance with them. He didn't know it was a hoax and understandably wanted to take it up.

In the women's 4 × 100 the Germans were favourites because they had broken the world record on the way to the final. Bullano in the Italian team remembered how cold the weather was and how, while she lay in the tunnel at the stadium waiting, Owens 'covered my legs with a blanket'.[45]

The race turned on the final change-over and by then the Germans had a substantial lead. Ilse Dörffeldt stood poised to run the anchor leg against Helen Stephens.

'It was,' Werner Schwieger says, 'the most fantastic event. I was sitting at the beginning of the section where the last baton pass would be – our women were about 8 metres ahead . . .'.

Marie Dollinger sprinted up to Dörffeldt but seemed to be coming too fast – and Dörffeldt did not seem to set off fast enough. Suddenly they were side by side, not one behind the other, and in the fumble the baton went down. Dörffeldt raised her arms in a gesture of complete despair then clutched her head.

Hitler, on his feet, sat down and thumped his gloves on his knee twice. Goebbels, next to him, said something. Hitler turned and said something to someone behind him.

Stephens strode home and America had a new Olympic record.

Audrey Brown, running the third leg for Great Britain, found the German team 'superbly drilled' and their dropping of the baton 'unbelievable'. She had often wonder if they would have won because Stephens 'was such an unknown quantity, running faster and faster each time she went out. Fortunately we managed to keep our heads and came in a creditable second.' Canada finished third.

The German women, crying, moved into a communal huddle.

Hitler summoned them and comforted them, saying that they shouldn't be so upset because they had proved they were the best in the world. *Der Angriff* supposed Hitler's comfort 'must have eased their sorrow and pain'.[46]

Brown said 'standing on the rostrum with the Canadians and Americans and looking round the vast stadium . . . was the most important moment in the Games for me, despite wearing rather ridiculous oakleaf laurels' (given to silver medallists).[47]

[Meanwhile] the press sought to demonstrate Germany's dominance by tallying up medals and points from the Games. Medal accumulation charts and graphs, which showed Germany's athletic supremacy over other nations, appeared in numerous publications. The press employed a confusing point system to add up top placements in the various Olympic events, as well. Foreign journalists questioned the fairness of this method, charging the Germans with manipulating statistics. Discrepancies certainly did appear. A post-Olympic book, for instance, calculated that Germany's women earned forty points in track and field while *Deutsche Sport Illustrierte* came up with fifty-eight. Instead of assigning points to the top three finishers, the magazine awarded Germany's 4 × 100-metre team the maximum points, on the basis of their world record time in the preliminaries, not their performance in the finals, in which they were disqualified.[48]

There remained the men's 4 × 400, Great Britain against America. On the first leg Britain's Frederick Wolff was slow and that loaded the pressure onto Godfrey Rampling.[49] Phil Edwards (Canada), a long-striding chunk of muscle, led, Robert Young (America) thrusting up to his shoulder and then on the bend, through the shadows of late afternoon, Rampling swept imperiously past both of them and strode away. He handed the baton to William Roberts, a short man moving urgently, while New Yorker Edward O'Brien – bigger, burlier – tracked him, counter-attacked, tried to go outside. For an instant they were abreast but now Roberts counter-attacked. The British anchor, Arthur Brown, did not squander his inheritance and as he crossed the line raised his arms in triumph.

Clutching the Californian telegram Owens took the bus back to the Village. He would do the exhibition tour, beginning at Cologne. The train left on the morrow, giving plenty of time to pack and say goodbye to people he'd met, particularly Luz. Instead Metcalfe 'rushed up' to him and said the train was leaving now: no time to pack except his running gear. Owens managed to leave a note for Albritton asking him to bring everything he'd left.[50] The Cologne meeting wasn't on the Tuesday but tomorrow.

As souvenirs the sprinters had been given special starting trowels, each in a leather case with *XI Olympiade Berlin 1936* inscribed on them. The sprinters liked them a lot and other competitors felt they were entitled to souvenirs, too. As a consequence the officials controlling the return of other equipment 'had difficulty in preventing the competitors from carrying off javelins, discuses, relay batons, etc.'.[51]

When the athletics finished in the stadium the gymnasts came on to do their exhibition, filling the time before the marathon runners came back. The gymnasts had been practising for two or three weeks. Werner Schwieger says that 'we had to go to the August-Bier-Platz [see map on page x] several times. Around the Olympic stadium there were lots of little sports grounds and fields, among them the August-Bier-Platz. There we practised all our presentations. They would check on the gymnastic kits. The white gym trousers were not supposed to be too long. We had to practise a lot, not only for the free exercises but also for the apparatus gymnastics on the horizontal and parallel bars, the horses, the trampoline and so on.'

The gymnasts entered through the tunnel for what was called *1,000 German Gymnasts* although it included the Swedes whose participation had provoked so much domestic controversy. 'We marched in in rows of three. There were little button-like markers in the ground and the one who was in the middle of the row of three had to step on these markers so it looked all a regular pattern. I was the one in the middle. We had practised this on August-Bier-Platz over and over again. And besides the free exercises, there were also presentations of apparatus gymnastics. Horizontal and parallel bars and other apparatus were put up in the middle of the field and we did the exercises.' When the presentation ended Schwieger and the others watched the climax of the marathon.[52]

In the background Sohn looked perfectly composed as he came back through the lanes of shadow into the stadium and sprinted for the line, reaching it at 2 hours 29 minutes 19 seconds. He moved away from people trying to help him, face expressionless, and sat, taking his shoes off. Huddled under a blanket he looked slightly lost, as if he didn't know how to handle winning the gold medal for the country oppressing his own; then he trotted off to the showers. He didn't see Harper come in second after holding off a strong challenge from Nam in the tunnel.[53] Sohn said, 'much credit for my victory must go to Mr. Harper of England. He kept telling me not to worry about Zabala but to let him run himself out so we paid no attention to him or any other runners and set our own pace.'[54] Reportedly Harper couldn't find the Great Britain team's changing rooms and no British official sought him out to tell him where they were. Barefoot and limping, he wandered the concrete corridors beneath the stadium vainly asking policemen but they couldn't understand him. He limped on, smoking a cigarette.

At the medal ceremony Sohn and Nam stood with their heads bowed.

Back at the Village Sohn lay on his bed, a blanket covering him, while a succession of tearful Japanese paid homage to him, some even laying their heads on his chest. One said, 'we have been preparing for this victory for 24 years'.[55]

The next day the Seoul daily newspaper *Dong a Ilbo* reported the marathon as a 'Korean victory in Berlin'. It carried a photograph of Sohn on the podium but the little Japanese flag had been removed from his tracksuit. Ten members of the newspaper staff were arrested and publication suspended for nine months. Sohn never ran again.[56]

In the swimming pool Mastenbroek beat Arendt in the first 100 metres freestyle semi-final, and Campbell won the other from another Dutch girl, 'Willy' den Ouden.

Owens had gone, Mastenbroek still very much here.

And that was the eighth day.

Chapter 9

LAST SHOT FIRED

I came all the way from California to do this.

The woman who kissed Hitler

The fine weather held as the Games moved into their second week. With the track and field events over, this second week would be a different mosaic of movement from the first, the competitions more varied and spread out; and always the raw politics of the mid-1930s crept, like a dark, distant shadow, closer and closer. This time the shadow came from Spain.

The American athletes left Berlin for a sequence of meetings whatever their feelings or exhaustion: on the Monday, one party to Dresden, another to Cologne; both parties in Prague on the Tuesday, some to a town called Bochum on the Wednesday and after that to London; on the Thursday another party from Hamburg to London for a Saturday competition. The prospect of their arrival excited anticipation, they filled stadiums and they filled column inches. The Berlin Olympics made them and Germany proved reluctant to let them go.

Hendrika Mastenbroek faced a week of incessant stress in the pool and she emerged from it with such stature that, fifty years later, someone said at a reunion for the Games Owens had been King and she Queen, but because the main weight of column inches was devoted to track and field events a lot of people scarcely noticed. Her week:

Monday	100 metres freestyle final
Tuesday	100 metres backstroke heats
Wednesday	4 × 100 relay heats
	100 metres backstroke semi-finals
Thursday	400 metres freestyle heats
	100 metres backstroke final
Friday	400 metres freestyle semi-finals
	4 × 100 relay final
Saturday	400 metres freestyle final

There were many pieces to the mosaic, including administrative. The International Amateur Athletic Federation met in Berlin and ratified the twenty-seven new records. It also took over running women's athletics from the International Womens' Sports Federation and in doing that stepped into delicate territory. The IAAF passed a resolution dealing with the 'man–woman' controversy although they couched it in careful language: 'Questions of a physical nature'. The Swedish secretary, Bo Ekelund, explained what it really meant. The resolution said that in the event of a protest the organisers of any meeting had to 'arrange for a physical inspection made by a medical expert'. The competitor had to undergo this test and accept its findings.

It would not be good news for Dora Ratjen although, as we shall see, she wasn't 'outed' by that but by her five o'clock shadow which made a couple of fellow passengers on her train curious . . .

Most competitors were quite normal and behaved quite normally. Pat Norton remembered: 'We were often escorted to open air restaurants by four good looking, heel clicking, Nazi officers for supper. The men were studiously polite and we got the impression they were there in the line of duty! The American girls didn't sit at home with nothing to do either. A bus would arrive after dinner with some of the American male athletes and they would all pile in and off they'd go – even one lass with her leg in plaster wasn't going to be left behind and was gratefully carried to the bus! One night we were joined by some German girls for singing. We Australians sang in a traditional way, light and pleasant, the Japanese with sweet nasally tinklings, and the Germans finished the night with robust marching songs.'[1]

In contrast Velma Dunn went into Berlin once. 'In 1932 I met – I don't know how – one of the British swimming judges and when I made the team in 1936 she sent me a congratulations telegram. I met her at the Games. The British girls team had hired a bus and she invited me to go along. Like all tours on a bus, you go by all these big buildings and everything, and you really don't know what's in them. That was the only time that I had a chance to get to Berlin. I didn't get off the bus. I do remember there were Swastica flags everywhere but when we had the Olympics here in the United States it was all decorated with our flags. To me it wasn't any different than it would be at home.'[2]

There was talk at the IAAF meeting of Owens losing his amateur status because he'd intimated he might turn professional. With coach Snyder he sought advice from one AAU official but met a policy of wait and see.

By the time the IAAF met, part of the American team – Albritton, Cunningham, Woodruff and Helen Stephens among them – had left for the meeting in Dresden, Snyder accompanying that group and saying the athletes looked 'dead tired'. They reached Dresden, which was already in Olympic mood since the torch passed through, by lunchtime, dined with the mayor and were shown the town.

In the 100 metres freestyle Arendt led at the turn from Campbell, Campbell ploughed a furrow past her but with some 25 metres to go Mastenbroek unleashed her power. Suddenly she was in a different race. Ten cleaving, scything strokes took her clear. Mastenbroeck: one gold. She had forced her time down to 1 minute 5.9 seconds. Campbell, second, and Arendt, third, beat the old record again.

Even so, Berlin could not escape that curious sense of emptiness and dispersal when the centrepiece – the athletics in the stadium – had gone, and the more minor sports existed in relative anonymity at so many different sites. The sense of emptiness heightened at 5.30 p.m. that evening when the Austria–Peru football re-match ought to have begun at the Post Stadium, barricaded and heavily guarded so no spectators could get in. The Austrian team arrived but the Peruvians didn't. The referee waited the statutory 15 minutes, blew his whistle and awarded the match to Austria.

In Vienna, the *Neue Freie Presse*, reflecting a more gentle and measured era, treated this extraordinary news item almost cursorily halfway down its page of Olympic coverage under the headline AUSTRIAN FOOTBALLERS IN SEMI-FINAL.

It simply was quite impossible to ignore the unbelievable incidents regarding the football struggle between Peru and Austria. The Austrian protest had to be heard and this is one of the very rare occasions when such a protest has been upheld during an Olympic Games. By this fact alone one can see that the Austrians were justified in making it. When the Peruvians heard they had to replay the match they flatly refused. Our team was already on the pitch when they learnt that the Peruvians would not be coming at all. Thus Austria won without playing and go into the semi-finals.

The Peruvian protest reached its climax when the football team withdrew and, under government pressure from Lima, the rest of their Olympic team did, too. They actively campaigned for the other South American teams to follow. That evening Goebbels held a meeting with the Peruvian ambassador and Olympic officials to try and reach a compromise, perhaps replaying the match on the Tuesday. The Peruvians said no.

They departed by train for Paris and at the station every Peruvian in Berlin turned up to cheer them off.

President Benavides meanwhile went down a well-trodden path, blaming communists for stoning the German Embassy.

The Chileans, in Berlin and at home, were in some confusion over whether to stay solid and leave with Peru. The Chilean press in Santiago urged all South American teams to withdraw, claiming that the Europeans looked down on them as unworthy competition.

In the first of the football semi-finals Italy beat Norway 2–1 after extra time. Austria would meet Poland the following day.

At the Dresden meeting autograph hunters swarmed. They saw Stephens beat Walsh and Krauss, equalling the time she'd done at the Games. Woodruff took the 800 metres with a late charge and Cunningham waltzed the 1,500. The winners received Dresden china for prizes.

Owens reached Cologne for the meeting there. He had shed 10lb in Berlin and now, starting at 6.30 in the evening, a crowd of 35,000 watched him win the long jump (albeit with 24 feet 4 inches/7 metres 43) and help win the 4 × 100 relay with LuValle, Bob Packard and Metcalfe, but he lost to Metcalfe in the 100 metres – Metcalfe did 10.3 seconds, equalling the world record. Owens was tired. He confessed to Snyder that at the start he looked across at Metcalfe, realised what was going to happen and 'just didn't care'. The event finished at around 8.30 p.m. and the banquet afterwards lasted until midnight.

And that was the tenth day.

The fine weather in Berlin reached its climax on the Tuesday, the sky virtually free of cloud and, with only moderate south-easterly winds, the day became genuinely hot.

At 8 a.m. the heats for the women's 100 metres backstroke began. Holm watched: she held the Olympic and world records. In the first heat Nida Senff (Holland) beat Holm's Olympic record and Mastenbroek finished only second in her heat. Holm, asked if she thought she'd have been able to beat Senff, said yes.

Owens caught a plane to join the other group, which had travelled the relatively short distance from Dresden to Prague, to compete against a Czechoslovak team that evening. Owens had virtually no dollars and no German marks at all, and a fellow passenger bought him a sandwich and a glass of milk, the only sustenance he would have.[3] He landed in Prague at 4.30 that afternoon after a long stopover and was taken straight to the stadium because the meeting started at 6 p.m. Checking in to the hotel would have to wait. The American athletes won every one of the nine events. Owens took the 100 metres but could go no faster than 10.7 seconds, and the long jump but with a mediocre distance.

Even as the Games moved into this second week the *Völkischer Beobachter* ran an article entitled 'The Olympic Guest Asks, "Racial Laws: Why?"' In the article the author observed how people of various physical statures and skin colors could be seen in Berlin. In step with Nazi racial hygienists, he argued that people fundamentally differed from each other because of race – not climate or culture. The next day the *Völkischer Beobachter* reiterated the point by featuring a photograph of American diver Dorothy Poynton Hill next to a Chinese diver with the caption, 'Blond and black.' . . .

Interestingly, when Germany lost, the press still employed versions of the races argument. *Der Angriff* and an internal party report, for instance, declared that fair competition with blacks was impossible because they were an entirely different race. Reporters used a modified form of the argument again when considering the Japanese. When [Martha] Genenger was placed second to Maehata of Japan in the breaststroke, the press complimented the Japanese swimmer and her team-mates for their sacrificial approach to competing for their country. More generally, members of the German media praised the healthy lifestyle and industrious training of the Japanese.[4]

That was the 200 metres breaststroke and Hideko Maehata became the first Japanese swimmer ever to win a gold in a race which captivated Japan, listening so intently to the radio. The commentator at the pool cried out '*Ganbare! [Come on! Come on!]*' more than twenty times over the final 50 metres.[5]

Behind Genenger came a twelve-year-old Dane, Inge Soerensen. Genenger was a schoolgirl, too.

In the second football semi-final Austria beat Poland 3–1.

And that was the eleventh day.

On the Wednesday the midday temperature remained lower than it had been for several days and towards evening the weather gradually became dull.

Owens came back to Berlin but only en route to the Ruhr town of Bochum and another meeting. The Berlin stopover proved long and the journey consumed the whole day.

In Grunau the rowers began their competitions.

In the swimming pool the Dutch team, including Mastenbroek and van Ouden, went very fast in the 4 × 100 metres relay heats, the Germans more than 2 seconds slower and the winners of the other heat, the Americans, 9 seconds slower still.

That evening Senff and Mastenbroek won their semi-finals in the 100 metres backstroke, Senff again decisively quicker.

Pat Norton finished sixth in the semi-final that Senff won.

My effort . . . was abysmal. It was a great disappoinment to me. Losing a week's training with a swollen gland, then to be confronted with my period on the day of the race did nothing for my morale. Menstruation was not a subject for general discussion among us girls ourselves, let alone with a male swimming coach! I was lethargic and slightly depressed and my limbs felt as if they had turned to lead. I managed to make the semi-final, but if I had repeated my Australian record I would have come third. Well, these things happen, and you only have one chance and that's that.[6]

The athletes reached Bochum at 4 p.m. During the flight turbulence shook the plane so badly that once on the ground some of them couldn't face their lunches. The meeting began at 6 p.m. and 8,000 spectators watched Owens win the 100 metres in 10.3 seconds, equalling his world record and leaving Borchmeyer in his wake – but he lost the long jump to an unknown German, Wilhelm Leichum.

In Berlin baseball became a demonstration sport, played by two American teams drawn from various sources. Under floodlights it attracted an audience of 100,000 and both teams gave the Nazi salute before the game began. A tri-lingual commentary outlined to spectators what they watched but inadequate floodlighting made the ball hard to see during the seven innings.[7]

When the Bochum meeting ended the Americans flew to Croydon, south of London and the city's first international airport. They didn't get there until almost midnight and, with everything closed, ate stale sandwiches and slept in a hangar.[8] They'd be competing at a meeting at the White City Stadium on the Saturday.

In Spain, the International Brigades, comprising volunteers from far and wide, joined the Republican side. They included a considerable number of Frenchmen as well as political refugees from Germany and Italy. In time they became a Republican army bolstered by the Soviet Union, and with Hitler and Mussolini backing the rebel Franco a murderous struggle of ideologies was played out. Hitler saw in Spain an ideal proving ground for new military technology and one tactic in particular, the indiscriminate bombing of towns. This the same man who travelled out to the stadium or the other venues virtually every day infused, supposedly, with the Olympic spirit. The same man who had comforted the German women's relay team would bomb the town of Guernica without a thought for all its women and children.

And that was the twelfth day.

In the early hours of the Thursday more American athletes arrived, from Hamburg, for the White City meeting.

It was cool in Berlin and a refreshing wind dragged cloud over on a day peppered by small, light showers.

From mid-morning Mastenbroek continued her campaign in the 400 metres freestyle heats. Ragnild Hveger (Denmark) went fast enough immediately to beat the Olympic record and was decisively faster than Mastenbroek's time in another heat.

At 5.10 that afternoon Senff won the 100 metres backstroke final from Mastenbroek. Eleanor Holm stood on her seat shouting 'Come on Edith!' to the American girl Edith Mottridge, fourth. Holm said that if she'd been swimming she'd have beaten Senff by '10 feet'. There is an irony here, and it is not that one. Senff made a mess of the turning point at 50 metres and lost the lead but swam with such force she regained it. So Mastenbroek had the silver: if Senff hadn't been able to regain the lead Mastenbroek would have ascended to the Owens plateau.

Owens at last had a moment to enjoy himself, not least because in London he could talk to people and wasn't actually competing that day. London was pleasantly hot, too, although he attracted the inevitable autograph hunters. He even spent time in a park and stopped to have his photograph taken while another member of the team hurdled over him.

Meanwhile, the Basque town of San Sebastian, in the Republican part of Spain, was being bombed and was the site of heavy fighting.

Goering threw a party in the garden of his ministry in Berlin, or rather in the extensive garden where he had had an eighteenth-century village recreated at a reduced scale. The wind which had dragged the cloud over now made the weather extremely cold and the guests in their summer clothing shivered and tried to warm themselves at coal braziers.

In the stadium that night 100,000 people watched a tattoo by all three arms of the German military, Hitler taking the salute. It began with bands playing Wagner and then the stadium was cast into darkness. Four searchlights played over the swastika at the east end, the Olympic flame at the Marathon Gate, the Olympic and Führer's standards at Hitler's box. The march-past came in a great, molten, controlled ripple from the tunnel beneath the Marathon Gate, soldiers goose-stepping and holding torches. They divided so that half moved round the track one way and half the other. When they met up they had created a circle of fire. Drums beat, trumpets blew from the Marathon Gate and the bands on the infield responded so that the stadium drowned in sound. The soldiers marched past Hitler to ecstatic applause. To use the Olympic Stadium *during* an Olympic Games for a military parade was an act which made all its own statements.

And that was the thirteenth day.

Towards 9 p.m. on the Friday the sun broke through briefly and around noon rain fell. It became a downpour and the Reich Sports Field showed that; and the temperature was very low.

In the morning Mastenbroek and Hveger won their 400-metre freestyle semi-finals, Hveger again the quicker of the two. Mastenbroek went on to win her second gold medal in the 4 × 100 metres freestyle relay. The Dutch team not only beat the Germans and Americans but broke the Olympic record. It was neither easy nor inevitable. Mastenbroek swam the anchor leg against Arendt and, although she was leading, gulped a mouthful of water just before the finish. She almost choked and, hardly able to breathe, her team-mates had to haul her out of the water: the winning margin, eight-tenths of a second.

Already it was time to be seeking perspective. A journalist, Frederick T. Birchall, explored the context of events in a carefully reasoned and reflective article for the *New York Times*. He argued that visitors to the Games would take with them the impression of a friendly, efficient Germany which might, just might, have been touched by what the visitors themselves brought: the Germans saw that 'all races' are good. He pointed out that anyone who had not been to Germany before, and who knew little of recent events, would conclude that Germany was a happy, prosperous country led by a great man and that her people were misunderstood. For the duration of the Games all the political and military controversies had been carefully obscured. He added that when the Games had gone and the streets returned to normal he hoped they'd stay obscured.

Broadcaster Shirer, so intimately acquainted with recent events, would have an interesting reflection of his own, and it would be rather different.

And that was the fourteenth day.

The weather became more pleasant on the Saturday although there was rain about, as Goebbels would discover.

Hitler attended the swimming and a small Californian woman wearing a white dress and broad red hat did what had been considered impossible. Hitler arrived amid a barrage of Nazi salutes from the 30,000-strong crowd and took his seat in the front row. She rose, went towards him, got through his bodyguards, flung her arms round his neck and kissed him. She asked for his autograph and when he signed it she kissed him on the cheek. She said 'I came all the way from California to do this.' She trotted back to her seat pursued by the bodyguards who caught her and led her out.

In direct contrast to Hitler's entry, former German Crown Prince Wilhelm bought an ordinary ticket for a day of the swimming, arrived and was recognised.[9] An attendant was ordered to take him to the VIP area but he declined, saying that he was quite happy with the seat he'd bought.

Mastenbroek faced Hveger in the 400 metres freestyle final. At some stage during the competition Hveger received a large box of chocolates from her supporters and Mastenbroek thought she might be given some. Hveger made a show of not giving her any and Mastenbroek thought *right, we'll see about that*. In the race she stayed with Hveger for the first 350 metres. Mastenbroek knew her own finish was of such power that nobody on earth could withstand it. She applied the power and as Hveger fell away she thought *this tastes better than chocolate*. Both beat the Olympic record but Mastenbroek had her third gold.[10] She was the first woman to win four medals at a single Games.

The Italian football team were a mighty force. They had won the 1934 World Cup and now, in sunshine, the final against Austria filled the stadium. The crowd were about to witness a match of its time: a physically robust game without histrionics, a masculine game of hard tackling, and a game of traditional tactics.

The Austrians were strong, too. Italy took the lead deep into the second half with an orthodox move down the wing, a cross and Annibale Frossi – curiously the right-winger – lurked close to goal. He stabbed the ball past the goalkeeper. The Italians embraced but in a restrained, manly way. The Austrians struck back with a header from Karl Kainberger taking the match into extra time. Almost immediately the Italians were everywhere, probing, attacking, and after a goalmouth scramble Frossi stabbed the ball in again. It was enough.

In London, the presence of Owens and so many other leading Americans drew a capacity crowd of 90,000 to the White City, site of the 1908 Games, and the gates had to be closed with thousands outside. Those inside saw the British Empire team soundly beaten with records broken in all directions and at several distances, notably the 4 × 100 *yards* relay.

Wykoff ran the first leg, then Glickman, Owens and Metcalfe, and while they warmed up a British supporter called out to Glickman 'Don't beat us too badly!' Wykoff accelerated at a tremendous pace and when Glickman handed the baton to Owens the British were a long way back. Metcalfe crossed the line with a lead of 10 yards and a new world record, albeit a slightly artificial one in a distance so rarely contested.

Owens never ran as an amateur again. He was, in any case, 'pretty sick of running'.[11]

That night Brundage contacted coach Snyder and asked what was going on, specifically about the supposed contracts offered to Owens, which inevitably would destroy his amateur status. Synder would not be drawn. Brundage also wanted to know if Owens was going to the meeting in Stockholm, even threatening 'dire consequences' if Owens wasn't there. Synder pointed out Owens had not signed an official entry form and under the rules could not be punished. The AAU and American Olympic Committee officials weren't having any of that. Athletes did what they were told and, anyway, there was money to be made for *them*.

Owens stayed in London.

Not to be outdone by Goering, or possibly to outdo Goering, Goebbels threw a party on an island in the River Havel to mark the end of the Games. Called the Pfaueninsel, the island had once had a dairy, a big dipper and a mansion but the ruling Hohenzollerns, treating it as their personal fiefdom, eventually lost interest in it and lovers went there for its privacy. It was ideal for Goebbels, who wanted a gigantic party. There were reasons.

It was 'the parties given by the three senior Nazi paladins, Goering, Goebbels and the future foreign minister Ribbentrop, that were the most keenly anticipated events in the social calendar' during the Games. 'The three men were not only political rivals but also bitter personal enemies and they could be relied upon to compete with each other in the extravagance of their entertaining.' Ribbentrop, who had been a wine merchant and had married money, would be lavish 'at the dinner and dance he gave at his house in the exclusive suburb of Dahlem. But Ribbentrop was a prize bore, and his party was utterly conventional.'[12]

Goering had outdone him and Goebbels intended to outdo both of them.

Trees were turned into luminous candelabra. The Reichswehr Pioneer Corps threw up a bridge of boats to link the island with the land and soldiers mounted a guard of honour, presenting their oars to the guests, who were shown to their places by a swarm of young girls dressed as Renaissance pages. At midnight there was a splendid firework display that reminded everyone of an artillery barrage.[13]

Helen Stephens met Goering during the Games and thought she'd had the first glass of beer in her life with him. She went to the party with room-mate Bland, the relay runner from St Louis. At the party Goering sent a message saying he wanted to see her upstairs. She reasoned it could be fun but told Harriet not to tell anybody afterwards. They went past a soldier guarding the door and inside were confronted with Goering sitting on a huge divan accompanied by two women in skimpy clothing. He offered them wine and as they demurred the telephone rang. He answered it. A young officer said that this was no place for girls like them and shepherded them out. Goering stood, said goodbye and blew Stephens a kiss.[14]

And that was the fourteenth day.

The weather remained pleasant on the Sunday although it began with a heavy mist and towards midday the sky became overcast. During the day more than 200,000 people were registered by the control gates at the railway stations, a record. Berlin buzzed.

The hard news, however, came from the AAU in Berlin and Owens and Snyder in London. A conference was called in mid-afternoon at the stadium when Brundage and Ferris learnt that Owens hadn't boarded the plane for Stockholm. 'We had no alternative under the circumstances but to disbar Owens,' Ferris said. 'It's an open-and-shut case of violating an agremeent. It means that Owens will not be able to engage in any competition controlled by the AAU or in college meets either so long as he is under the ban.'[15]

Owens was informed of his suspension by telegram.

Snyder struck back accusing the AAU of sacrificing anybody 'to get its 10 per cent'.

Owens said: 'There's nothing I can gain out of this trip. This suspension is very unfair to me. All we athletes get out of this Olympic business is a view out of a train or an airplane window. It gets very tiresome, it really does. This track business is becoming one of the greatest rackets in the world. It doesn't mean a darn thing to us athletes. The AAU gets the money.'

At the 1936 Games, only one competition remained to be decided, the timed jumping in the equestrian event. The rest was already settling into memory, and not just the track and field centrepiece. There had been the four-day pentathlon with its riding, fencing, swimming and cross-country running won by Germany's Gotthard Handrick.

There had been the men's swimming fought out between the Japanese and the Americans but a Hungarian medical student, Ferenc Csík, took the 100 metres freestyle beating the world record holder, Peter Fick (USA), and three leading Japanese.

There had been the gymnastics with their graceful yet somehow curious movements and scoring. In the open Dietrich Eckart Stadium sometimes sunlight caught these movements and cast eerie, elongated shadows from them. The German men and women won.

There had been the men's diving where among Marshall Wayne's opponents was the Japanese he had watched practising so diligently and then, with Dick Degener, psyched him out. In the springboard final the Japanese, Tsueno Shibahara, landed firmly on his bottom on his first dive. The officials felt that someone in the crowd had made a noise distracting him – perhaps dropping a bottle – and approached Wayne and Degener to see if they'd object to him retaking the dive. They applied the psychology again: *Let him dive all day and you pick his best dive out of that.* Degener won the springboard from Wayne, Shibahara was fourth. Wayne won the highboard from room-mate Root.

There'd been the women's diving. 'I got a silver medal, three-tenths of a point away, that's all,' Velma Dunn says. 'To me it was close and it wasn't bad – three-tenths of a point in the entire world. I was very proud because I figured that that was a very good result. I wasn't disappointed at that time because I thought of Tokyo in 1940. I practised hard for that. I was seventeen in 1936 so I would still only have been twenty-one in 1940 – and Dorothy [Poynton-Hill, gold] was older than that.'[16]

There had been another American diver at the threshold of a career, thirteen-year-old Marjorie Gestring, who became the youngest Olympic gold medal winner of all when, with Hitler watching, she took the springboard diving. She was only twenty-six when she tried to qualify for the 1948 Games – but didn't.

There had been the men's fencing with Italians taking the foil – Giulio Gaudini, and the épée – Franco Riccardi. A Hungarian, Endre Kabos, took the sabre. He'd started fencing when he'd been given a fencing outfit for his birthday but, embarrassed, hid it in his wardrobe. A friend discovered it and teased him. Kabos joined a fencing club the following day. By 1932 he had become good enough to win gold in the team competition. Now he added the individual gold and won twenty-four of his twenty-five matches in Berlin. The Hungarian team returned to Budapest undefeated.[17]

There had been the wrestling and boxing: the one grunt and grab, the domain of the Hungarians, the Finns, Americans and Swedes; the other noisy, totally direct and mostly the domain of the Germans and the French. The rules said boxers had to be weighed every day, which made those struggling to make their weights suffer agonies with so much food available in the Village. The daily agony became so intense that one report suggested the British and American teams threatened to go home and regretted that they did not.

There had been the weight-lifting where an Egyptian, Khadr El Touni, won gold in the middleweight division by 35 kilograms, a world record and so impressive that his name was etched on an official plaque outside the stadium. Mythology cloaks him. Some claim that to keep himself interested during training at home he sat his four wives at different corners of the stage; some claim Hitler said to him 'I wish you could have been a German.' Egypt took five medals.[18]

There had been the rowing, sculling and canoeing at Grunau, Germans, Austrians, Czechs strong here. There had been the yachting at Kiel, stately little galleons line astern and tacking.

There had been the cycling, either on a banked track or the road race out into the Grünewald, and some lively action woven into it. In the 1,000 metres sprint Toni Merkens (Germany) swerved in front of Arie van Vliet to keep him in second place. The Dutch protested, leading to a 100 mark fine for Merkens – but he kept the gold. The individual road race reached a desperate climax with one Frenchman, Robert Charpentier, preparing a final assault against another, Guy Lapébie, considered the stronger sprinter. Charpentier launched his attack and as he did so he leant across and gripped Lapébie's saddle, literally holding him back. Lapébie said 'I'd have had to hit him to make him let go.' Charpentier got the gold, Lapébie, 0.2 of a second behind, the silver. Charpentier was one of the men of the Games, apart from this: he won golds in the team road race and the team pursuit.

There had been the shooting at Wanssee – that exacting test of controlling the nervous system, intense concentration and remaining motionless.

There had been the hockey where the Indians won – magical, magisterial, mystical in their skills. Victorious as they had been in 1928 and 1932 and would be again in 1948, 1952 and 1956, a complete dynasty of triumph.

After their initial practice match – the one which they had lost 4–1 to Germany – they sent for reinforcements in the shape of a great player, A.I.S. Dara, although he wouldn't arrive until the semi-finals. As they waited for him to come the team moved with gathering strength in their other practice matches: 5–1 against Berlin Hockey Club, 13–3 against Berlin Select, 15–0 against Brandenburg, 5–1 against Stettin, 8–2 against Afghanistan, 9–1 and 15–0 against America. They began the competition by beating Hungary comfortably 4–0, and afterwards they and the rest of the Indian party went to Hotel Adlon where the Maharaja and Maharani of Baroda received them 'graciously. The Maharaja was dressed in a navy blue suit and the Maharani had a gold-bordered blue sari on.'[19]

Their hockey team dealt with America 7–0 and Japan 9–0.

In the semi-finals Germany beat Holland 3–0 just before India, plus Dara at inside right, beat France 10–0. It meant they had scored 31 goals and conceded none. Now they faced Germany, of course, in the final – a match put back a day because of torrential rain. While in the dressing room, a crowd of 40,000, the largest attendance at an Olympic hockey match, waited, among them the 'ruler of Baroda, the princess of Bhopal. All the players reverently saluted the tricolour of the Indian National Congress, which their Assistant Manager had taken with him to Berlin.'[20]

The Germans held this immensely strong Indian side until 3 minutes before the interval but after it the Indians cut loose. From a penalty corner 7 minutes into the second half they made it 2–0, urgently adding a third and fourth. That was 12 minutes after the interval. A minute later they scored again and added a sixth.

The Germans now decided to play rough. Going for Dhyan Chand, the German goalkeeper removed one of his teeth. Coming back after receiving first aid, the bare-footed Dhyan Chand instructed his team to go easy on goals. 'We must teach them a lesson in ball control,' he said. As the stunned crowd watched, the Indians repeatedly took the ball up to the German circle and then backpassed to dumbfound their opponents.[21]

India won 8–1 and afterwards when Dhyan Chand told Hitler, who had watched the match, that he was a sepoy (ordinary soldier) in the army Hitler is said to have replied: 'If you were a German, I would have made you at least a major general.'

There had been the water polo where the Hungarians retained their gold medal but the Austrians won the crowd by shouting 'Heil Hitler' when they jumped into the water, the salute being held in mid-air.

There had been the polo – Argentina won, beating Great Britain and Mexico. There had been basketball, that game of the gentle giants, now an official Olympic sport. America won (and would be undefeated until 1972 when the USSR took the gold).

All these events must have seemed very close, just yesterday or the day before, and yet very far away – gone forever – as the Closing Ceremony began at 9 p.m. that evening when the timed jumping in the equestrian event had finally been decided. And that decision caught the mood of the whole Games (although much earlier the cross-country course had proved horrific with three horses being killed and twenty failing to complete it). One of the German team, Lieutenant Konrad von Wangenheim, had fallen in the steeplechase the day before, breaking his collarbone. He remounted and finished the course. If he withdrew because of his injury Germany would lose the team medal so he arrived at the stadium with his arm in a sling. As each German rider entered the arena they gave the Nazi salute and Hitler returned it. Von Wangenheim reached the first fence but fell again and his horse came down on top of him. The horse got up and he did, too. He completed the course and Germany had the gold, giving a final flourish to the medal table.

	Gold	Silver	Bronze
Germany	33	26	30
United States	24	20	12
Hungary	10	1	5

Floodlights came on to illuminate the stadium, haunting spotlights rising to form an arch of light. The nations paraded by, speeches were made, thunderous music played.

The big scoreboard carried the legend THE LAST SHOT IS FIRED.

Shirer recorded that for this Closing Ceremony he had had to use his wits to 'smuggle' Mrs William Randolph Hearst, wife of the newspaper tycoon, and a couple of her friends into the ceremony. They'd arrived the night before with no tickets. Shirer persuaded the SS guards to let them have diplomats' seats from where they could see Hitler.[22]

Shirer, who enjoyed the Games but found covering them a nuisance, was concerned that the Nazi propaganda had seduced foreign visitors, especially Americans and especially big businessmen. Shirer and a colleague, Ralph Barnes of the *Herald Tribune*, had been asked to meet some and discovered they had indeed formed favourable impressions. These businessmen met Goering who complained that the American reporters in Berlin were being unfair to the Nazis. Shirer asked the businessmen if Goering had discussed, for example, the Nazi suppression of the churches. Yes, they replied, and said that he had insisted there was no truth in what was being written. Shirer and his colleague reacted strongly to this but didn't feel they were convincing the businessmen.

In the stadium, Baillet-Latour thanked Hitler and the Germans with 'deepest gratitude' and summoned the youth of the world to Tokyo in 1940.

The Olympic flame flickered and died, the arch of light dimmed and 100,000 stood in silence for a long minute.

Pat Norton caught the mood. 'The Games finished and we thought, no more until 1940, Japan! The Closing Ceremony had a sad ring to it as the flags of all the nations were marched round the arena accompanied by the sound of rolling guns firing, followed by a choir singing "Song of the Flags." It was saying goodbye to the friends we made at *Friesenhaus* that saddened us. Jeanette from the Argentine, who just waved "goodbye" and did not look back, our giggly little Japanese girls and South Americans. Somehow it didn't seem right – we were very subdued realising we would never see them again.'[23]

And that was the fifteenth day.

It was over.

Chapter 10

VILLAGE PEOPLE

The way I see it now as an old man, you only become a true Olympic
champion when you add your credibility to the role of an idol, which
you may acquire through winning Olympic medals. Berlin gave me
the role of the idol; I have done my best to fill this role with my
personal credibility. And thus there exists between Berlin and me an
inseparable bond of reflection and feeling.

Jesse Owens, Berlin 2000 Olympic bid

Those August days, before the great gathering dispersed and dreamed of
Tokyo – the next celebration of a peaceful world at play – some of the
American athletes went into Berlin to have a drink, Cornelius Johnson
among them. According to Archie Williams, the 400 metres gold medal
winner in Berlin, 'ol' Corny was doing pretty good'. which must be affec-
tionate shorthand for had had a beer or two. They got into a taxi and when
they arrived at wherever they were going – presumably somewhere to catch a
bus back to the station to catch a train back to the Village – had to pass the
hat round to raise the fare. Ol' Corny was nobody's fool. Ol' Corny slept right
through.[1]

These young men, whose average age Williams estimated at twenty-one or
twenty-two, could look forward to Tokyo and the Games after that, 1944,
wherever they would be. They could not know Hitler nursed an urge to
appropriate the Olympic movement, as so much else. Speer designed a
stadium to accommodate 400,000 and Hitler came to Speer's offices to
examine a large, precise model of it.[2] Conversation moved to the Olympics
and Speer pointed out, as he had done before, that his track and field area did
not conform to Olympic measurements. Hitler, voice unaltered and by
definition matter-of-fact, explained that after Tokyo *every* Games would be in
Germany, and they would decide the measurements. To those who wield it,
this is what power means. The building schedule projected completion of the
stadium in time for the Nazi Party Rally planned for 1945.

What makes Hitler so bewildering a subject is that when not planning to seize the world, and seize the Olympic movement along the way, he could be utterly charming. The German pin-up javelin thrower Tilly Fleischer remembered, 'I was his table companion with Leni Riefenstahl at the closing banquet and he was very natural, knew a lot about sport and at the meal he ate Mixpikals [cold vegetables] and drank only water.'[3]

Rie Mastenbroek went back to Rotterdam by train where a huge crowd turned out to greet her, but there was a darker side. Her coach tried to adopt her and they fell out, her career over.

The Australian team left on 17 August, travelling to London. There they were given afternoon tea at Australia House, went to the Cenotaph and placed a wreath to commemorate Australia's war dead. They had done the same in Berlin.

The day after, following a banquet in Berlin where Von und zu Gilsa was praised for his work in ensuring the success of the Games, Wolfgang Fürstner returned to his barracks and, using his service pistol, shot himself. Since he was an officer, the German Army insisted on 'a funeral with full military honours'.[4] This must have enraged the Nazis, who wanted the whole thing hushed up, because foreign correspondents found out and wrote about it. Soon enough the walls of the Village became a canvas scrawled with obscenities about Fürstner the Jew.

The Village itself became the Olympia-Lazarett Döberitz, a military hospital, and the Heeres-Infanterieschule, a Wehrmacht training centre.

Owens and Snyder left London for New York. By then Owens had $200 in his hand because his former employer in Cleveland and the black owner of a barber's shop had heard of his financial plight and sent him an international bankers' draft. They put in $100 each.[5] Owens had been receiving all manner of commercial offers and one can only wonder what impact they had on him, a man who had never known money, when they all turned out to be worthless.

The Canadian team went to London and, reportedly, at their hotel other residents 'began raising a fuss because they were uncomfortable with the thought of staying in the same hotel as a black man', in the words of Phil Edwards. The team moved elsewhere. One of the women fencers, Cathleen Hughes-Hallett, said, 'If this hotel is too good for him, it's too good for me.'[6]

The main body of the American team left Hamburg on the *President Roosevelt*.

Velma Dunn Ploessel 'went to the University of Southern California. I enrolled immediately. Some of the athletes went on little tours up to Scandinavia and so on but I went right to college. I was a physical education major and at the end of the first week of classes the head of the physical education department called me into her office and said "I hope you are not going to continue competing because it is so unladylike." So you can see things have changed a little bit. I mean, what I was doing is one of the most ladylike things a woman can do.'

The Australian team sailed for home two days after the Americans.

The American athletes chosen for the tour to Scandinavia arrived at Oslo airport and saw a huge sign

WELCOME JESSE OWENS

In vain did they explain, then insist, that Owens wasn't coming and at one point Archie Williams signed himself 'Owens' to smooth over a difficult moment. In the athletics meeting Towns found the track fast, made a tremendous start to the 110-metre hurdles and led by the first hurdle. As he crossed the line he glanced back and saw the next hurdler *still* at the final hurdle. He heard a lot of talking but that, of course, was in Norwegian. Eventually someone told him in English that he had broken the world record and for a moment he imagined a time of 14.0 seconds, 0.2 quicker than Berlin. In fact, he had done an astonishing 13.7, so astonishing it stood for fourteen years and no Olympian beat it until Melbourne, 1956.

Meanwhile, Williams & Co. persuaded someone to ring the team hotel and explain to Towns that there had been a terrible mistake – instead of ten hurdles, only nine had been put up so his record didn't count. So shaken was Towns by the news that he remained in a state of shock until the next day, when the truth emerged. He'd got ten out of ten; there was no mistake.[7]

The final contingent of the American team sailed from Hamburg on 26 August on the *Manhattan*.

Glickman had been busy and it seems that he did not feel tired at all. Following the White City meeting he journeyed to Scotland where he took part in a relay and a faintly outrageous 100-yard handicap. He had to start so far back he stood on the grass beyond the track. From there even he could not win. He went to a meeting in Hamburg where he beat Draper and Borchmeyer, went to a triangular meeting in Paris against France and Japan, and beat Wykoff.[8]

Because his father and mother were working, when the *Manhattan* docked in New York Glickman caught the subway from the pier to his home in Brooklyn. He'd cover that in three words: no big deal.

Soon after, a ticker-tape parade in New York welcomed the Olympic heroes, Owens in the leading car with the mayor, LaGuardia. It was, Glickman would insist, a happy day nicely rounded off because they all went to a nightclub.

'When I came home,' John Woodruff recalls, 'they gave a parade for me in my hometown celebrating my victory.'[9] Yet even the tremendous achievements of the black athletes did not alter the general climate of discrimination. Much later, Woodruff was due to run at a meeting in Dallas and the athletes went by train, of course, but officials said 'that we black athletes couldn't eat in the dining car. Well, we got together and told them that, if we couldn't eat in the dining car with the rest of the people, we were not going. They lifted that requirement.' When they reached Dallas they couldn't stay in a regular hotel but instead 'had to go to the local black YMCA'.

Glickman and Owens drifted apart. It happens. They had their lives to lead. Glickman did know, of course, that Owens was still subjected to racial indignities. He had to sit in the back of buses and could not get into Midtown hotels in New York, although the Paramount let him in provided he used the freight elevator to go to his room. Glickman was distressed to see Owens, now professional, running exhibitions – sometimes against horses. Glickman did know about Owens's 'sexual activities' because whenever he met him Owens always had a date or headed off on one.

Avery Brundage gave an extensive Official Report based around what he claimed were 'so many misleading stories and malicious reports'. He began by explaining that the selection of a large group of human beings in haste and regardless of any factor other than competitive ability is bound to throw up problems with some of them. A day after the *Manhattan* sailed for Germany everyone had been assembled and reminded of their responsibilities, especially since the world would be watching them. Some, however, strayed. One of those indulged in 'continued excessive drinking and insubordination, despite repeated warnings' and as a consequence the Olympic Committee decided unanimously to dismiss them. (Brundage did not say *her* for whatever reason. Everybody must have known perfectly well it was Eleanor Holm.) To prevent this distracting the other competitors, a veil of silence had been drawn over the affair by all the team officials and no more than a basic statement released. Brundage explained that 'the Committee's action was misinterpreted and became the signal for a torrent of criticism'.

Brundage then cleared up the mystery of the two boxers who were also dismissed when the team arrived, although this was glossed over as homesickness. That had been 'invented to protect the boxers who, while collecting souvenirs, had appropriated several expensive cameras'. The police became involved and the Committee had done well to get the boxers out of Germany.

Brundage then turned to the 4 × 400 relay and said vehemently that an 'erroneous' report suggested Glickman and Stoller – again Brundage did not name them – were not selected for religious reasons. 'This report was absurd.' The sprinters, Brundage suggested, only went to Berlin as substitutes since the four selected finished first, second, third and fourth in the Randall's Island trials. That they broke the world record in Berlin vindicated the policy completely.[10]

The nine Chinese *wushu* demonstrators toured Denmark, Sweden, Czechoslovakia, Hungary, Austria and Italy where 'they were highly acclaimed for their performances with bare hands or such ancient weapons as swords, cudgels and spears. Some of the performers later became well-known *wushu* masters, professors or leaders of national organisations.'

The thirty-nine Chinese observers, many physical education teachers, toured Europe too, looking at sports facilities, sports management and methods of training, knowledge they used when they got home. The Chinese team, of course, 'failed to collect a single medal. All were eliminated in the preliminaries except Fu Baolu in the pole vault, holder of the then national record of 4.015 metres, whose best performance fell below 4 metres at the Berlin Olympics, and who joined the air force soon after his return home and was killed during the War of Resistance against Japan. The Chinese made an even poorer showing in other events, finishing the marathon race, for instance, one hour behind the winner. "We were a far cry from many countries in the results and athletic abilities," wrote the Chinese Delegation in its report. "We were ridiculed as having brought back nothing but a *duck's egg*."'[11]

The Indian hockey team went on a post-Olympic tour and got back to Bombay on 29 September. In Germany they'd generated so much enthusiasm they needed chaperones at the railway stations to prevent the crowds overwhelming them. Now on the Ballard Pier they saw a welcoming committee of only two people. As the team came ashore plump raindrops fell – like tears, someone thought.

Many did turn their gaze towards Tokyo in 1940, but the twin themes flowed again. The month before the Berlin Olympics, Japan and Germany had opened negotiations towards an Anti-Comintern Pact, the Comintern an international organisation working for a communist ascendancy. The two countries signed the agreement in November 1936.

The Pact was an important contribution to the Second World War, as was Mussolini's declaration of the emergence of the Rome–Berlin axis three weeks earlier. The Berlin Olympics, then, may have provided a springboard for this diplomatic process. In fact, Tokyo might not have become the host city of the next Olympics had not Japan secured support from Italy and

Germany. Rome was Tokyo's strongest rival but Mussolini agreed to Japan's request that Rome withdraw in February 1935.

Germany supported Tokyo at the general meeting of the IOC in Berlin in July 1936, which disappointed the Finnish consul. Six months previously, Hiroshi Oshima, Japan's ambassador to Italy, had attempted to conclude negotiations on the Anti-Comintern Pact. At this time, he had also spoken to the chairman of the Olympic Organisation Committee in Berlin about the possibility that Tokyo might hold the 1940 games.[12]

It begs a question. Because the domestic coverage of the Games produced 'national frenzy' in Japan, did they cement political relations with Nazi Germany? Generally, 'the Japanese media often focused on Hitler and reported on the success of the Games. The Olympics were seen as a particularly wonderful festival for Japan, the next host country. However, most Japanese media did not directly praise Nazism itself, nor did they portray Nazi Germany as Japan's best friend. Germany was simply a great host country of the Olympics.'[13] The natural focus, just like in every other country, remained firmly on their own competitors.

It begs a further question. If the Berlin Olympics were deliberately orchestrated as a paean of praise for the Nazi regime, did participation have a similar effect in Japan?

We can say with a fair degree of certainty that the Olympics worked to integrate Japanese people into the Imperial system through nationalistic symbols and ceremonies, such as the national flag, national anthem, financial aid from the Emperor himself to the Japanese Olympic Team, and the Team's worshipping at the Imperial Palace and Shinto Shrines.

On the other hand, the Olympics played an exactly opposite role in Korea under Japanese occupation. Both Korean marathon runners who won medals . . . were hailed as national heroes in Korea. [Sohn's] contribution surely encouraged Korean national pride and excited hostility toward Japan.[14]

Once the 1936 Olympics had ended, and the great gathering dispersed, the Nazis could give free rein to their racial and gender obsessions without any thought for treading on Olympic sensibilities. One German writer, Richard Ungewitter, composed a long report advancing the argument that competitive sport was no place for a woman. He dispatched this to, among others, von Tschammer und Osten, von Schirac, Minister of the Interior Frick and Rudolf Hess as well as 'several doctors, and racial hygienists'.

Ungewitter expressed alarm that the women's athletic achievements were too close to the men's, charging it was 'unnatural' and threatened motherhood. Comparing world records in several events, he wrote, 'Discus: Men 50.48, women 47.63 m . . . 100m: Men Negro 10.4, Women 11.5 sec . . . Freestyle swim: Men 1:05:9, Women 1:06:6 min.' He declared that black men had surpassed too many records set by 'Aryans' and proposed that in future competitions blacks be banned.[15]

He went further, maintaining that 'women's voices grew deeper, breasts became flatter, pelvises became narrower, and stomach muscles became tighter from strenuous athletic training. He touted these changes as proof that masculine traits developed in women who participated in intense athletics. Furthermore, Ungewitter charged that these physical changes made childbirth more difficult.'[16] However, one contributor to the publication *Die Frau* responded by pointing out that women were not trying to compete with men but with other women and that the two sexes divided naturally, complementing each other.[17]

Women have competed in the Olympics ever since.

The fencer Helene Mayer returned to the United States and became an American citizen. In 1937 she won the World Championships in Paris, defeating Elek-Schacherer.

Gretel Bergmann knew, in those ominous August days, that she had 'to get away from all this. There was a big Jewish population in Laupheim and everybody felt sorry for me blah blah blah. So I went away for two weeks – under an assumed name, of course, because Jews couldn't go into any hotels. There I decided I have to get out.' She left Germany in May 1937 for America and she didn't look back.

'Here I am, come to the land of the free and these poor people [the blacks] were so discriminated against it was unbelievable. We made it our business to really fight that. Jesse Owens experienced it. Can you believe that? We met the 800 metre winner Woodruff a couple of times and he kept telling us he went to the University of Pittsburgh – they weren't allowed in any restaurants even after he won the medal. His professor was being nasty to him because he missed a couple of weeks of school – but that was because he won a medal for America! I mean, you can't believe it.'[18]

Bergmann won the US high jump and shot-put in 1937, the high jump again in 1938. She helped get a fellow Jewish athlete Bruno Lambert – a sprinter, although not evidently top class – out of Germany and they married and so she became Margaret Lambert (Gretel is a nickname). She brought in money by working at a women's weight-loss salon in Manhattan, and swears she worked so hard as a masseuse she lost more weight than the customers.

Pierre de Coubertin remained a controversial figure. It seems he tried to orchestrate a Nobel Peace Prize for himself in 1928 and 1929, getting Theodor Lewald to support the attempt as well as the German minister of foreign affairs, Gustav Stresemann. A further campaign followed towards the end of 1935, launched by a member of the French government who sought support from Mussolini's finance minister, a Japanese senator and the German press. The boycott campaigns from November 1933 certainly harmed the attempt and the Nobel Prize went instead to Carl von Ossietzky, a German journalist subsequently sent to a concentration camp because of his opposition to Hitler.

It's hardly surprising that the Axis newspapers celebrated de Coubertin in September 1937 when he died. *La Stampa*, the Turin paper, described him as 'the authentic founder of the modern Olympics, with lofty spirit, a man of action'.

The *Corriere della Sera* pointed out that he had recorded a message to those who were going to run with the flame from Greece to Berlin: 'No nation, no class, no profession is excluded.'

De Coubertin responded to a magazine article in *L'Auto* on 4 September 1936 which denounced the Games as 'disfigured' and spoke of the 'farce of the Olympic oath'. He said, 'What, the Games disfigured, the Olympic idea sacrificed to propaganda? It's entirely false! The great [*grandoise*] success of the Games in Berlin has magnificently served the Olympic ideal. Don't people come and talk to me about a Games accessible to women . . . and adolescents. For them there is a second kind of sport, physical education which will make them healthy. But for the Games, my Games, I want to hear a long cry of passion. At Berlin people thrilled to an idea which we must not judge but which excited the passion which I constantly seek. In another way, the Germans organised the technical side with all the care you could wish and you cannot reproach them at all for disloyalty to sport. In such circumstances, how do you want me to repudiate the Games?'

The glorification of the Nazi regime, he added, proved the catalyst for the Games to develop as they did – opening the way, by implication, to the extent of their success.[19] A month later de Coubertin was saying he didn't want to give any more interviews 'because of the reactions of the French press which had not been sufficiently loyal or courteous'.

Did de Coubertin really feel no remorse for having held the Games in Nazi Germany?

According to one source, we have his 'declarations from the years 1935–37, that is to say from the time of the racial Nuremberg laws and the re-militarisation of the Rhineland'. They are 'those of a man caught up in the ideology of sports neutrality which he himself had helped to forge, and to a point obsessed with the perpetuation of his Olympic work so it overshadowed the singular criminality of the Nazi regime. Abandoned by his compatriots, separated from the International Olympic Committee since 1925, ruined by his Olympic expense and the destruction in the course of the Great War of the property in Alsace of his in-laws, but also victim of bad financial investments, overwhelmed by the illnesses of his children, manipulated by the German sports directors Carl Diem and Theodor Lewald whom he'd met before 1914, he had the naivety to believe that the Games in Berlin would better serve the cause of Olympic pacifism than that of the Nazis, and that the [political] rivalry between nations did not merit a boycott.'[20]

Leni Riefenstahl's extraordinary film 'documentary' of the Games had its premiere in the spring of 1938. In 1934 she had done something similar with the Nuremberg Rally, making *Triumph of the Will*, an eerie, militaristic masterpiece with Hitler at its centre. She had used innovative techniques (cameramen on roller skates to capture movement) and did so again with the Olympics. Her *Olympia* used seven leading cameramen and 'many others'. It had a big production staff – five editors, alone – and used so much film they needed until 1938 to get it into a manageable state. Even then it came in two parts: *Festival of the People* (126 minutes) and *Festival of Beauty* (100 minutes). It was revolutionary by comparison with the static newsreels of the day, capturing the moods and human emotions of the Games. Some of the footage lingering over men's bodies was deliberately sensual, if not overtly sexual.

By then Hitler had entered Vienna in triumph, incorporating Austria into the Reich.

On 22 June 1938 Max Schmeling fought Joe Louis in New York for the heavyweight championship of the world again. It lasted 2 minutes and 4 seconds. In that time Schmeling went down three times and afterwards, so the legend goes, they found some of Schmeling's teeth in Louis's glove. His face looked like a landfill site.

Because of the Sino–Japanese War, on 15 July 1938 Tokyo and Sapporo renounced their holding of the 1940 Games so there would be time to find other hosts for them. Two months later the high-jumper Dora Ratjen broke the world record at the European Championships in Vienna and afterwards, says Gretel Bergmann, 'it came out she was not a man and not a woman. I heard this from the discus winner, Mauermayer. I was in touch with her for a while and she wrote me that Ratjen was "in between".'

'I know how he got caught – the shaving. He was on a train coming back from Vienna [and the European Championships]. At Magdeburg two women saw this person in women's clothing with a five o'clock shadow and you know in Germany to denounce somebody was a great sport. So at the next stop these two women got the police and the police pulled her/him off the train and took him to the police station. Then he was told, or she was told – I don't know [chuckle] – *it* was told that there would be a medical examination. *Then* he admitted he was a male. His genitalia were set back, evidently. The funny part of it, I always say, is that there were three girls in that family already and when Dora was born the midwife told the parents "You have another girl" because there was this *thing* that wasn't quite right down there. And that's how they brought him up as a girl. But if you wipe a baby's bottom you know whether it's a boy or a girl!'

The German Athletic Federation banned her/him from women's competitions.

In October Germany occupied the Sudetenland in Czechoslovakia through which, only three years earlier, the Olympic torch had come.

In May 1939, Werner Schwieger had to take part in a three-month exercise with the German Luftwaffe (an anti-aircraft unit). Through part of our story he has been a representative of many others. Now he became representative of millions. The darkness was very close.

In January 1939 Franco captured Barcelona and in March took Madrid without resistance. The Spanish Civil War, one of many ominous backdrops to the Olympics, finally drew to a close. In March, Hitler entered Prague, Czechoslovakia dismembered. The darkness was much closer.

Hitler's war began on 3 September 1939 when Britain declared war after he had invaded Poland on the 1st.

With Sapporo withdrawn the Winter Games were awarded to St Mortitz but, after a dispute about Swiss ski instructors and their amateur status, they went to Garmisch. The choice of Garmisch remained even after the invasion of Poland but once Britain and France declared war the Games had to be abandoned.

Lewald, the half Jew, was forced to resign. Karl Ritter von Halt, a Nazi, replaced him on the IOC's executive committee. It was he who told Baillet-Latour of the cancellation of Garmisch. As with everything else, the Nazis sought to control the IOC, or as von Tschammer und Osten put it, 'reorganise' it. Baillet-Latour was 'the most obvious lever' for the Nazis to use, 'but it is nevertheless striking that he should have been invited to act as a puppet of Hitler's Germany'. He died in 1942.[21]

The long-jumper Luz Long was wounded fighting in Sicily in 1943 and died in a British military hospital. He was awarded the de Coubertin medal for sportsmanship posthumously. What he had done for Jesse Owens was not forgotten.

Von Tschammer und Osten died in 1943 of pneumonia.

American sprinter Foy Draper joined the US Army Air Corps and served in North Africa. In 1943 he flew on a mission to attack German and Italian troops in Tunisia and never returned.[22]

The Hungarian Ferenc Csík, who had taken the 100 metres freestyle and added a bronze in the 800 metres freestyle relay, became a doctor. In 1945, aged thirty-two, he died in the town of Sporon during an Allied bombing raid. He was treating patients.[23]

As the Soviet armies overran East Prussia and Silesia they pushed before them a tide of refugees fleeing these eastern German provinces. Some were temporarily housed in the cottages at the Olympic Village.

In March 1945, members of the Hitler Youth, some aged as young as 12, were being fed mindlessly into the killing machine to die for nothing – the war lost except to the insane. Five hundred of these Hitler Youth were addressed at the May Field. These children were exhorted to sacrifice their lives in a way which, more than half a century after, made one participant physically ill to recall. A little while later some of the Hitler Youth were ordered to reassemble there to watch the execution of members who had gone absent without leave: shot or hanged – it's not clear which – as an example. That these brutal acts were carried out on the May Field, or perhaps even close by, where in those August days the eager youth of the world had assembled to compete in peace, remains grotesque and eloquent and almost unbearable in its poignancy.

Tilly Fleischer was evacuated from her village near Frankfurt after heavy bombing in 1944 and went to the city of Halle, which would later be in the Soviet zone of Germany. Her husband came and took her back to Frankfurt 'just before the Russians arrived'. In April 1945 American soldiers did arrive and briefly occupied the village before pressing on. She remembered how they cooked ham and eggs, a seemingly impossible luxury in what had become a broken land.[24]

The Olympic Village fell into the Soviet zone of occupation. On 20 April there was a bombing raid on a shunting yard nearby, the next day the last person living in the Village was evacuated. The Red Army arrived that evening, on 24 or 25 April. On 28 April they took control of the Olympic Stadium as the Russians tightened their grip on the whole city.

When Hitler's war ended on 7 May 1945 Berlin lay destroyed almost beyond recognition. William Shirer, who had known it so intimately, returned and at moments was unsure where he was actually standing. Perhaps he reflected ruefully on those visiting American businessmen who, during the Olympics, had assured him what a splendid place Germany was and what a good job Hitler was doing.

Werner Albrecht von und zu Gilsa, who took the credit for the Olympic Village, became a general and the last combat commander of Dresden. He committed suicide.

Hitler himself, who had journeyed from Wilhelmstrasse almost every day to fete and be feted by the Olympic Games now lay in a shallow grave in the area behind the Chancellory. He shot himself in the bunker below and his body, brought up, had been burnt. Goebbels, who not so long ago had given that memorable party for 2,000 guests on the island in the Havel, took poison in the bunker as did his wife Magda. They ensured it was also administered to their children.

A great jungle of wrecked machinery littered Unter den Linden, the stone-clad buildings pock-marked by shell, mortar and small arms fire from the street-to-street fighting as the Soviet army conquered it. Most of the buildings themselves stood like rows of rotting teeth, bombed to the point where only external walls remained. The population, traumatised, faced a long summer at the mercy of the Soviet conquerors and then a bitter cold winter, a killing winter.

The Olympic stadium, protected from the bombing and street fighting because of its distance from the city, survived. That gave it a curious atmosphere of its own because it stood in such direct contrast to the devastation everywhere else.

Hitler's plan with Speer to recast the whole centre of the city on a monumental scale, making it the centre of the world, lay dead in the rubble. Some of what Hitler did build lived on as ghosts, altered forever. In the eastern sector a vast concrete bomb shelter was dynamited, but instead of shattering it sank and remained, grotesque, on the edge of a public park. The East Germans did blow up the catacomb of Hitler's bunkers behind the Chancellory in Wilhelmstrasse, entombing them and levelling the earth above them. Nobody would be able to locate where he died or where his body was burnt afterwards. The area fell within no man's land when the East Germans built the wall in 1961: no possibility of a shrine, of pilgrims, of memorials, of a place for a rebirth. There, in fact, no possibility of *anything*.

Goering's Air Ministry came through so unscathed that East German politicans used it and, because the Wall ran alongside it, one person used the roof to throw a line over and, when friends secured it on the western side, he and his family went down the rope to freedom on a home-made pulley.

From 1945, the soon-to-be affluent West completely rebuilt its half of the city; the impoverished east couldn't afford that, so whole districts remained as they had been in those August days except that virtually every building carried the scars of the street fighting that marked the closing chapter of Nazi Berlin. When the city had been divided between the Soviet Union, America, France and Great Britain the stadium fell into the British sector. Once upon a time, so the legend goes, they played a cricket match there. It attracted no spectators.

In August 1945 Korea regained its independence from a defeated Japan. At that moment Kitei Son reverted to Sohn Kee-chung. He would become a senior and influential Olympic figure.

Doris Carter, the Australian high-jumper, went back to the Reich Sports Field in 1946. 'The stadium was little damaged but other buildings were wrecked. Trees and window frames had been burnt for firewood. What was left of the Bell Tower that called the "youth of the world" to the Games contained damaged machinery that I imagine [had once] provided the air conditioning for all those tunnels.'[25]

At the Nuremberg Trials, Goering – he who had staged those three preposterous parties of self-aggrandisement during the Olympics – refused to plead against charges of crimes against humanity. When films of the death camps were shown in court he turned away, unable or unwilling to watch. He was sentenced to death by hanging but poisoned himself.

Cornelius Johnson, co-holder of the world high jump record and winner of the Olympic gold, was working as a baker on a ship when, in February 1946, he was suddenly taken ill. He died on his way to hospital in California, aged thirty-two.[26]

In June 1948 the Soviet Union imposed a blockade on West Berlin. The Cold War was replacing the darkness.

Throughout these desperate years the International Olympic Committee tried to hold the middle ground, to maintain normality. When the 1940 Games could not be held in Tokyo they were transferred to Helsinki but the Soviet invasion of Finland in November 1939 ended that. The IOC awarded the 1944 Games to London over bids from Detroit, Lausanne and Rome. In fact, normality did not return until July 1948 when London, itself battered by the bombing of the war, finally hosted the Games. Fifty-nine countries and 4,099 competitors came. Germany and Japan were not invited.

The fencer Ilona Elek was twenty-nine in 1936, her first Olympics. When the Games resumed she became one of only two competitors to defend her title successfully. She went to Helsinki four years later and won silver.

Don Finlay, the Briton who finished second in the 110 metres hurdles in Berlin, took the athlete's oath in London. The United States dominated with 38 gold medals, Sweden 16, France and Hungary 10. Czechoslovakia and Austria, restored to nationhood, had 6 and 1 respectively. The Indians won the hockey, of course.

In May 1949 the Berlin blockade ended and West Germany came into existence as the Federal Republic. West Berlin remained under the control of America, Britain and France. In response the Soviets made their zone of Germany into the German Democratic Republic, calling their sector of Berlin the capital. The Western powers did not recognise that, or the Democratic Republic, which began to tighten the 'border' between the two Germanies and round West Berlin. The Olympic Village fell just inside the Democratic Republic.

A strained kind of normality was achieved because in 1952 Germany went to the Helsinki Games as a single team and continued like that until 1968. Japan came back at Helsinki, too.

The fencer Helene Mayer, who visited her native Offenbach in 1938, returned to Germany from America but died from cancer. She was forty-three.

On 13 August 1961 the German Democratic Republic, in a bid to stop the haemorrhaging of her citizens to the growing prosperity of the Federal Republic, closed the border round West Berlin. The planning was carried out in absolute secrecy and nobody in the West knew until 1.54 a.m. when a train went into the east and did not come back. Then the Wall went up.

Carl Diem died in 1962. Immediately after the war he worked in physical education in Berlin and two years later, with the British military administration, helped create the German sports university in Cologne.

Dean Cromwell, who coached the United States Olympic team to London and then retired, died that same year. He'd coached ten Olympic gold medal winners.

The 1964 Winter Games went to Sapporo, the Summer Games to Tokyo. The Japanese rehabilitation was complete.

In 1966 the Berlin stadium became a central part in a spy film, *The Quiller Memorandum*. A young American (George Segal) goes there to meet a British spymaster (Alec Guinness). As Segal enters, the camera pans round the ranks of stone terracing. Guinness is sitting having his lunch and Segal joins him. 'Impressive, isn't it?' Guinness asks rhetorically. He points to the place from where Hitler watched. Guinness explains that a new generation of Nazis has grown up, difficult to recognise because – and he looks again at where Hitler watched from – they don't wear uniforms any more. The scene, brief and played deadpan, the terracing constantly in the background, contained something unavailable anywhere else, a sense of proximity to what had been.

In New York City, Gretel Bergmann sat nervously in a dentist's waiting room. She picked up a copy of *Time* magazine and read an article saying that in future the IOC decreed all female competitors would have to pass a sex test. To illustrate this the magazine carried a photograph of Dora Ratjen, now also known as Hermann. She burst out laughing. As we have seen, Bergmann, half mischievously – as captured in a video of her life – but also recapturing the oppressiveness of the anti-Semitic situation,[27] suggested that Ratjen was ordered to be her room-mate because he would never dare touch a Jew. 'I tried to get in contact with him but he never answered and nobody – nobody – knew about him. He went completely out of the picture,' Bergmann says.[28]

He may have spent two years in prison, presumably for deception.

After the war some say he called himself Horst rather than Hermann. He may have lived in Hamburg and worked as a waiter. The extent of the public exposure is uncertain because in either 1955 or 1957 he 'came out', confessing he had only lived as a woman for about three years, and the Hitler Youth had forced him to conceal his sex.

At the 1968 Summer Games in Mexico, the German Democratic Republic – that direct creation of the consequences of Hitler's war – won nine gold medals. They would win many more, exploiting the Games just as shamelessly as Hitler, Goebbels and the Reich ever did. They did not select men in the women's events but they did make some of their competitors take performance-enhancing drugs which gave them masculine characteristics.

Sprinter Phil Edwards served in the Canadian army as a captain during the Second World War. He died at Montreal in 1971.

Esther Myers, by then Esther Wenzel, visited Germany in 1972 and went to the Olympic stadium but divided Berlin made a profound impression on her. 'The glittering city on the West was beautiful when we were there – beautiful [but in the East] not a smile did you see on anyone's face, not a smile. Oh, it was the most depressing place I've ever seen in my life.' [29]

On Baillet-Latour's death during the war his vice president, Sigfried Edström, replaced him and in 1945 Avery Brundage beame his vice president, succeeding him in 1952. It was he who took the decision that the 1972 Munich Games must continue after terrorists attacked the Israeli team. He died in Garmisch in 1975.

Ralph Metcalfe's career ended after the 1936 Olympics and he went into politics, serving on the Chicago City Council from 1949 to 1971 and as a US Congressman from 1971 until he died in 1978. The Ralph H. Metcalfe Federal Building in Chicago is named after him.

Jesse Owens returned to Berlin in 1978 and said: 'The way I see it now as an old man, you only become a true Olympic champion when you add your credibility to the role of an idol, which you may acquire through winning Olympic medals. Berlin gave me the role of the idol; I have done my best to fill this role with my personal credibility. And thus there exists between Berlin and me an inseparable bond of reflection and feeling.'

Dhyan Chand became and remains a player of mystical skills. Some talk of his stick being broken one time in Holland to see if he had an adhesive device in it, some talk of the Japanese deciding he did – glue. When he finished playing he coached for a time, fished, hunted, cooked. He had little money: you didn't get rich playing hockey. When the liver cancer which eventually claimed him took hold, he was taken to a Delhi hospital and put in a general ward. Nobody recognised him. Reportedly, it took a newspaper article to get him into a special room. He died in 1979.

A lifelong heavy smoker, Owens died in 1980 of lung cancer. Glickman went to the funeral in Chicago and, arriving late, found the cathedral full. Members of the 1936 team were there and they signalled him to come up front and join them. Glickman was the only white member and found himself disappointed about that, but somehow gratified that the white person was a Jew.

Because Owens is so central to the whole story of Berlin 1936 I asked his biographer, William J. Baker, to explore the mythology.

'One time in the 1950s Owens' daughter Marlene was named Homecoming Queen of Ohio State University and he of course was there to present to her the crown before 80,000 people. According to a local newspaper Jesse said to Marlene as they were walking out to take the crown "Remember, dear, this could only happen in America." If I were doing my book again I think I would probably have entitled it "Only In America." It is only in America that a kid could be exploited the way he was, and achieve what he did, that whole mix of good and bad.'

I asked whether Baker believed there had been a deliberate attempt to construct a mythology by Owens and others.

I don't think people ever start out intentionally creating mythologies as a rule, except in the most Machiavellian situations. Mythology by definition is a kind of take on the world that makes sense to people and it gives meaning to people. The Jesse Owens mythology came out of some hard facts, good hard facts, honest hard facts. He won four gold medals, he really did come from a very, very poor sharecroppers' background in Alabama, Hitler did not shake his hand – that's where mythology happens.

You assign virtue or vice to facts and to circumstance, and coincidence becomes pattern in mythology.

With Jesse Owens the mythology is that he is this poor black boy come from the South and, by the flexibility of American life, this black boy moves north and goes to college and makes a success, goes to Berlin and wins these medals, and America honours him for that. As in all mythologies it changes in mid-stream: by the 1970s it was the 'in' thing to talk about black abuse at the hands of white society so Jesse was talking about 'Hitler didn't shake my hand but then FDR didn't either when I came back' – that sort of thing, to emphasise the exploitation, the abuse. Before that people had heard of him, forgotten him. Between 1937 and 1950 there was scarcely mention of Jesse Owens in the American mainstream press. Only in the black press can you find out anything about him. Then suddenly it became chic to have this background and it fits in with the American myth of log cabin to the White House, or in this case shanty in Alabama to Berlin.

Part of the myth was to make his image pure as a kid and that's what this Paul Neimark book was about.[30] They are cleansing history. It's hagiography. You remove the clay feet from the hero and you give him golden heels. And of course Jesse can't bear up under that scrutiny. He had lots of flaws.

He went back and back to Berlin and was feted more and honoured more. The Germans adored him. Always it was this myth that 'Hitler rejected him but we loved him even in 1936 and now we love him the more and honour him the more – because he is Mr Freedom and he is Mr Right for us, and that's a reflection on us: that's who *we* are. We're not Hitlerian Germans, we're not Nazis, we are good Germans.'

It's *all* mythology.

I did an essay called 'Jesse Owens and the Germans, a political love story'. There was this passionate love affair between the German people and Owens, initially for athletic reasons and then for political reasons.

In December 1980 Stella Walsh, an innocent bystander at the robbery in Cleveland, Ohio, was fatally shot. The woman who had accused Helen Stephens of being a man was now revealed at the autopsy to have both male and female sex organs. The deputy coroner was baffled. She was divorced. Her former husband said they'd only had sex a couple of times and 'she wouldn't let me have the lights on'. She was sixty-nine and although she'd lived in the United States since the age of two, she always ran for Poland.

Larry Snyder remained head track coach at Ohio State University until 1965 and during his career the people he coached broke fourteen world records. He was head coach to the 1960 United States Olympic team in Rome. He died in 1982.[31]

In March 1984 West Berlin's Mayor, Eberhard Diepgen, said that in those August days Jesse Owens 'jumped his way right into the hearts of the Berliners.' With IOC President Juan Antonio Samaranch watching, Diepgen dedicated a street near the stadium to his memory:

JESSE-OWENS-ALLEE

His widow said she was 'deeply moved by the dignity of the commemorative act and by the gratitude that the democratic Berlin feels towards Jesse, because, looking back on the events of 1936 from today's perspective, the towering figure of Jesse and the admiration for him do eclipse Hitler'.

Marty Glickman served in the Pacific where he saw a story in a newspaper about the death of a Japanese lieutenant, Suzuki, which made him wonder. Glickman thought he had raced him in Paris one time after the Olympics.

In 1985 Glickman returned to Berlin. He went, of course, to the stadium. He walked into it as he had done in another life, for him and Berlin. He felt anger rising and the sense of injustice, still raw, openly shocked him.

Thereby hangs an explanation for what may have happened in Berlin. At the 2005 World Athletics Championships in Helsinki the great American runner Michael Johnson, commentating for BBC television, said that a member of the American team had been saying the right things about his team-mates 'but I never looked at any of those athletes that I competed against as my team-mates, because those are the guys I had to beat out for medals. It was extremely competitive. US athletes don't really look at it as a team. *Those are the guys I've got to beat.* That's one of the things you grow up with as an athlete. You come up through the ranks in an environment that is extremely competitive and we are all fighting for the same things within our country. We're fighting for sponsorship, for the best scholarships out of high school even, we're fighting for a spot on the US team eventually. So by the time you get here you know how to fight.'

Surely the same ethos governed the team of 1936. Publicly, of course, in those days the world was a much politer, more reticent, more diplomatic place. People habitually spoke in platitudes. Behind the platitudes, Johnson's theory of extreme competitiveness must have existed in more or less the same form in 1936, especially when – as now – America produced whole clutches of world-beating sprinters. That may be the final solution to the Jewish relay mystery: in a ruthlessly competitive environment you *always* pick the best you have, and Owens was the best they had. The rest –

racism, anti-Semitism, what might have offended Hitler and what might not – didn't figure.

Put it another way. If you'd had the chance to select Jesse Owens for your relay team what would you have done?

In 1986 during celebrations to mark the fiftieth anniversary of the Games Rie Mastenbroek, Sohn of the marathon and John Woodruff were invited to Berlin. Willy Daume, President of the German Olympic Committee spoke: 'Ladies and gentlemen, as you know Jesse Owens was the Emperor of the Berlin Olympics in 1936 but there was also a young girl and she became the Empress of Berlin . . .'.

The Berlin Wall fell on 9 November 1989 and Germany, reunited at last after Hitler's war, competed as one team at Barcelona in 1992. Franco was long gone and the Spanish Civil War receding into memory. The Soviet Union no longer existed.

Germany got 33 gold medals.

M.N. Masood, a member of the 1936 Indian hockey team, went on to become the first Asian appointed as a UNESCO Mission Chief (Indonesia, 1952–7), and India's ambassador to Saudi Arabia (1961–4). He died in 1991.

Glickman had become a well-known broadcaster on the New York Knicks and football Giants. He'd kept in touch with Sam Stoller. They had dinner together in New York in 1947 but they hadn't talked about the Olympics because, as Glickman reflected, what more was there to say between them? Then they lost touch but in 1983 a *New York Times* reporter rang Glickman to say he had tracked down an address in Fort Lauderdale for Stoller – Glickman heard he had died some time before but went there nevertheless, hoping he was wrong. A woman, presumably Stoller's widow, spoke on the intercom from an apartment and told Glickman she was not prepared to discuss Stoller or the Olympics.[32] Glickman died in December 1992.

Archie Williams got his degree in mechanical engineering and although his running career ended with a leg injury he became a commercial pilot, flying for the US Air Force during the Second World War. He also held degrees in aeronautical engineering. He taught mathematics and computing at high school level in California. He died in 1993.

Helen Stephens went through her career, which ended soon after the Games, unbeaten. She played baseball and softball at a professional level and, between 1938 and 1952, ran her own basketball team. She died in St Louis in 1994.

Dave Albritton was 'one of the first high-jumpers to use the straddle technique'. Like Owens he was born in Danville, Alabama and went to the same technical school. He held the world record with Cornelius Johnson.

He won national outdoor competitions from 1936 to 1950 and then entered politics, serving in the Ohio House of Representatives. He died in 1994.[33]

Don Lash, the distance runner, won twelve national titles by 1940 including seven consecutive cross-countries. The war swept away any chance of an Olympic medal. He joined the Indiana State Police and became an FBI agent, later an estate agent. He died in 1994.[34]

Gisela Mauermayer's career ended in 1942. She taught sport in Munich until the end of the war but because, at eighteen, she had joined the NSDAP (*Nationalsozialistische Deutsche Arbeiterpartei*, the Nazi Party) she couldn't continue teaching. She studied biology and from 1954 to 1975 was chief librarian at the Munich zoological collection.

Because she had been friendly before the Games, Gretel Bergmann decided to get in touch with her. 'There was an article in the paper about her. I got her address and I wrote her. I said, "Did you know that I was Jewish because you were always so nice to me?" she said, "Of course we knew you were Jewish but it didn't make any difference to us because you were an athlete like we were athletes."' Mauermayer died in 1995.[35]

Gretel Bergmann's husband Bruno fought with the US Army in the war. They had sons in 1947 and 1951. In 1980 she was inducted into the Jewish Hall of Fame. The German Athletic Association saluted her, too. She was caught in a great moral dilemma and resolved it in this way: 'It would be unfair to transfer that hatred to those who had absolutely nothing to do with the events of the Hitler time.' She would say this often.[36] 'I don't think you can hold the next generation responsible. I got a lot of lip from the American Jewish people. I made a speech and I said that. I keep telling them. I must say that the town of Laupheim has conducted itself beautifully.'

In 1996 the German Olympic Committee invited Bergmann to be a guest of honour at the Atlanta Games.

The envelope from Frankfurt was franked *Der Präsident, Nationales Olympisches Komitee für Deutschland* and delivered to a 'two-storey brick house' in Queens, New York. The letter, in English, read: 'It is my honor and pleasure to inform you that the National Olympic Committee for Germany has decided to invite you to be our guest of honor during the Olympic Centennial Games in Atlanta. This is on the grounds of our relations over the last year, and the discussion we had in New York. As you were not in a position to accept our invitation to Germany for reasons we understand and honor, we feel that this invitation might be an equivalence.'[37]

Again she 'decided that I could not blame this generation for what their fathers and grandfathers did. I mean, if my father killed somebody, I should not be held responsible.'

When she arrived at Atlanta airport – a tall, white-haired woman in a blue blouse and slacks – two girls approached and asked for her autograph. She could hardly believe they knew who she was. They did. She asked them if they'd heard of Hitler and when they said yes she said *If one ever surfaces in America kick him in the pants.*

'We feel that Mrs Lambert was not treated adequately at the time of the Berlin Olympics,' Walter Troger, President of the German Olympic Committee, explained. 'She was an Olympic candidate who did not get a fair chance. We wanted to do something for her. We felt she deserved it.'

Over the years she received several invitations to visit Germany, but wouldn't go. In 1937 she had promised herself she would never return and it became a matter of principle. This led a German television company to wonder if accepting the German invitation to Atlanta and refusing to go back did not represent a contradiction. She explained again how she had resolved the dilemma. 'The German Olympic Committee was making an attempt at making amends, and I thought I can't hold the sins of the fathers and grandfathers against the new generation. After all, many of them hate what Hitler and the Nazis did, too. So as long as the Olympics are in my country now, I'll meet them halfway. If that's considered a contradiction by anyone, well then, I can't help it and I make no apologies.'

In 1999 Bergmann faced a further dilemma when she was invited back to Germany to receive a shower of honours, including a sports centre named after her. Now she reasoned that the present and future generations would be curious to know who she was, and the only way to let them find out would be for her to tell them what had happened in those distant August days and why. It was so long since she had spoken German that she needed an interpreter.[38]

'I felt it was important to remember, and so I agreed to return to the place I swore I'd never go again. But I had stopped speaking German and didn't even try when I was there. It seemed that there was a new and completely different atmosphere in Germany. I'm sure there's still anti-Semitism in Germany, but there's anti-Semitism in America, too.'

She had some specific memories of that trip. 'We were in one of the best hotels in Frankfurt. My son was with me and we went in the elevator and there were two swastikas scratched into the elevator. I went to complain and nobody gave me any satisfaction. I wrote to them and still nobody gave me any satisfaction. Then I wrote to Walter Tröger, the head of the German Olympic Committee, who got to be very friendly. I told him about it and he did something. I got a letter of apology from the hotel. I was so upset: some kids did it and they'd let it go. When they wrote to me they said they'd tried to get the swastikas out but they couldn't so finally they put a plaque over them.

'I was so comfortable in Laupheim because all those people who made life so miserable for us are all down under the ground.'[39]

And a final glimpse of the sanity which eventually emerged from the madness. Gretel Bergmann was sent a colour photograph from Laupheim. It was of the entrance to the town's track; over the entrance the sign read:

GRETEL-BERGMANN-STADION

In 1933, she recalled, 'I was nineteen, the Nazis came and I was forbidden to enter that track even to watch.[40] The height I jumped just before the Games was the same height as the gold medal at the Games . . . .'

Marathon winner Sohn went to the 1947 Boston Marathon as a coach and remained active within athletics, helping Seoul with the bid for the 1988 Olympics and acting as chairman of the Olympics Organising Committee. He died in November 2002.

In 1936 Judith Deutsch was the leading Austrian swimmer but as a Jew she decided not to go to Berlin and 'a land which so shamefully persecutes my people'. She emigrated to what was then Palestine. Her records were erased and the Austrians banned her from competing for life. In 1995 she was finally invited to Vienna for a ceremony reinstating them but wouldn't go because, she said, she'd had to wait far too long. Undeterred, the Austrians flew to Israel and held the ceremony there. In 2003 a reunion was organised in Vienna. Judith's sister went with some contemporary swimmers but reportedly Judith was by now too frail for such a journey.

In old age Rie Mastenbroek lived in a small Dutch town where she kept a wheelchair handy, the legacy of a car accident in 1968. She died in November 2003.

Leni Riefenstahl never joined the Nazi Party and subsequently claimed naivety about their motives. She'd been an actress and could have skiied in the German cross-country team at Garmisch in 1936 but chose to make the film instead. After the war she became a photographer. She died in 2003, aged 101.

Eleanor Holm did not, as one might imagine, fade into obscurity. Once her swimming career ended she made a film in 1938 with another Olympic athlete, Glenn Morris. He played Tarzan to her Jane in *Tarzan's Revenge*. She stayed briefly in films, divorced Art Jarrett and married an impresario. She married a third time and died in Miami, at ninety, in 2004.[41]

Tilly Fleischer, who was given a car by her home town of Frankfurt, in honour of her Olympic achievements, ran several leather businesses after the war. In the autumn of 1988 her oak tree for winning in 1936 finally died.

She planted another one immediately at the Frankfurt Stadium. Fleisher died in the summer of 2005.

Fritz Schilgen, who had padded into the stadium and lit the flame, died near Frankfurt in September 2005, aged ninety-nine.

Doris Runzheimer who, under her maiden name of Eckert, finished sixth in the 80 metres hurdles, died at the end of October 2005.

The University of Southern California received two oak trees, one from Ken Carpenter and the other from the 4 x 100 relay team. They provided two of its members and, anyway, Owens already had three trees of his own. Carpenter's still stands (in 2005), but the relay tree came down – the victim of root rot – in the summer of 2002. A mature oak has been rededicated.

I'm indebted to the research of Jerry Papazian, Past President, USC Alumni Association, which appears on the FrankWykoff2.com website, for the known locations of other trees (2005): Owens's at his high school in Cleveland, Ohio and at Ohio State University (the fate of the third, at his mother's home, also in Cleveland, is not known); Cornelius Johnson's 'in the backyard of a home on Hobart Street in Korea town'; Forest Towns's on the University of Georgia Campus.[42]

On his return, John Woodruff's sapling was cleared in Washington, DC for unwanted bugs and planted at his home town of Connellsville, Pennsylvania, in the grounds of the Carnegie Library. Later, Connellsville had a new stadium and the tree went there. A plaque told people about it.

Velma Dunn Ploessel's single chance, like so many others, came and went in Berlin. Of course Tokyo never happened, nor were any Games held in 1944 and 'very few people could make that long transition from 1936 to the next Games in 1948. I got married in 1943. I have a boy and a girl, both teachers, and I have three grandsons from my son. They are all college graduates. My son was a swimmer at college and my grandsons are all swimmers or water polo players and I think some kind of sport is the thing to do. Have I still got the silver medal? I sure have!

'I'm eighty-seven, I just took my drivers' test again [October 2005] and I've got a licence for five more years but I really don't expect to drive that much longer.'[43]

Louis Zamperini led an astonishing life, or rather lives, but reflected ruefully that he had shaken hands with 'the worst tyrant the world has ever known'. He remembered Hitler as 'like a dangerous comedian'. He served as a bomber pilot in the Pacific during the Second World War, spent forty-seven days on a life-raft in shark-infested waters and was taken prisoner by the Japanese. Believed dead, his parents collected his life insurance and when he turned up the US government would not take it back. He found religion and went back to Japan preaching forgiveness. There's even talk of a Hollywood film.[44]

When the war started, Werner Schwieger was not conscripted but continued his job in a foundry until 1940 when he joined the Luftwaffe as an instructor. He returned to the foundry and worked there until he was called up by the army in September 1944. In January 1945 he was fighting the Americans in Alsace but the retreat took him to Bavaria where in May he was taken prisoner. Transferred to the French military he became a prisoner working on French farms. On his release in November 1947 he returned to Berlin and started studying at the teachers' training college. He eventually became a vocational teacher.

He still reminisces a lot and he still (2005) has the medal which every participant got. 'There is a bell on it. There used to be a swastika beneath the bell but I scratched it out.' Asked whether the 1936 Olympics were exciting, he answers emphatically: 'Oh, yes.'

John Woodruff of the tumultuous 800 metres graduated in sociology and fought as a second lieutenant from 1941. Later he saw action in Korea then worked at the New York City Children's Aid Society, became a teacher, worked with the New York police athletics league, and served as a parole officer. A 5-kilometre Run and Walk is held each year in Connellsville in his memory.[45] At time of writing he is resident in a senior living community in Arizona and, although slightly deaf, his memory is sharp. He can relive the 800 metres, the ebb and flow of it, how he found himself trapped.

'I still think about it, oh yes. It was the type of race I did not intend to run. If I'd have tried to break out of the "box", with my stride I would have fouled somebody and I would have been disqualified. So the only thing that I could do in order to try and win the race was to stop without incident, go into the third lane and let the other athletes precede me. And then I ran around all of them, and that's why I came in at 1 minute 52.9: it was a very slow race. 800 metres? Going round the outside I must have covered nearly a kilometre . . . .'

In 2005 he was ninety. 'I was ninety on July 5. I still keep interested in things.' He sounds a man without any form of bitterness and when I ask him about the discrimination of the time he says: 'Well, I can envision why something like that happened, because there was a lot of discrimination everywhere.'

And now the seventh decade since those August days has come.

Fritz Wandt, the autograph hunter who became a farmer, was called up into the army in 1942. He fought in France and Italy, where he received wounds severe enough to keep him in hospital for a year. He was sent to the front and wounded again so that as Hitler's war moved through its final convulsions, and the Soviets advanced, he found himself in a castle-cum-hospital at Rostock. The Soviets moved through on 1 May but left him and the staff unmolested. One of the doctors said that anyone who thought they were fit enough could go. So he went. His parents still had the farm near the Village.

The farm became part of a collective in East Germany. Wandt was happy and liked the people and later he experienced all the mixed emotions of his fellow East Germans when the Wall came down.

The interview was carried out by my intrepid Berlin helper, Birgit Kubisch, on a November evening. When she reached Dyrotz, where Wandt lives, he stood in the street wearing a brown hat but no jacket, waiting. Inside the farmhouse there was steaming coffee and stollen, the traditional German Christmas cake, already laid out on the kitchen table. They sat and he started talking in a warm Berlin accent.

After I visited the Village in 1936 on the guided tour I never went again afterwards. It was a military training centre, with guards in front. Why should we have gone there? In 1998, however, the Historia Elstal Association was founded. [Döberitz the name of the original barracks; Elstal the name of the place where the Village was situated; Dyrotz a nearby hamlet]. Since I have always been interested in history in general and local history and geography in particular, and since the Olympic Village was part of this, I registered as a member of the Association. The Association employed a historian – at that time, after 1990, you would still get public funds for such things – and she dealt very thoroughly with all the stories of this community. I have met a lot of very interesting people – television, student journalists – and it's fun when people thank you and say they liked it. Normally they come to the Olympic Village for guided tours. Sometimes television or radio stations make appointments to visit us and take recordings for their programmes. We normally meet at the Olympic Village, because they want to see it, of course, and then we do the interviews there. The last guided tour this year was at the end of November.

He still has his autograph book and its sixty signatures. 'Here is a Finn . . . he was often world champion . . . Volmaro Iso-Hollo. Here is Robert Clark . . . second in the decathlon . . . and this looks like Willy Johnson . . . must be an American as well. H. Uhland? Well those names, you know, it's difficult to read them. And this is the name of someone I'm told is still alive . . . an Egyptian. I can even remember that one. There were several of us German boys standing there and one of them tried to teach this Egyptian the German letters. There were five shops in the reception building – a photographer's shop, a stationer's, a sportsgoods shop, I think a fruit and vegetable shop and one selling sweets. This Egyptian took the boy who had taught him the letters to the photographer's shop and bought him some present. Some wrote the sports they were in, like boxing. An American wrote "1,500-metre-runner". . . here is an Indian . . . the captain of their hockey team . . . Dhyan Chand.'[46]

On another winter morning, moving towards the seventh decade, the mist of dawn lingers, shrouding each shape in a gentle, timeless embrace so that somehow they are all still there; yet, of course, they cannot still be there.

The athletes' achievements live on, but that most malign of shadows is just that. . . .

Imagine a huge area of flat parkland decorated by carefully planted trees. Imagine, at strategic points across this parkland, the structures of heavy stone which still harmonise with the distant city of heavy stone.

The stadium, now with a roof for the 2006 World Football Cup, remains genuinely breathtaking in its symmetry and scale, the walls – like freshly cleaned granite – curving in an endless cliff face. The trekkers on 1 August 1936 had exactly the same reaction when they were confronted with it and the knowledge that Hitler really was coming.

Temporary fencing guards it as teams of construction workers in hard hats continue the renovations and alterations: there's an air of quiet, controlled activity, more work in progress than building site.

The bell tower is so tall it looms above the mist but weeds grow in the tiers of stone seats beside it. The *Platz* where the motorcade drew up retains its original configuration but the gates through which Hitler entered have long since gone.

The bell, cracked and with a shell hole in it, has been taken to the House of German Sport half a mile the other side of the stadium where it stands beside some steps. The House is three-sided with a grassy area in the middle – and, inevitably, heroic statues on plinths – with the Cupola Hall at one end. Renovation is going on here, too, making it hard to recapture the living dramas of the fencing.

The Friesenhaus, where the women stayed, is joined to it and is also made of heavy stone. Here Hertha BSC, the football club that uses the Olympic stadium for its home matches, has offices. The entrance and reception are decked out with pennants and pictures of the players. What were once ground-floor bedrooms are now offices with their mandatory computer screens.

The entrance to the hockey stadium, off the Olympia Platz, is padlocked. The Platz, broad and level and leading to the stadium, still has the columns of tall, white poles which bore the flags of so many nations. This November day the Platz's central reservation is being used as a training ground for motor-cyclists and their instructors. It's big enough to accommodate them easily.

These shapes and spaces in the mist retain a studious grandeur; they have classical proportions and they still fulfil their original, cumulative purpose: to take your breath away. The stadium continues to have this impact regardless of the fact that the world has grown accustomed to immense stadiums so that now this is only one among many. It's difficult to say quite why the impact remains: perhaps it has to do with the perfect proportions; perhaps the imposing stonework; perhaps the knowledge that in August 1936 the world of sport had seen nothing to equal it; perhaps because here a poor black American sharecropper's son brought the potential of the human body to an astonishing, immortal climax. Or perhaps because with hindsight we know what cataclysmic events came afterwards. Or maybe because Hitler built it and strode into it at a time when he truly stood at the centre of the world.

Well, all of those things.

Just off the Olympic Platz a narrow path, trees and bushes to one side, stretches away to the railway station. Camouflaged by the growth of the bushes it's easy to miss the old, white sign *HERREN* and round a corner the old, blue sign *DAMEN*: two of the public toilets just as they were – closed these many decades and now daubed with graffiti, bringing them into the modern era. Curious.

Here on the narrow path you feel close to 1936 in a way you cannot anywhere else. Here is the human dimension.

This winter's day you can follow the route from the stadium out to the Olympic Village, the same route the buses took as they transported the competitors to and fro on the old Hamburg road. Once you are clear of Charlottenburg you go to Staaken and after Staaken there's a necklace of snug, solid hamlets strung along the highway. Because they fell into the Soviet Zone time passed them by: main streets of cobblestones and sharp cambers, modest houses, hardly a shop anywhere, men on old bicycles, tractors leaving their tyre prints in drying mud. If any competitors in 1936 gazed from the buses this is what they must have seen, and sentimental Westerners, returning when the Wall came down, said *Yes, this is the Germany I remember from my childhood.*

Once upon a time the 'original landscape . . . with its elevations, pine, oak and birch trees, the picturesque valley of an old watercourse and the meadow-like open fields . . . provided the most favourable conditions imaginable for its planning, and the wooded hills surrounding the small valley offered natural confines.'[47] The Soviet Army built ranks of prefabricated four-storey apartments in the open fields between the cottages and lived in them until, in 1991–2, the soldiers were withdrawn to Volgograd as Germany reunited. They took everything they could (well, it did belong to them), leaving only the empty shells of the apartment blocks to the ravages of time.

When you pull off the highway you're in woodland and, suddenly, an estate of orange-painted apartment blocks comes into view – they were the barracks temporarily vacated to accommodate the sportsmen who couldn't be housed in the Village. Behind them there's a perimeter fence and more woodland. Through it you can see grey shapes among the trees, the apartments and cottages of the Village.

Everything is where it was and nothing is the same as it was. This is ghostland, nature reclaiming what was taken from it – weeds grow between the joints of the concrete blocks which made, and make, the roadways, undergrowth creeps towards the cottages in one final advance. All the windows are boarded up as if they are blind now. The pathways, once so neat, still wend their way through the trees, linking cottage to cottage, but they're bruised and broken.

Nothing stirs, nothing moves.

Something is moving in the background, however, as well as the good work of the Historia Elstal Association. The Deutsche Kreditbank AG has set up a foundation which now owns the Village – it must have been interesting to ascertain who owned it before, since it passed from Nazi Germany to Soviet then East German control (where private property was abolished), never mind the Soviet Army who requisitioned it.

Barbara Eisenhuth of the Bank explains, 'We are going to install a museum of Olympic history and sport. We want to show this area to as many people as possible and we are organising some events in 2006. We hope many tourists will come to the Village.' But even if extensive renovation is carried out every tourist will need imagination.

The 3,000 young men from fifty-one countries who walked these very paths under these very trees, now grown so tall, and gazed through these same windows, who played in those clearings and trained on that very track, made this secluded, pastoral and wooded meeting point somewhere, in the history of human sporting endeavour, precious.

In the Village any of the 3,000 could approach anyone else and spend as long as they liked with them. 'We did not talk on these occasions. We used the most primitive method of signs and gestures. These were quite sufficient for us to carry on our simple, healthy conversations.'[48]

Now, empty and silent, it is a private place; anyone who goes there is alone with his thoughts, with images and echoes from the seven decades past.

It ought to be timeless, but not for any of those reasons.

Here, when it could not have been more public, the youth of the world prepared to board the shuttle buses – pug-nosed *Wehrmacht* buses, commandeered for the purpose. Those buses pulled up just over there and went via the necklace of hamlets, on past Staaken and then all those long since departed competitors confronted, in peaceful combat, their destinies: the few – like Jesse Owens – to be touched by greatness, the majority to return on those same buses as anonymous as when they had left those few hours before; and would be anonymous forever, their unique moment gone, the great darkness of war drawing ever closer.

This place knew Hitler on one of those June days before August – in uniform of course, striding along inspecting, his entourage in tow, also in uniform, of course. Here, on another of those June days, Goebbels would come, looking shifty in raincoat and homburg hat and wondering, no doubt, how best the Village might be exploited. It knew the tide of refugees Hitler's war brought to it and the eventual brutal division of Germany into two independent countries created by arbitrary boundaries which – fantastically (and only officially) – hated each other, *this* side of Staaken and that side. It knew occupation by Hitler's 'sub-humans' from the east. It saw the breathless embrace of reunification when the Wall fell and then the retreat to Volgograd as the 1990s dawned and the last of the Soviet military vehicles lumbered away. It knew, finally, precious privacy.

Today the Village stands as a memory of all those things, but it also stands for something to set against all those things, too: that people from every corner of the world and every background – race, creed, colour, religion – really could, and really can, meet and compete at the most intense level, and nobody dies.

The Hindenburghaus near the entrance acted as a social meeting point for everybody. The Indian team can be regarded as representative, not because they won the hockey gold medal but because they were a group of such varied backgrounds united by the Olympic circumstances. They remembered how 'we were entertained to pictures and occasional dancing, acrobatic feats or jugglery. Every evening after dinner, we used to pass two hours in the house, with our sweatsuits on or any other informal dress, cheering, clapping and joking. The Italians were the most noisy and none could beat them in this respect. A sight of a pretty girl dancing gracefully was always enough to rouse our Italian friends to the highest pitch of enjoyment. . . .'[49]

If you stand by yourself on any of the overgrown paths and listen, I swear you can still hear the echoes from those August days vaulting across the bitter decades, can hear the sound the youth of the world made.

It is laughter.

NOTES

ONE: Man at the Centre of the World

1. The XIth Olympic Games, Berlin, 1936 Official Report.
2. Hitler had his own army, *Sturmabteilung* (Storm Section). They were also known as the storm troopers and Brown Shirts.
3. Paul Yogi Mayer, *Jews and the Olympic Games* (London, Vallentine Mitchell, 2004), p. 102. Hitler won the Iron Cross, Germany's highest award for bravery, during the First World War.

TWO: Poisoned Chalice

1. Duff Hart-Davis, *Hitler's Games* (London, Century Hutchinson, 1986), p. 43.
2. www.athensenvironmental.org/modern_olympics/modern_olympics06.asp (visited 5 May 2005).
3. 'Jewish Women in Gymnastics and Sport in Germany 1898–1938', *Journal of Sport History*, Vol. 26, No. 2 (Summer 1999); (visited 5 May 2005).
4. William L. Shirer, *The Rise and Fall of the Third Reich* (London, Pan Books, 1971), p. 171.
5. *Los Angeles Times*, 3 August 1932, p. 9.
6. The XIth Olympic Games, Berlin, 1936 Official Report.
7. Milly Mogulof, *Foiled* (Oakland, CA, RDR Books, 2002), p. 61.
8. Shirer, *The Rise and Fall of the Third Reich*, p. 236.
9. The XIth Olympic Games, Berlin, 1936 Official Report.
10. IOC Official Bulletin, 1933.
11. The XIth Olympic Games, Berlin, 1936 Official Report.
12. The XIth Olympic Games, Berlin, 1936 Official Report.
13. There is confusion about chronology because March presented the new stadium plans but a long time *afterwards* Hitler reacted violently when construction began. According to Albert Speer in his *Inside the Third Reich* (London, Sphere Books, 1979 reprint), p. 129, Hitler 'went to inspect the site and came back in a state of anger and agitation'. March's design was a 'concrete structure with glass partition walls' like one in Vienna but Hitler stormed that he would 'never

set foot inside a modern glass box like that'. Speer remembered Hitler ordering Pfundtner to cancel the Games because, as head of state, he – Hitler – had to declare them open and he wouldn't do it in such a stadium. Overnight, Speer added, he himself sketched how natural stone cladding could be attached to the steel skeleton now up. The glass partitions went, bringing Hitler back. Speer wondered irreverently whether Hitler really would have cancelled the Games or whether he used a 'flash of pique' to get his way, a tactic he deployed often.

14. The XIth Olympic Games, Berlin, 1936 Official Report.

15. *Ibid.*

16, *Ibid.*

17. *Ibid.*

18. *New York Times*, 8 March 1934.

19. Gretel Bergmann; interview with author.

20. Paul Yogi Mayer, *Jews and the Olympic Games* (London, Valentine Mitchell, 2004), p. 15.

21. Gretel Bergmann; interview with author.

22. *Ibid.*

23. I am indebted to my neighbour Inge Donnell for pointing out that although *Führer* does mean leader – and could be used quite innocently, as for the leader of a trade union or a troupe of boy scouts – Hitler decreed that it only be used about him, and as a consequence it became intimately associated with him, and acquired a strength and force through the connection.

24. Part of the triumph of the Olympic ideal is how, as a global movement, it has been able to accommodate the conflicting demands of member nation-states – ostensibly by offering itself as a totally unpolitical movement and therefore both above politics and not concerned with them. This has not always proved possible and the 1980s were particularly bad, with the United States and some allies boycotting Moscow in 1980, the Soviet Union and some of its allies boycotting Los Angeles in 1984. For a fuller discussion of this, and its relevance to Berlin in 1936, see Chapter 10, 'Aftermath'.

25. The XIth Olympic Games, Berlin, 1936 Official Report.

26. *Ibid.*

27. The Brandenburg Gate stood then and stands now as a symbol of Berlin comparable to the Statue of Liberty, the Eiffel Tower or Buckingham Palace. By an almost impossible irony it lay almost exactly on the line that partitioned East and West Berlin – it was just on the eastern side – and, when the Berlin Wall went up, became a symbol of that. (It was so tall it could, of course, be seen from both sides even though the Easterners were kept well away from it by an inner wall.) Instinctively, the night the Wall came down, and even though there was no checkpoint there, the world's television crews gathered at the

Gate's western side. They had the perfect backdrop, the same one that adorned the 1936 poster.

28.   The XIth Olympic Games, Berlin, 1936 Official Report.

THREE: No Jews or Dogs Allowed

1.   William Shirer, *Berlin Diary* (London, Hamish Hamilton, 1941), p. 30.
2.   IOC Bulletin, February 1935.
3.   Danzig, at various times in it history German, was now a Free City on the Baltic between the German provinces of Pomerania and East Prussia and they had a corridor of Polish land between them, too. Hitler fully intended to bring Danzig back into the Reich.
4.   Lewis H. Carlson and John J. Fogarty, *Tales of Gold* (Chicago, IL, Contemporary Books, 1987), p. 135.
5.   Deborah E. Lipstadt, *Beyond Belief* (New York, The Free Press, 1986) p. 66.
6.   *New York Times*, 2 August 1935; quoted in Lipstadt, *Beyond Belief*, p. 66.
7.   Lipstadt, *Beyond Belief*, p. 66.
8.   William Johnson, *All That Glitters Is Not Gold* (New York, Putnam, 1972); quoted in Lipstadt, *Beyond Belief*, p. 66.
9.   Quoted in Milly Mogulof, *Foiled* (Oakland, CA, RDR Books, 2002), p. 98.
10.   *La Suisse «face aux Jeux Olympiques de Berlin 1936»*, 2004, éditions de l'Université de Fribourg, in www.lexpress.ch/loisirs/livres/2004/jo.htm (visited 14 April 2005).
11.   Margaret Bergmann Lambert, *By Leaps and Bounds* (United States Holocaust Memorial Museum, Washington DC, 2005).
12.   Quoted in Lipstadt, *Beyond Belief*, p. 66.
13.   Even with all imaginable caveats this is an astonishingly naive speech. For the effects of legalised anti-Semitism – down to Jewish mothers unable to buy milk for their children in some places – see William L. Shirer, *The Rise and Fall of the Third Reich* (London, Pan Books, 1971), p. 291.
14.   Shirer, *Berlin Diary*, p. 68.
15.   Lipstadt, *Beyond Belief*, p. 67.
16.   Quoted *ibid*.
17.   Based on Mogulof, *Foiled*, pp. 112–15.
18.   www.shoreac.org/THE%20COLUMBIA%20COMET.htm (visited 3 August 2005). Incidentally, Johnson did not go to Berlin. A torn hamstring kept him out of competition for almost all of 1936.
19.   Mogulof, *Foiled*, p. 118.
20.   *Ibid.*, p. 118.
21.   *Ibid.*, p. 112.
22.   *Ibid.*, p. 126.

23. Fritz Wandt; interview with Birgit Kubisch.

24. Marty Glickman with Stan Isaacs, *Fastest Kid on the Block* (Syracuse, NY, Syracuse University Press, 1996), p. 13.

25. The resolution against going to Berlin:

> Whereas, on Nov 20, 1933, the Amateur Athletic Union of the United States in annual meeting assembled, adopted a resolution calling upon the American Olympic Association to notify the International Olympic Committee and the German Government that American athletes would not be certified to the Olympic Games of 1936 unless German-Jewish athletes were permitted and encouraged in fact, as well as in theory to train, prepare for and participate in these games; and
>
> Whereas the German sports authorities thereupon renewed their pledges to observe the Olympic code and not to discriminate against German-Jewish athletes in the selection of the German team directly to the Amateur Athletic Union of the United States and subsequently to the president of the American Olympic Committee; and
>
> Whereas acceptance of the invitation by the American Olympic Committee to participate in these Games was made conditional upon the keeping to these pledges; and
>
> Whereas in spite of their pledges the German sports authorities in the two years that have since elapsed have not permitted or encouraged German-Jewish athletes to train, prepare for and participate in the Games, but on the contrary have denied them as a group solely because of their race, not only an equal opportunity with non-Jewish athletes but also a fair and adequate opportunity to train and compete for places on the German Olympic team; and
>
> Whereas the German sports authorities have thus made race a test of eligibility for the German Olympic team; and
>
> Whereas, in order to further the war which it is waging upon Christianity and the Christian churches and for the purpose of gaining complete control over the minds and souls as well as the bodies of German youth, the German Government has made it impossible for Catholic and Protestant athletes to engage in sports and athletics except as members of Nazi organisations; and
>
> Whereas, these measures have resulted in the denial of opportunity to train and compete for places on the German Olympic team to devout Catholic and Protestant athletes who for reasons of conscience have been unwilling to deliver themselves over to those hostile to their religion and their churches; and
>
> Whereas, the German sports authorities have thus made religion a test of eligibility for the German Olympic team; and

Whereas, the German sports authorities have declared their intention of promoting the racial and anti-Semitic, the pagan and anti-Christian and other political policies of the German Government and the Nazi party in the regulation of sport and in the selection of the German Olympic team; and in the selection of the German team; and

Whereas, the German sports authorities have thus introduced political considerations into sports and the Olympics; and

Whereas, the injection of these considerations is a contravention of the purpose of amateur sport and the Olympic ideal of fair play; and

Whereas, the participation of American athletes in the Olympic Games under these conditions will represent and will be interpreted to the German people by the German Government as American endorsement of its sports and other policies and will thus give support to the Nazi efforts to destroy those principles of liberty and equality for the preservation of which the American Republic was established;

Therefore be it resolved, that the Amateur Athletic Union of the United States declare itself against America's participation in the Olympic Games in 1936 if held in Berlin and solemnly calls upon American athletes to refuse to participate in the Eleventh Olympiad, if it is held in Germany, and requests the American Olympic Committee to revoke its conditional acceptance of the German Olympic Committee's invitation to an American team to the Games and calls upon the International Olympic Committee to remove the 1936 Olympic Games to another country where it is possible for them to be held in accordance with the Olympic ideal of chivalry and fair play; and

Be it further resolved, that the Amateur Athletic Union of the United States calls upon the American Olympic Association and the American Olympic Committee to convene special meetings of these bodies as soon as possible for the purpose of reconsidering the question of American participation in the Games, if they are held in Germany, in the light of developments since the American Olympic Committee conditionally accepted the invitation of the German Olympic Committee.

Be it further resolved that the Amateur Athletic Union of the United States instructs its delegates to such meetings to vote against American participation in the Eleventh Olympiad, if it is held in Germany.

Be it further resolved that the A.A.U. of the United States calls upon the A.O.C and the American representatives on the International Olympic Committee to request the I.O.C to convene itself as soon as possible in special session to consider the question of the removal of the Eleventh Olympiad from Germany in the light of the evidence of the failure of the German authorities to conform to the Olympic code and to their numerous pledges.

Be it further resolved that the Amateur Athletic Union of the United States calls upon American athletes, upon amateur athletes and upon all who love fair play to govern themselves in accordance with the letter and the spirit of these resolutions to give no support or encouragement to the formation of an American team to compete in the Games and to take no part in the Games either as spectators or competitors, if they are held in Germany.

26. The XIth Olympic Games, Berlin, 1936 Official Report.
27. *Ibid.*
28. IOC Bulletin, February 1936.
29. www.sok.se/?open&f=F16&id=98F96&mid=200 (visited 12 August 2005).
30. Werner Schwieger; interview with Birgit Kubisch.
31. Fritz Wandt; interview with Birgit Kubisch.
32. The XIth Olympic Games, Berlin, 1936 Official Report.

FOUR: Stormy Waters

1. John Thomas Lang (1876–1975) was a prominent Australian politician during the early twentieth century. He was a member of the Australian Labor Party, and the Premier of New South Wales for two terms, from 1925 to 1927, and again from 1930 to 1932. He is the only Premier of any Australian state to have been dismissed by the State Governor (the representative of the British monarch) without there being an election or parliamentary vote of no confidence. This was due to his refusal to pay interest on government loans borrowed from financiers in the United Kingdom at the height of the Great Depression.
2. Stephanie Daniels and Anita Tedder, 'A Proper Spectacle' – Women Olympians 1900–1936 (Houghton Conquest, Beds., ZeNaNa Press, 2000), p. 100.
3. Australian Olympic Report.
4. *Ibid.*
5. The XIth Olympic Games, Berlin, 1936 Official Report.
6. Giles MacDonogh, *Berlin* (London, Sinclair-Stevenson, 1997), p. 64.
7. N.M. Masood, *The World's Hockey Champions* (Delhi, Model Press, 1937) in www.bharatiyahockey.org (visited 21 November 2005).
8. Australian Olympic Report.
9. Daniels and Tedder, 'A Proper Spectacle', p. 100.
10. Australian Olympic Report.
11. According to Owens's biographer William J. Baker: 'Crucial to Jesse Owens's fame in August in Berlin was the fall of Joe Louis in June just a few weeks before. All the team sports were segregated in America and Joe Louis and Jesse Owens were the only two really visible black athletes. With the fall of Louis the

king had died, long live the king! Jesse Owens becomes king. His glamour, his acclaim is all the greater, I contend, because the king was dead.'

12. Jesse Owens and Paul Neimark, *JESSE: The Man Who Outran Hitler* (New York, Fawcett Gold Medal, 1978).

13. *Ibid.*

14. usatf.org/athletes/hof/snyder.asp (visited 18 May 2005).

15. William J. Baker, *Jesse Owens, An American Life* (New York, The Free Press, 1986), p. 54.

16. www.ubcsportshalloffame.com/cgi-bin/search.cgi?person (visited 25 April 2005).

17. The XIth Olympic Games, Berlin, 1936 Official Report.

18. Masood, *The World's Hockey Champions.*

19. Presumably the Australians were described as the first team to arrive because, prior to that, only the five Japanese had come rather than the entire Japanese team.

20. www.jewishvirtuallibrary.org/jsource/Holocaust/olympics.html (visited 16 November 2005).

21. Masood, *The World's Hockey Champions.*

22. Daniels and Tedder, '*A Proper Spectacle*', p. 106.

23. Masood, *The World's Hockey Champions.*

24. *New York Times*, June 1996.

25. www.bharatiyahockey.org/granthalaya/goal/1936/page5.htm
One report suggests that during the voyage the Indian hockey team practised so assiduously on deck that hundreds of balls were lost – hit into the sea.

26. iwitnesstohistory.org/ResidentPages/Wenzel/Wenzel%2036%20olympics.htm (visited 10 October 2005).

27. www.bharatiyahockey.org/granthalaya/goal/1936/page5.htm

28. The XIth Olympic Games, Berlin, 1936 Official Report.

29. www.canadianboxing.com/profiles_content.htm (visited 23 April 2006).

30. The American selectors can afford to be ruthless because they have such strength in depth: if you don't make the qualification on the day you don't go. Other countries simply couldn't do this – witness the British controversy over whether Sebastian Coe should have gone to Los Angeles in 1984 on reputation and known world-class achievement rather than present form. Britain was simply not strong enough in talent to leave him at home. See also below, Michael Johnson, Chapter 10, 'Village People'.

31. *New York Times*, 12 July 1936.

32. Mack's brother Jackie made a profound social impact when he became the first African-American to play in a major league baseball match, for the Brooklyn Dodgers, in 1947. www.walteromalley.com (visited 16 November 2005).

33. Marty Glickman with Stan Isaacs, *The Fastest Kid on the Block* (Syracuse, NY, Syracuse University Press, 1996).

34. Masood, *The World's Hockey Champions*.

35. www.bharatiyahockey.org/granthalaya/goal/1936/page5.htm (visited 4 November 2005).

36. Christine Duerksen Sant, '"Genuine German Girls": The Nazi Portrayal of its Sportswomen of the 1936 Berlin Olympics', unpublished doctoral thesis. Winston Salem, Wake Forest University, 2000, p. 67.

37. *Ibid.*

38. Sant, '"Genuine German Girls"', p. 89. NB: blond used in America for women, blonde in Britain.

39. Gretel Bergmann; interview with author.

40. Sant, '"Genuine German Girls"', p. 69.

41. The story of the United States in Olympic football needs a book of its own. Suffice it to say, that the $7,000 enabled them to go to Berlin to lose to Italy 1–0, and get home again.

42. Lewis H. Carlson and John J. Fogarty, *Tales of Gold* (Chicago, IL, Contemporary Books, 1987), p. 171.

43. Sharon Kinney Hanson, *The Fulton Flash* (Carbondale, IL, Southern Illinois University Press, 2004).

44. Velma Dunn; interview with author.

45. Carlson and Fogarty, *Tales of Gold*, p. 150.

46. *Ibid.*, p. 146.

47. Baker, *Jesse Owens*, p. 78.

48. Owens and Neimark, *The Man Who Outran Hitler*, p. 67.

49. *The Man Who Outran Hitler* reads like a post-event justification for many things and at crucial moments does not seem to ring true – something we shall meet again. I have used what is recorded in the book with caution.

50. Smallwood, in fact, recovered sufficiently to qualify for the 400-metre semi-finals in Berlin, only to fall ill again. He finally had his appendix removed in a Berlin hospital.

51. Baker, *Jesse Owens*, p. 79.

52. Carlson and Fogarty, *Tales of Gold*, p. 173.

53. John Woodruff; interview with author.

54. Hanson, *The Fulton Flash*, p. 64.

55. Gretel Bergmann; interview with author.

56. *Ibid.*

57. My neighbour Inge Donnell spent a long time with her magnifying glass trying to decipher the signature and it really is a scrawl. By a careful examination of each individual letter – and some deduction! – we concluded it had to be Tschammer's.

58. Gretel Bergmann; interview with author. Interestingly, Christine Sant wrote in
     '"Genuine German Girls"': 'Tolerating Bergmann at training courses and some
     track meets, although in conflict with Nazi racial principles, was a small price to
     pay in order to keep the aim of hosting the Olympics alive. But in the final
     moments, priorities shifted again. Allowing Bergmann actually to compete in the
     Olympics would have appeared an egregious violation of Nazi racial policies.
     A victory by her most likely would have been taken as an embarrassing blow to
     the political leadership, who sought to impress the huge national and inter-
     national audience. In the case of Bergmann, racism clearly won out over the
     chance for a medal for Germany and the promises of fair competition.' (p. 60).
59. *Ibid.*, p. 63.
60. Official US Report of the Games.
61. Baker, *Jesse Owens*, p. 78.
62. www.usc.edu/dept/pubrel/trojan_family/summer03/F_Zamperini.html (visited
     26 September 2005).
63. Baker, *Jesse Owens*, p. 79.
64. Daniels and Tedder, *'A Proper Spectacle'*.
65. Velma Dunn; interview with author.
66. Hanson, *The Fulton Flash*.
67. Fritz Wandt; interview with Birgit Kubisch.
68. www.swimming.org (visited 13 April 2005).
69. Velma Dunn; interview with author.
70. Masood, *The World's Hockey Champions*.
71. Baker, *Jesse Owens*, p. 78.
72. The XIth Olympic Games, Berlin, 1936 Official Report.
73. *Ibid.*
74. Duff Hart-Davis, *Hitler's Games* (London, Century Hutchinson 1986).
75. The XIth Olympic Games, Berlin, 1936 Official Report.

FIVE: Light My Fire

1. Albert Speer, *Inside the Third Reich* (London, Sphere, 1979), p. 119.
2. Sharon Kinney Hanson, *The Fulton Flash* (Carbondale, IL, Southern Illinois
    University Press, 2004).
3. The XIth Olympic Games, Berlin, 1936 Official Report.
4. Richard D. Mandell, *The Nazi Olympics* (London, Souvenir Press, 1971), p. 246.
5. Hanson, *The Fulton Flash*.
6. Lewis H. Carlson and John J. Fogarty, *Tales of Gold* (Chicago, IL, Contemporary
    Books, 1987), p. 138.
7. en.olympic.cn/games/summer/2004-03-27/121663.html (visited 22 September
    2005).

8. *New York Times*, Thursday 23 July.

9. Official US Olympic report.

10. Velma Dunn; interview with author.

11. Marty Glickman with Stan Isaacs, *The Fastest Kid on the Block* (Syracuse, NY, Syracuse University Press, 1996).

12. Official US Olympic report.

13. William J. Baker, *Jesse Owens, An American Life* (New York, The Free Press, 1986), p. 82.

14. Jesse Owens with Paul Neimark, *Jesse: The Man Who Outran Hitler* (New York, Fawcett Gold Medal, 1978), p. 71.

15. Hanson, *The Fulton Flash*.

16. www.usc.edu/dept/pubrel/trojan_family/summer03/F_Zamperini.html (visited 26 September 2005).

17. Carlson and Fogarty, *Tales of Gold*, pp. 162–3.

18. www.jewishvirtuallibrary.org/jsource/Holocaust/olympics.html

19. Stephanie Daniels and Anita Tedder, *'A Proper Spectacle'* – Women Olympians *1900–1936* (Houghton Conquest, Beds., ZeNaNa Press, 2000), p. 103.

20. Fritz Wandt; interview with Birgit Kubisch.

21. A record player with trumpet.

22. Carlson and Fogarty, *Tales of Gold*, p. 161.

23. *New York Times*, 25 July 1936.

24. Hanson, *The Fulton Flash*.

25. Esther Myers; interview by Matthew Walker of *I, Witness to History*, Wichita, Kansas for this book.

26. The XIth Olympic Games, Berlin, 1936 Official Report.

27. en.wikipedia.org/wiki/Luigi_Beccali (visited 11 August 2005).

28. *New York Times*, 26 July 1936.

29. Owens with Neimark, *The Man Who Outran Hitler*.

30. The XIth Olympic Games, Berlin, 1936 Official Report.

31. *Ibid*.

32. Hanson, *The Fulton Flash*.

33. *New York Times*, 26 July 1936.

34. Canadian Olympic Committee, *Canada at the XI Olympiad 1936 Germany*.

35. Fritz Wandt; interview with Birgit Kubisch.

36. The XIth Olympic Games, Berlin, 1936 Official Report.

37. Horst Wessel was a 23-year-old Nazi Party member murdered in 1930, supposedly by communists, and made into a martyr. His song was adopted by the Nazis as their anthem.

38. *New York Times*, 29 July 1936.

39. Daniels and Tedder, *'A Proper Spectacle'*, p. 107.

40.   Hanson, *The Fulton Flash*.

41.   Baker, *Jesse Owens*, pp. 83–4.

42.   *Ibid*, p. 84.

43.   Hanson, *The Fulton Flash*.

44.   The XIth Olympic Games, Berlin, 1936 Official Report.

45.   Duff Hart-Davis, *Hitler's Games* (London, Century Hutchinson, 1986), p. 135.

46.   The XIth Olympic Games, Berlin, 1936 Official Report.

47.   *Ibid*.

48.   Fritz Wandt; interview with Birgit Kubisch.

49.   British Olympic Association, *The Official Report of the XIth Olympiad, Berlin 1936*.

50.   Daniels and Tedder, 'A Proper Spectacle', p. 106.

51.   Velma Dunn; interview with author.

52.   Carlson and Fogarty, *Tales of Gold*, p. 140.

53.   Hanson, *The Fulton Flash*.

SIX: War Games

1.   *Daily Express*, 1 August 1936.

2.   Hedda Adlon, *Hotel Adlon* (London, Barrie Books, 1958), p. 211. Princess Mafalda, born in Rome and the second child of King Victor Emmanuel III of Italy, married a Nazi, but during the war Hitler suspected her of treachery. She died in Buchenwald concentration camp.

3.   The XIth Olympic Games, Berlin, 1936 Official Report.

4.   *Ibid*.

5.   *Ibid*. The organisers tried to cater for individual nations' preferences. They sent out a questionnaire and this is what came back (in the MENUS OF THE NATIONS I have used only selected examples):

> Argentina: three meat dishes daily with large portions. Australia: English cooking; beef, mutton and veal preferred; three meat dishes daily. Austria: biomalt. Finland: ample quantities of milk. France: hors d'oeuvres instead of soup or broth at lunch. Germany: tomato juice, cream cheese with linseed oil; Ovaltine, Dextropur, Dextroenergen. Greece: cold or warm Ovaltine at all meals. Holland: warm meals only in the evening; ample quantities of vegetables, potato and fresh salads; for breakfast, Dutch cheese; for lunch, cold cuts of various kinds, sausages, eggs, Dutch cheese, bread and butter. India: curry, meats including mutton, veal, lamb and fowl but no beef, pork or beef suet. Poland: cold or warm Ovaltine for breakfast and dinner. Switzerland: Ovaltine at every meal. U.S.A.: Ovaltine, Dextroenergen. Yugoslavia: dishes cooked in oil.

The Official Berlin Report comments:

> Since the meals provided at the international physical education students'
> encampment did not agree with the Indian and Chinese representatives, the
> camp authorities approached the household department of the North
> German Lloyd Company with the request that lunch be prepared at the
> Olympic Village for about 30 Chinese and 30 Indians, the food then being
> transported each day to the students' encampment in special containers.
> The menus at Frisian House [Friesenhaus] and in Kopenick were in general
> the same as those at the Olympic Village, and the dishes were prepared in a
> similar manner.

THE MENUS OF THE NATIONS

Afghanistan: no pork and no sausages with a high fat content; fish and fowl
demanded daily; ample quantities of fruit, principally bananas; rice and
fresh vegetables.

Australia and New Zealand: beefsteaks, fowl and lamb but no pork;
mostly grilled meat; salads; milk and tea as principal beverages.

Brazil: large quantities of meat, especially beef and pork; veal and lamb
less popular; black beans daily (with dry rice); little butter but large
quantities of olive oil; six oranges daily and one pound of bananas per
person; strong coffee.

Canada: considerable quantities of beefsteak prepared in the English
fashion, also roast beef and spare ribs; cold cuts seldom requested; American
breakfast with all extras; salads; vegetables cooked only in water; lamb and
veal as well as fowl prepared in the usual fashion, but preferably roasted;
stewed fruit, tomatoes and fresh fruit constantly demanded; large quantities
of honey and cream cheese.

Chile: the Chileans were moderate eaters, preferring beef and pork as well
as fowl. Beefsteaks half done were popular; rice, noodles or spaghetti at
every meal; large quantities of marmalade.

China: the Chinese were also moderate in their requests, pork and fowl
being preferred as meats although beefsteaks were also demanded
occasionally; no lamb; fish requested now and then; curry as a principal
spice; large quantities of salad and fresh fruit, but few vegetables; 300
grammes of rice daily per person; iced tea and orange juice as beverages.

France: the French sportsman is also an epicure, paying less attention to
practical nourishment than to tasty and varied dishes. English steaks
Chateaubriand fashion with white bread and red wine preferred for the

weight-lifters; all kinds of meat requested, this being prepared in the form of steaks, fillets, cutlets, roasts and ragouts; delicacies such as mushrooms, anchovies, sardines, corn on the cob, green peppers, etc. popular; stewed fruit with every meal; vegetables steamed in butter but without sauces; cheese, fruit and coffee after the principal meals.

Germany: the weight-lifters received beefsteak Tatar, chopped raw liver, cream cheese with oil and considerable quantities of eggs, often four per meal. Light refreshment before training and more substantial food afterwards. The athletes required normal meals, steaks, cutlets, pork chops, roast beef and fowl being principally requested. Large quantities of fruit; vegetables prepared with flour, potatoes but practically no rice; tomatoes and salads popular; milk with grape-sugar and fruit juices preferred as a drink; various kinds of bread with large quantities of butter.

Great Britain: moderate eaters; grilled meat, 'medium' done, especially popular three to four eggs, oatmeal, tea, milk, fruit and toast for breakfast; Horlicks malted milk; plainly cooked vegetables.

India: no beef or pork; principally fowl or lamb prepared in curry and eaten with rice only; few vegetables and salads; four to five eggs daily; large quantities of fruit and fruit salads. Several sportsmen were vegetarians.

Italy: the Italians' diet was prescribed by their sporting physician. Principally soups, spaghetti, macaroni and large quantities of Parmesan cheese; noodles, ravioli and strudles of all kinds; starchy foods at every meal; the weight-lifters ate considerable quantities of meat, while the boxers consumed only bouillon with egg two days before competing; daily portions of meat average in size; normal quantities of fruit; coffee and chianti wine preferred as beverages; large quantities of rolls.

Japan: for breakfast, soup with meat, vegetables, soy and rice, then eggs, fruit and bread; for lunch, meat (pork preferred), vegetables, rice, potatoes and often a sweet dessert; for dinner, steaks, ragouts, and other similar dishes with rice; vegetables and salads always mixed with soy; preserves which the Japanese brought with them also popular.

South Africa: grilled steaks and fowl; menu in general similar to that of the English.

Switzerland: it was difficult in the beginning to prepare a menu suitable to all the members of the Swiss team, different groups preferring Italian, French and German dishes. As soon as all the kitchens were in operation however, special wishes could be gratified without difficulty.

U.S.A.: beefsteaks as well as lamb and veal daily for lunch and dinner; no form of fried meat except fowl; underdone steaks before competition; for breakfast, eggs with ham, bacon, oatmeal or hominy and orange juice; large quantities of fresh and stewed fruit; no kippered herrings; vegetables and baked potatoes with principal meals; sweet dishes including custards and ice cream.

6. *Canada at the XI Olympiad 1936 Germany.*
7. Werner Schwieger; interview with Birgit Kubisch.
8. *Canada at the XI Olympiad 1936 Germany.*
9. *Ibid.*
10. Esther Myers; interview by Matthew Walker of *I, Witness to History*, Wichita, Kansas for this book.
11. www.wichita.edu/dt/shockermag/show/dept.asp?_s=138&_d=11 – (visited 10 October 2005).
12. The XIth Olympic Games, Berlin, 1936 Official Report.
13. *Canada at the XI Olympiad 1936 Germany.*
14. *Ibid.*
15. Velma Dunn; interview with author.
16. *Canada at the XI Olympiad 1936 Germany.*
17. Stephanie Daniels and Anita Tedder, 'A Proper Spectacle' – *Women Olympians 1900–1936* (Houghton Conquest, Beds., ZeNaNa Press, 2000), p. 109.
18. *Ibid.*
19. Esther Myers; interview by Walker of *I, Witness to History* for this book.
20. 'A Proper Spectacle', p. 109.
21. *Canada at the XI Olympiad 1936 Germany.*
22. *Ibid.*
23. *Ibid.*
24. *Ibid.*
25. www.athletics.mcgill.ca/varsity_ sports_player_profile.ch2?athlete_id=959 - 39K (visited 19 October 2005).
26. Official US Olympic report.
27. Marty Glickman and Stan Isaacs, *The Fastest Kid on the Block* (Syracuse, NY, Syracuse University Press, 1996).
28. www.olympicwomen.co.uk/Berline.htm (visited 22 September 2005).
29. Velma Dunn; interview with author.
30. The *New York Times* (3 August 1936) reported that there was a 'foolish controversy' over whether the Americans gave the salute or lowered their flag. This may have been fuelled by the singular fact that the Americans in the crowd whistled – which to an American means venting approval and enthusiasm, but to a European signals derision.

   The paper added that the talk of the town since the Opening Ceremony had been who did and who did not give the salute. The Germans were delighted because they thought – 'erroneously' – that the French did. The paper sought to clarify the situation. The Nazi salute involved throwing the right arm forward, the Olympic involved lifting the arm sideways to shoulder height. However, it added, to people on the move telling the difference is not easy.

31. This reconstruction of the parade is of necessity speculative in places. We know what some teams did (and did not do). Of others there is no record. The Official Berlin Report naturally stayed away from that in its text but did carry photographs of the teams passing by and, presumably, their photographers took pictures of any giving the Nazi salute. From that, I have deduced that the photographs showing no salute reflect the fact that those depicted did not give one. The Riefenstahl film is grainy, incomplete and taken from a distance.

The reader may regard this as arcane, but *nothing* about Hitler in the 1930s was that, and here, in microcosm, were how so many of the family of nations were trying to cope with him, standing there in his box looking down on them, and his Germany.

Incidentally, Russia – to become an Olympic powerhouse as the USSR after Hitler's war – competed in the 1912 Games, but after the October Revolution the Communists regarded them as bourgeois and stayed away until Helsinki, 1952. No doubt the absence was partly due to the pathological fear of Soviet citizens being exposed to contact with foreigners, especially from the West. Even in Finland they had their own Olympic village, near the Russian border, and chaperones kept foreign contacts to an absolute minimum where they could not be completely avoided.

32. www.cishsydney2005.org/images/ST25-PAPER%20FOR%20ICHSC%20(SAKAUE).doc -

33. *The Times*, London, 1 August 1936.

34. www.tvhistory.tv/1936%20German%20Olympics%20TV%20Program.htm (visited 25 October 2005).

35. Paul Yogi Mayer, *Jews and the Olympic Games* (London, Vallentine Mitchell, 2005), p. 103.

36. The Official Report on the Games is, as we have seen, an astonishingly comprehensive and detailed record but – to use the word astonishing again – there are errors in the relay run statistics. I am indebted to a friend, Reg Plummer, for casting his knowing eye over them. To be pedantic (and why not, just this once?): the total for 24 July is out by 3 kilometres; a distance on 25 July needs to be increased by 10 kilometres to match the time allocated for its completion; 26 July is out by 0.2 of a kilometre; 29–30 July figures are out by 9 kilometres. I have, however, left the original totals alone for authenticity and simplicity – both valuable commodities when examining Hitler's Reich.

SEVEN: The Führer and the Runner

1. Werner Schwieger; interview with Birgit Kubisch.
2. Velma Dunn; interview with author.
3. The XIth Olympic Games, Berlin, 1936 Official Report.
4. *Ibid.*
5. *Ibid.*
6. *Ibid.*
7. *Ibid.*
8. *Daily Express*, 3 August 1936.
9. *Ibid.*
10. www.fay-west.com/connellsville/historic/woodruff.php (visited 13 August 2005).
11. *New York Times*, 3 August 1936.
12. *Daily Express*, 3 August 1936.
13. *New York Times*, 3 August 1936.
14. Stan Greenberg, *Olympic Fact Book* (Enfield, Guinness Publishing, 1991), p. 39.
15. Sharon Kinney Hanson, *The Fulton Flash* (Carbondale, IL, Southern Illinois University Press, 2004).
16. Lewis H. Carlson and John J. Fogarty, *Tales of Gold* (Chicago, IL, Contemporary Books, 1987), p. 139.
17. Stephanie Daniels and Anita Tedder, '*A Proper Spectacle*' – *Women Olympians 1900–1936* (Houghton Conquest, Beds., ZeNaNa Press, 2000), p. 117. Brown is clearly being discreet, hence the six asterisks. The other runners in the heat were Krauss, Meagher, Romanič of Romania and Testoni. Only two of these surnames have six letters. . . .
18. William J. Baker, *Jesse Owens, An American Life* (New York, The Free Press, 1986), p. 93.
19. Hanson, *The Fulton Flash*.
20. Duff Hart-Davis, *Hitler's Games* (London, Century Hutchinson, 1986), p. 177.
21. Daniels and Tedder, '*A Proper Spectacle*', p. 112.
22. Albert Speer, *Inside the Third Reich* (London, Sphere, 1979), p. 119.
23. Werner Schwieger; interview with Birgit Kubisch.
24. Daniels and Tedder, '*A Proper Spectacle*', p. 102.
25. Carlson and Fogarty, *Tales of Gold*, p. 187.
26. *Canada at the XI Olympiad 1936 Germany.*
27. *New York Times*, 13 August 1936.
28. Guy Oliver, *World Soccer*, 2nd edn (Enfield, Guinness Publishing, 1995), p. 85.
29. www.fifa.com/en/comp/olympicsmen/0,3664,114-OLY-1936,00.html (visited 16 August 2005).

30. Milly Mogulof, *Foiled* (Oakland, CA, RDR Books, 2002), p. 155.
31. *Ibid*, p. 157.
32. Baker, *Jesse Owens*, pp. 97–8.
33. Hanson, *The Fulton Flash*.
34. Carlson and Fogarty, *Tales of Gold*, p. 139.
35. Hanson, *The Fulton Flash*.
36. *Ibid*.
37. *New York Times*, 4 August 1936.
38. Carlson and Fogarty, *Tales of Gold*, p. 183.
39. Mogulof, *Foiled*, p. 157.
40. Baker, *Jesse Owens*, p. 98.

EIGHT: Bitter Taste

1. Christine Duerksen Sant, '"Genuine German Girls": The Nazi Portrayal of its Sportswomen of the 1936 Berlin Olympics', p. 99. Unpublished doctoral thesis, Winston-Salem, Wake Forest University, 2000.
2. Stephanie Daniels and Anita Tedder, 'A Proper Spectacle' – *Women Olympians 1900–1936* (Houghton Conquest, ZeNaNa Press, 2000), p. 105.
3. *New York Times*, 5 August 1936.
4. Deborah E. Lipstadt, *Beyond Belief* (New York, The Free Press, 1986).
5. William J. Baker, *Jesse Owens, An American Life* (New York, The Free Press, 1986), p. 100.
6. Neil Duncanson, *The Fastest Men on Earth* (London, Willow Books, 1988).
7. Lewis H. Carlson and John J. Fogarty, *Tales of Gold* (Chicago, IL, Contemporary Books, 1987), p. 181.
8. *Ibid.*, p. 174.
9. Daniels and Tedder, 'A Proper Spectacle', p. 102.
10. *Ibid.*, pp. 102–3.
11. Velma Dunn; interview with author.
12. Carlson and Fogarty, *Tales of Gold*, p. 188.
13. iwitnesstohistory.org/ResidentPages/Wenzel/Wenzel%2036%20olympics.htm (visited 10 October 2005).
14. www.answers.com/topic/trebisonda-valla marathon (visited 1 October 2005).
15. Carlson and Fogarty, *Tales of Gold*, p. 151.
16. www.athletics.org.nz/lovelock2.html (visited 23 November 2005).
17. *New York Times*, 5 August 1936.
18. It seems that Riefenstahl staged a recreation of this for her film on the Games. Viewing it today, it certainly looks and feels like a reconstruction. No doubt the darkness hampered her filming of the original event.
19. Carlson and Fogarty, *Tales of Gold*, p. 148.

20. Marty Glickman with Stan Isaacs, *Fastest Kid on the Block* (Syracuse, NY, Syracuse University Press, 1996).

21. Harold Abrahams, British sprinter who won the 100 metres gold at Paris in 1924 (and became one of the subjects of the film *Chariots of Fire*). Ironically, in the context of the Berlin Games, he was Jewish.

22. www.library.otago.ac.nz/exhibitions/rhodes_scholars/jack_lovelock.html (visited 1 October 2005).

23. www.library.otago.ac.nz/exhibitions/rhodes_scholars/jack_lovelock.html (visited 1 October 2005).

24. Associated Press quoted in the *New York Times*, 6 August 1936.

25. Baker, *Jesse Owens*, p. 103.

26. Carlson and Fogarty, *Tales of Gold*, p. 153.

27. www.usc.edu/dept/pubrel/trojan_family/summer03/F_Zamperini.html (visited 29 September 2005).

28. Carlson and Fogarty, *Tales of Gold*, p. 150.

29. *Ibid.*, p. 146.

30. Werner Schwieger; interview with Birgit Kubisch.

31. Glickman with Isaacs, *Fastest Kid on the Block*.

32. Baker, *Jesse Owens*, p. 104.

33. *Ibid.*, p. 102.

34. *Ibid.*, p. 105.

35. Daniels and Tedder, '*A Proper Spectacle*', p. 101.

36. www.sport.nl/boek.php3?artid=2691 (visited 20 August 2005).

37. Anthony Read and David Fisher, *Berlin: The Biography of a City* (London, Hutchinson, 1994), p. 214.

38. *The Times*, London, 11 August 1936.

39. *New York Times*, 9 August 1936.

40. www.olympic.org/uk/athletes/heroes/bio_uk.asp?PAR_I_ID=88103 (visited 15 August 2005).

41. marathoninfo.free.fr/jo/berlin1936.htm (visited 2 October 2005).

42. Daniels and Tedder, '*A Proper Spectacle*', p. 120.

43. *Ibid.*, p. 111.

44. Baker, *Jesse Owens*, p. 110.

45. Daniels and Tedder, '*A Proper Spectacle*', p. 112.

46. Such coverage lent itself nicely to critics of women's sports who claimed that women were emotionally ill-suited for serious competition. Most assuredly, the press and Nazi leadership would have refrained from drawing such attention to any male athletes who similarly let their emotions show. members.fortunecity.com/dikigoros/intersexism.htm (visited 18 April 2005).

47. Daniels and Tedder, '*A Proper Spectacle*', p. 117.

48. Sant, '"Genuine German Girls"', p. 89.
49. Father of Charlotte Rampling, the film actress.
50. Baker, *Jesse Owens*, p. 111.
51. The XIth Olympic Games, Berlin, 1936 Official Report.
52. Werner Schwieger; interview with Birgit Kubisch.
53. marathoninfo.free.fr/jo/berlin1936.htm (visited 2 October 2005).
54. *New York Times*, 9 August 1936.
55. *Ibid.*
56. marathoninfo.free.fr/jo/berlin1936.htm (visited 2 October 2005).

NINE: Last Shot Fired

1. Stephanie Daniels and Anita Tedder, *'A Proper Spectacle' – Women Olympians 1900–1936* (Houghton Conquest, Beds., ZeNaNa Press, 2000), pp. 116–17.
2. Velma Dunn; interview with author.
3. William J. Baker, *Jesse Owens, An American Life* (New York, The Free Press, 1986), p. 112.
4. Christine Duerksen Sant, '"Genuine German Girls": The Nazi Portrayal of its Sportswomen of the 1936 Berlin Olympics', pp. 90–1. Unpublished doctoral thesis, Winston-Salem, Wake Forest University, 2000.
5. www.cishsydney2005.org/images/ST25-PAPER%20FOR%20ICHSC%20(SAKAUE).doc -
6. Daniels and Tedder, *'A Proper Spectacle'*, p. 121.
7. *New York Times*, 12 August 1936.
8. Baker, *Jesse Owens*, p. 113.
9. Crown Prince Wilhelm (1882–1951) was the eldest of Kaiser Wilhelm II's five sons. He fought in the First World War but afterwards went into exile in Holland. Promising to stay out of politics, he returned to Germany in 1923 and lived the rest of his life as a private citizen. www.firstworldwar.com/bio/princewilhelm.ht (visited 20 August 2005).
10. www.sport.nl/boek.php3?artid=2691 (visited 20 August 2005).
11. Baker, *Jesse Owens*, p. 116.
12. Anthony Read and David Fisher, *Berlin: The Biography of a City* (London, Hutchinson, 1994), p. 213.
13. Quoted in Giles MacDonogh, *Berlin* (London, Sinclair-Stevenson, 1997), p. 159.
14. Lewis H. Carlson and John J. Fogarty, *Tales of Gold* (Chicago, IL, Contemporary Books, 1987), p. 142.
15. *New York Times*, 16 August 1936.
16. Velma Dunn; interview with author.
17. www.webenetics.com/hungary/olympic_1936.htm (visited 18 April 2005).

18. www.athens2004.com/en/ParticipantBiography?noc=EGY&rsc=ARM070000 (visited 21 August 2005).

19. M.N. Masood, *The World's Hockey Champions* (Dehli, Model Press, 1937).

20. sify.com/sports/hockey/fullstory.php?id=13392134 (visited 21 August 2005).

21. *Ibid.*

22. William Shirer, *Berlin Diary* (London, Hamish Hamilton, 1941), p. 59.

23. Daniels and Tedder, 'A Proper Spectacle', p. 126.

TEN: Village People

1. Lewis H. Carlson and John J. Fogarty, *Tales of Gold* (Chicago, IL, Contemporary Books, 1987), p. 152.

2. Albert Speer, *Inside the Third Reich* (London, Sphere, 1979), p. 116.

3. Stephanie Daniels and Anita Tedder, 'A Proper Spectacle' – *Women Olympians 1900–1936* (Houghton Conquest, Beds., ZeNaNa Press, 2000), p. 101.

4. Paul Yogi Mayer, *Jews in the Olympic Games* (London, Valentine Mitchell, 2004), p. 107.

5. William J. Baker, *Jesse Owens, An American Life* (New York, The Free Press, 1986), p. 118.

6. www.athletics.mcgill.ca/varsity_ sports_player_profile.ch2?athlete_id=959 (visited 19 October 2005).

7. Carlson and Fogarty, *Tales of Gold*, pp. 151, 175

8. Marty Glickman with Stan Isaacs, *The Fastest Kid on the Block* (Syracuse, NY, Syracuse University Press, 1996).

9. John Woodruff; interview with author.

10. US Official Olympic report.

11. en.olympic.cn/games/summer/2004-03-27/121663.html (visited 22 September 2005).

12. www.cishsydney2005.org/images/ST25-PAPER%20FOR%20ICHSC%20(SAKAUE).doc (visited 24 October 2005).

13. *Ibid.*

14. *Ibid.*

15. Christine Duerksen Sant, '"Genuine German Girls": The Nazi Portrayal of its Sportswomen of the 1936 Berlin Olympics', p. 115. Unpublished doctoral thesis, Winston-Salem, Wake Forest University, 2000.

16. *Ibid.*

17. *Ibid.*, p. 116.

18. Gretel Bergmann; interview with author.

19. www.adpf.asso.fr/adpf-publi/folio/olympisme/hommages.html (visited 14 April 2005).

20. *Ibid.*

21. www.aafla.org/SportsLibrary/Olympika/Olympika_1994/olympika0301g.pdf

22. frankwykoff2.com/foy_draper2.htm (visited 22 October 2005).

23. www.webenetics.com/hungary/olympic_1936.htm (visited 18 April 2005).

24. Daniels and Tedder, '*A Proper Spectacle*', p. 127.

25. *Ibid.*

26. usatf.org/athletes/hof/johnson_c.asp (visited 25 August 2005).

27. *Hitler's Pawn*, Clear Channel Entertainment Television/Black Canyon Productions, New York.

28. Gretel Bergmann; interview with author.

29. webs.wichita.edu/dt/shockermag/show/dept.asp?_s=138&_d=11 (visited 10 October 2005).

30. Jesse Owens with Paul Neimark, *JESSE: The Man Who Outran Hitler* (New York, Fawcett Gold Medal, 1978).

31. usatf.org/athletes/hof/snyder.asp (visited 25 August 2005).

32. Glickman with Isaacs, *The Fastest Kid on the Block*.

33. usatf.org/athletes/hof/albritton.asp (visited on 10 May 2006).

34. usatf.org/athletes/hof/lash.asp (visited 11 August 2005).

35. de.wikipedia.org/wiki/Gisela_Mauermayer (visited 12 August 2005).

36. *Ibid.*

37. *New York Times*, 18 June 1996.

38. www.jewsinsports.org/Olympics. asp?sport=olympics&ID=2 - 9k (visited 19 November 2005).

39. Gretel Bergmann; interview with author.

40. *New York Times*, 28 October 2002.

41. eleanor-holm.biography.ms/ (visited 21 August 2005).

42. frankwykoff2.com/olympic_oak_tree.htm (visited 25 October 2005).

43. Velma Dunn Ploessel; interview with author.

44. www.usc.edu/dept/pubrel/trojan_family/summer03/F_Zamperini.html (visited 29 September 2005).

45. en.wikipedia.org/wiki/John_Woodruff (visited 12 August 2005).

46. Fritz Wandt; interview with Birgit Kubisch.

47. The XIth Olympic Games Berlin, 1936 Official Report.

48. M.N. Masood, *The World's Hockey Champions* (Delhi, Model Press, 1937).

49. *Ibid.*

STATISTICS

Here are all the medal winners from Berlin with, for interest, the winning times from Track and Field in the 1896 and 2004 Athens Games. (Track and Field has been the centrepiece all the way through, and comparisons can be made). In every event at Berlin the winner won gold, second silver and third bronze.

Men

Track and Field

100m J. Owens (USA) 10.3s, R. Metcalfe (USA) 10.4, M. Osendarp (Hol) 10.5. Athens 1896 12.0, Athens 2004, 9.85.

200m: J. Owens (USA) 20.7s, M. Robinson (USA) 21.1, M. Osendarp (Hol) 21.3. Athens 22.2/ 19.79.

400m: A. Williams (USA) 46.5s, G. Brown (GB) 46.7, J. LuValle (USA) 46.8. Athens 54.2/ 44.0.

800m: J. Woodruff (USA) 1m 52.9s, M. Lanzi (Ita) 1:53.3, P. Edwards (Can) 1:53.6. Athens 2:11.0/ 1:44.45.

1,500m: J. Lovelock (NZ) 3m 47.8s, G. Cunningham (USA) 3:48.4, L. Beccali (Ita) 3:49.2. Athens 4:33.2/ 3.34.18.

5,000m: G. Höckert (Fin) 14m 22.2s, L. Lehtinen (Fin) 14:25.8, H. Jonsson (Swe) 14:29.0. Athens: not held/ 13:14.39.

10,000m: I. Salminen (Fin) 30m 15.4s, A. Askola (Fin) 30:15.6, V. Iso-Hollo (Fin) 30:20.2. Athens: not held/ 27:05.10.

Marathon: S. Kee-Chung (Jap) 2h 29m 19.2s, E. Harper (GB) 2h 31:23.2, N. Seong-Yong (Jap) 2h 31:42.0. Athens 2h 58.50/ 2h 10:55.0.

3,000m steeplechase: V. Iso-Hollo (Fin) 9m 03.8s, K. Tuominen (Fin) 9:06.8, A. Dompert (Ger) 9:07.2. Athens: not held/ 8:05/81.

110m hurdles: F. Towns (USA) 14.2s, D. Finlay (GB) 14.4, F. Pollard (USA) 14.4. Athens 17.6/ 12.91.

400m hurdles: G. Hardin (USA) 52.4s, J. Loaring (Can) 52.7, M. White (Phi) 52.8. Athens: not held/ 47.63.

4 × 100 relay: USA 39.8s, Italy 41.1, Germany 41.2, GB 41.3. Athens: not held/ 38.08.

4 × 400 relay: GB 3m 09.0s, USA 3:11.0, Germany 3:11.8. Athens: not held/ 2:55.91.

50km road walk: H. Whitlock (GB) 4h 30m 41.1s, A. Schwalb (Switz) 4h 32:09.2, A. Bubenko (Lat) 4h 32:42.2. Athens: not held/ 3h 38:46.0.

High jump: C. Johnson (USA) 2.03m, D. Albritton (USA) 2.00m, D. Thurber (USA) 2.00m. Athens 1.81m/ 2.36m.

Pole vault: E. Meadows (USA) 4.35m, S. Nishida (Jap) 4.25m, S. Oe (Jap) 4.25m. Athens 3.30m/ 5.95m.

Long jump: J. Owens (USA) 8.06m, L. Long (Ger) 7.87m, N. Tajima (Jap) 7.74m. Athens 6.35m/ 8.95m.

Triple jump: N. Tajima (Jap) 16.00m, M. Harada (Jap) 15.66m, J. Metcalfe (Austral) 15.50m. Athens 13.71m/ 17.79m.

Shot-put: H. Woellke (Ger) 16.20m, S. Bärlund (Fin) 16.12m, G. Stock (Ger) 15.66m. Athens 11.22m/ 21.15m.

Discus: K. Carpenter (USA) 50.48m, G. Dunn (USA) 49.36m, G. Oberweger (Ita) 49.23m. Athens 29.15m/ 69.89m.

Hammer: K. Hein (Ger) 56.49m, E. Blask (Ger) 55.04m, F. Warngard (Swe) 54.83m. Athens: not held/ 82.91m.

Javelin: G. Stock (Ger) 71.84m, Y. Nikkanen (Fin) 70.77m, K. Toivonen (Fin) 70.72m. Athens: not held/ 86.50m.

Decathlon: G. Morris (USA) 7,254 pts, R. Clark (USA) 7,063 pts, J. Parker (USA) 6,760 pts. Athens: not held/ 8,893 pts.

Basketball

America, Canada, Mexico.

Boxing

Flyweight: W. Kaiser (Ger), G. Matta (Ita), L. Laurie (USA).

Bantamweight: U. Sergo (Ita), J. Wilson (USA), F. Ortiz (Mex).

Featherweight: O. Casanovas (Arg), C. Catterall (S Af), J. Miner (Ger).

Lightweight: I. Harangi (Hun), N. Stepulov (Est), E. Agren (Swe).

Welterweight: S. Suvio (Fin), M. Murach (Ger), G. Petersen (Den).

Middleweight: J. Despeaux (Fra), H. Tiller (Nor), R. Villareal (Arg).

Light-heavyweight: R. Michelot (Fra), R. Vogt (Ger), F. Risiglione (Arg).

Heavyweight: H. Runge (Ger), G. Loveli (Arg), E. Nilsen (Nor).

Canoeing

1,000 metres kayak singles: G. Hradetsky (Aus) 4m 22.9s, H. Cämmerer (Ger) 4:25.6, J. Kraaier (Hol) 4:35.1.

10,000 metres kayak singles: E. Krebs (Ger) 46m 01.6s, F. Landerfinger (Aus) 46:14.7, E. Riedel (USA) 47:23.9.

1,000 metres kayak pairs: Austria 4m 03.8s, Germany 4:08.9, Holland 4:12.2.

10,000 metres kayak pairs: Germany 41m 45.0s, Austria 42:05.4, Sweden 43:06.1.

1,000 metres Canadian singles: F. Arnyot (Can) 5m 32.1s, B. Karlik (Czh) 5:36.9, E. Koshik (Ger) 5:39.0.

1,000 metres Canadian pairs: Czechoslovakia 4m 50.1, Austria 4:53.8, Canada 4:56.7.

10,000 metres Canadian pairs: Czechoslovakia 50m 33.5s, Canada 51m 15.8, Austria 51:28.0.

10,000 metres folding kayak singles: G. Hradetzky (Aus) 50:01.2, H. Eberhardt (Fra) 50:04.2, X. Hörmann (Ger) 50:06.5.

10,000 metres folding kayak pairs: Sweden 45:48.9, Germany 45:49.2, Holland 46:12.4.

Cycling

1,000 metres time-trial: A.Vliet (Hol) 1m 12.0s, P. Georger (Fra) 1:12.8, R. Karsch (Ger) 1:13.2.

1,000 metres sprint: T. Merkens (Ger) 11m 8s, A.Vliet (Hol), L. Chaillot (Fra).

4,000 metres team pursuit: France 4m 45.0s, Italy 4:51.0, Great Britain 4:52.6.

2,000 metres tandem: Germany 11.8s, Netherlands, France.

Team road race: France 7h 39m 16.2s Switzerland 7 39:20.4, Belgium 7 39:21.0.

Individual road race: R. Charpentier (Fra) 2h 33m 05.0s, G. Lapebie (Fra) 2 33:05.2, E. Nievergeit (Switz) 2 33:05.8

Equestrian

Jumping: K. Hasse (Ger) 4 faults, H. Rang (Rom) 4, J. von Platthy (Hun) 8
Team: Germany 44 faults, Holland 51.5, Portugal 56.

Dressage: H. Pollay (Ger) 1,760 pts, F. Gerhard (Ger) 1,745.4 pts, A. Podhajsky (Aus) 1,721.5.
Team: Germany 5,074 pts, France 4,846 pts, Sweden 4,660.5 pts.

Three-day event: L. Stubbendorf (Ger) 37.7 faults, E. Thomson (USA) 99.9, H. Lunding (Den) 102.2.
Team: Germany 676.75 pts, Poland 991.70 pts, Great Britain 9,195.90 pts.

Fencing

Foil: G. Gaudini (Ita) 7 wins, F. Gardère (Fra) 6, G. Bocchino (Ita) 4.
Team: Italy, France, Germany.

Épée: F. Riccardi (Ita) 13 wins, S. Ragno (Ita) 12, G. Cornaggia-Medici (Ita) 12.
Team: Italy, Sweden, France.

Sabre: E. Kabos (Hun) 7 wins, G. Marzi (Ita) 6, A. Gerevich (Hun) 6.
Team: Hungary, Italy, Germany.

Football

Semi-finals: Italy 2, Norway 1; Austria 3, Poland 1.
Final: Italy 2, Austria 1.

Gymnastics

Team: Germany 657.430 pts, Switzerland 654.802 pts, Finland 638.468 pts.

Individual combined exercises: A. Schwarzmann (Ger) 113.100 pts, E. Mack (Switz), 112.334 pts, K. Frey (Ger) 111.532 pts.

Floor exercises: G. Miez (Switz) 18.666, J. Walter (Switz) 18.5, K. Frey (Ger)/ E. Mack (Switz) 18.466.

Parallel bars: K. Frey (Ger)19.067, M. Reusch (Switz) 19.034, A. Schwarzmann (Ger) 18.967.

Pommel horse: K. Frey (Ger) 19.333, E. Mack (Switz) 19.167, A. Bachmann (Switz) 19.067.

Rings: A. Hudec (Czh) 19.433, L. Škutelj (Yug) 18.867, M. Volz (Ger) 18.667.

Horizontal bar: A. Saarvala (Fin) 19.367, K. Frey (Ger) 19.267, A. Schwarzmann (Ger) 19.233.

Horse vault: A. Schwarzmann (Ger) 19.200, E. Mack (Switz) 18.967, M. Volz (Ger) 18.467.

Handball

Germany, Austria, Switzerland.

Hockey

India, Germany, Holland.

Modern Pentathlon

G. Handrick (Ger) 31.5, C. Leonard (USA) 39.5, S. Abba (Ita) 45.5.

Rowing

Single sculls: G. Schäfer (Ger) 8m 21.5s, J. Hasenöhri (Aus) 8:25.8, D. Barrow (USA) 8:28.0.
Double sculls: Great Britain 7m 20.8s, Germany 7:26.2, Poland 7:36.2.
Coxless pairs: Germany 8m 16.1s, Denmark 8:19.2, Argentina 8:23.0
Coxed pairs: Germany 8m 36.9s, Italy 8:49.7, France 8:54.0.
Coxless fours: Germany 7m 01.8s, Great Britain 7:06.5, Switzerland 7:10.6.
Coxed fours: Germany 7m 16.2s, Switzerland 7:24.3, France 7:33.3.
Eights: United States 6m 25.4s, Italy 6:26.0, Germany 6:26.4.

Shooting

Free pistol: T. Ullman (Swe) 559, E. Krempel (Ger) 544, C. des Jammonières (Fra) 540.
Rapid-fire pistol: C. van Oyen (Ger) 36, H. Hax (Ger) 35, T. Ullman (Swe) 34.
Small-bore rifle: W. Rögeberg (Nor) 300, R. Berzsenyi (Hun) 296, W. Karás (Pol) 296.

Swimming

100m freestyle: F. Csík (Hun) 57.6s, M. Yusa (Jap) 57.9, S. Arai (Jap) 58.0.

400m freestyle: J. Medica (USA) 4m 44.5s, S. Uto (Jap) 4:45.6, S. Makino (Jap) 4:28.1.

1,500m freestyle: N. Terada (Jap) 19m 13.7s, J. Medica (USA) 19:34.0, S. Uto (Jap) 19:34.5.

200m breaststroke: T. Hamuro (Jap) 2m 42.5s, E. Sietas (Ger) 2:42.9, R. Koike (Jap) 2:42.2.

100m backstroke: A. Keifer (USA) 1m 05.9s, A. van de Weghe (USA) 1:07.7, M. Kiyokawa (Jap) 1:08.4.

4 × 200m freestyle relay: Japan 8m 51.5s, USA 9:03.0, Hungary 9:12.3.

Springboard diving: R. Deneger (USA) 163.57, M. Wayne (USA) 159.56, A. Greene (USA) 146.29.

Highboard diving: M. Wayne (USA) 113.58, E. Root (USA) 110.60, H. Stork (Ger) 110.31.

Water polo: Hungary, Germany, Belgium.

Weight-lifting

Featherweight: A. Terlazzo (USA) 312.5kg, S.M. Soliman (Egy) 305kg, I. Shams (Egy) 300kg.

Lightweight: A.M. Mesbah (Egy) 342.5kg / R. Fein (USA) 342.5kg,[*] K. Jansen (Ger) 327.5kg.

Middleweight: K.E. Thouni (Egy) 387.5kg, R. Ismayr (Ger) 352.5kg, A. Wagner (Ger) 352.5kg.

Light-heavyweight: L. Hostin (Fra) 372.5kg, E. Deutsch (Ger) 365kg, I. Wasif (Egy) 360kg.

Heavyweight: J. Manger (Aus) 410kg, V. Psenicka (Czh) 402.5kg, A. Luhaäär (Est) 400kg.

Wrestling

Free-style bantamweight: O. Zombori (Hun), R. Flood (USA), J. Herbert (Ger).

Free-style featherweight: K. Pihlajamaki (Fin), F. Millard (USA), G. Josson (Swe).

Free-style lightweight: K. Karpati (Hun), W. Ehrl (Ger), H. Pihlajamaki (Fin).

Free-style welterweight: F. Lewis (USA), T. Andersson (Swe), J. Schlleimer (Can).

Free-style middleweight: E. Poilve (Fra), R. Voliva (USA), A. Kireicci (Tur).

Free-style light heavyweight: K. Fridell (Swe), A. Neo (Est), E. Siebert (Ger).

Free-style heavyweight: K. Palusalu (Est), J. Kalpuch (Czh), H. Nystrom (Fin).

Graeco-Roman bantamweight: M. Lorincz (Hun), E. Svensson (Swe), J. Brendel (Ger).

Graeco-Roman featherweight: Y. Erkan (Tur), A. Reini (Fin), E. Karlsson (Swe).

Graeco-Roman lightweight: L. Koskela (Fin), J. Herda (Czh), V. Vali (Est).

Graeco-Roman welterweight: R. Svedberg (Swe), F. Schafer (Ger), E. Virtanen (Fin).

Graeco-Roman middleweight: I. Johansson (Swe), L. Schweikeert (Ger), J. Palotas (Hun).

Graeco-Roman light heavyweight: A. Cadier (Swe), E. Bietags (Lat), A. Néo (Est).

Graeco-Roman heavyweight: K. Palusalu (Est), J. Nyman (Swe), K. Hornfischer (Ger).

Yachting

Olympic monotype: D. Kagchelland (Hol), W. Grogramm (Ger), P. Scot (GB).

International star: Germany, Sweden, Holland.

6 metres: Great Britain, Norway, Sweden.[**]

8 metres: Italy, Norway, Germany.

Women

Track and Field (no women competed at Athens, 1896, so the comparison relates to 2004).

100m: H. Stephens (USA) 11.5s, S. Walsh (Pol) 11.7, K. Krauss (Ger) 11.9. Athens 10.93.

80m hurdles: T. Valla (Ita) 11.7s, A. Steuer (Ger) 11.7, E. Taylor (Can) 11.7. Athens: not held.

4 × 100m relay: USA 46.9s, GB 47.6, Canada 47.8. Athens 41.73.

High jump: I. Csák (Hun) 1.60m, D. Odam (GB) 1.60, E. Kaun (Ger) 1.60. Athens 2.06.

Discus: G. Mauermeyer (Ger) 47.63m, J. Wajsówns (Pol) 46.22, P. Mollenmauer (Ger) 39.80. Athens 67.02.

Javelin: T. Fleisher (Ger) 45.18s, L. Krüger (Ger) 43.29, M. Kawsniewska (Pol) 41.80. Athens 71.53.

Fencing

Foil: I. Elek-Schacherer (Hun) 6 wins, H. Mayer (Ger) 5, E. Preis (Aus) 5.

Gymnastics

Team: Germany 506.50 pts, Czechoslovakia 503.60, Hungary 499.0.

Swimming

100m freestyle: H. Mastenbroek (Hol) 1m 05.9s, J. Campbell (Arg) 1:06.4, G. Arendt (Ger) 1:06.6.

400m freestyle: H. Mastenbroek (Hol) 5m 26.4s, R. Hveger (Den) 5:27.5, L. Kight-Wingard (USA) 5:29.0.

200m breaststroke: H. Maehata (Jap) 3m 03.6s, M. Genenger (Ger) 3:04.2, I. Soensen (Den) 3:07.8.

100m backstroke: D. Senff (Hol) 1m 18.9s, H. Mastenbroek (Hol) 1:19.2, A. Bridges (USA) 1:19.4.

4 × 100 freestyle relay: Holland 4m 36.0s, Germany 4:36.8, USA 4:40.2.

Springboard diving: M. Gestring (USA) 89.27, K. Rawis (USA) 88.35, D. Poynton-Hill (USA) 82.36.

Highboard diving: D. Poynton-Hill (USA) 33.93, V. Dunn (USA) 33.63, K. Köhler (Ger) 33.43.

* Tie-breaker by bodyweight did not exist then.

** Discontinued Olympic sport.

BIBLIOGRAPHY

Adlon, Hedda, *Hotel Adlon*, London, Barrie Books, 1958

Baker, William J., *Jesse Owens, An American Life*, New York, The Free Press, 1986

Bringmann, Gilbert, *Fussball-Almanach 1900–1943*, Kassel, Kasseler Sportverlag, 1992

Carlson, Lewis H. and Fogarty, John J., *Tales of Gold*, Chicago, IL, Contemporary Books, 1987

Daniels, Stephanie and Tedder, Anita, *'A Proper Spectacle' – Women Olympians 1900–1936*, Houghton Conquest, ZeNaNa Press, 2000

Dost, Susanne, *Das Olympische Dorf 1936 im Wandel der Zeit*, Berlin, VBN Verlag Bernd Neddermeyer GmbH, 2004

Duncanson, Neil, *The Fastest Men on Earth*, London, Willow Books, 1988

Girardi, Wolfgang, *Olympic Games*, London, Collins, 1972

Glickman, Marty with Isaacs, Stan, *The Fastest Kid on the Block*, Syracuse, NY, Syracuse University Press, 1996

Greenberg, Stan, *Olympics Fact Book*, Enfield, Guinness Publishing, 1991

Hanson, Sharon Kinney, *The Fulton Flash*, Carbondale, IL, Southern Illinois University Press, 2004

Hart-Davis, Duff, *Hitler's Games*, London, Century Hutchinson, 1986

Lambert, Margaret Bergmann, *By Leaps and Bounds*, Washington DC, the United States Holocaust Memorial Museum and the Holocaust Survivors' Memoirs Project, 2005

Le Tissier, Tony, *Berlin Then and Now*, London, Battle of Britain Prints, 1992

Lipstadt, Deborah E., *Beyond Belief*, New York, The Free Press, 1986

MacDonogh, Giles, *Berlin*, London, Sinclair-Stevenson, 1997

Mandell, Richard D., *The Nazi Olympics*, London, Souvenir Press, 1971

Masood, M.N., *The World's Hockey Champions*, Delhi, Model Press, 1937

Matthews, Peter, *International Athletics Annual, 1985*, London, Sports World Publications, 1985

Mayer, Paul Yogi, *Jews and the Olympic Games*, London, Vallentine Mitchell, 2004

Melzer, Joachim, *Haupstadt Berlin: Fotografien 1930–1940*, Berlin, Verlag Jürgen Schacht, 1991

Mogulof, Milly, *Foiled: Hitler's Jewish Olympian* Oakland, CA, RDR Books, 2002

Nawrocki, Dr. Axel, editor for Berlin 2000 Olympia GmbH, *Berlin 2000*, Berlin 1993

Oliver, Guy, *World Soccer, Second Edition*, Enfield, Guinness Publishing, 1995

Owens, Jesse, with Neimark, Paul, *JESSE: The Man Who Outran Hitler*, New York, Fawcett Gold Medal, 1978

Read, Anthony and Fisher, David, *Berlin: The Biography of a City*, London, Hutchinson, 1994

Richter, Walter, *Olympics 1936, Band 1*, Hamburg, Cigaretten-Bilderdienst Altona-Bahrenfeld, 1936

Sakue, Professor Yasuhiro, 'Sport, Politics and Business', paper presented at the International Committee of Historical Sciences Congress, Sydney, July 2005

Sant, Christine Duerksen, '"Genuine German Girls": The Nazi Portrayal of its Sportswomen of the 1936 Berlin Olympics', unpublished doctoral thesis, Winston-Salem, Wake Forest University, 2000

Shirer, William, *Berlin Diary*, 5th edn, London, Hamish Hamilton, 1941

—— *The Rise and Fall of the Third Reich*, 8th edn, London, Pan, 1971

Speer, Albert, *Inside the Third Reich*, 4th edn, London, Sphere, 1979

Wallechinsky, David, *The Complete Book of the Winter Olympics, 1994 Edition*, London, Aurum Press, 1993

INDEX

Note: References to countries are mainly to teams. **Bold** entries indicate medal winners